ROUTLEDGE LIBF
19TH CENTUR   ...GION

Volume 9

CHARLES HADDON SPURGEON

CHARLES HADDON SPURGEON
A Preacher's Progress

PATRICIA STALLINGS KRUPPA

Routledge
Taylor & Francis Group

LONDON AND NEW YORK

First published in 1982 by Garland Publishing, Inc.

This edition first published in 2018
by Routledge
2 Park Square, Milton Park, Abingdon, Oxon OX14 4RN

and by Routledge
711 Third Avenue, New York, NY 10017

Routledge is an imprint of the Taylor & Francis Group, an informa business

British Library Cataloguing in Publication Data
A catalogue record for this book is available from the British Library

ISBN: 978-1-138-06800-1 (Set)
ISBN: 978-1-315-10089-0 (Set) (ebk)
ISBN: 978-1-138-11880-5 (Volume 9) (hbk)
ISBN: 978-1-138-11881-2 (Volume 9) (pbk)
ISBN: 978-1-315-10119-4 (Volume 9) (ebk)

Publisher's Note
The publisher has gone to great lengths to ensure the quality of this reprint but
points out that some imperfections in the original copies may be apparent.

Disclaimer
The publisher has made every effort to trace copyright holders and would welcome
correspondence from those they have been unable to trace.

CHARLES HADDON SPURGEON ★ A Preacher's Progress

Patricia Stallings Kruppa

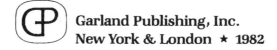
Garland Publishing, Inc.
New York & London ★ 1982

Library of Congress Cataloging in Publication Data

Kruppa, Patricia Stallings, 1936–
    Charles Haddon Spurgeon : a preacher's progress.

    (Modern British history)
    Bibliography: p.
    Includes index.
    1. Spurgeon, Charles Haddon, 1834–1892.   2. Baptists—
Clergy—Biography.   3. Clergy—England—Biography.
I. Title.   II. Series.
BX6495.S7K78   1982   286'.1'0924 [B]   81-48362
ISBN 0-8240-5158-0

All volumes in this series are printed on acid-free,
250-year-life paper.
Printed in the United States of America

TABLE OF CONTENTS

		Page
ACKNOWLEDGMENTS		i
INTRODUCTION		1
I.	THE EDUCATION OF A PREACHER	8
II.	THE PREACHING SENSATION OF LONDON . . .	67
III.	THE PASTOR OF THE TABERNACLE	147
IV.	EVANGELIST TO THE WORLD	233
V.	RITUALISM AND REGENERATION	254
VI.	A POLITICAL DISSENTER	282
VII.	DEFENDER OF THE FAITH	362
VIII.	THE DOWNGRADE CONTROVERSY	404
IX.	LAST YEARS	445
CONCLUSION		468
BIBLIOGRAPHY		481
NOTES ON ADDITIONAL BIBLIOGRAPHY		496
INDEX		500

ACKNOWLEDGMENTS

I have received a great deal of assistance in my research for this study, and I would like to express my gratitude to the librarians and scholars who have answered my questions, helped me locate materials, and shared their knowledge with me. I am particularly grateful to Opal Carlin and her staff at William Jewell College in Liberty, Missouri, who guided me through Spurgeon's library, and to the Reverend Dr. G. R. Beasley-Murray, the Principal of Spurgeon's College, London, who allowed me full access to the large collection of Spurgeon manuscripts and memorabilia housed in the College. Dr. Ernest Payne, Secretary of the Baptist Union of Great Britain, permitted me to read the unpublished text of his paper on "The Downgrade Controversy," and discussed his views of the controversy with me. My manuscript has been read in whole or part by Robert D. Cross, Nancy N. Barker, Standish Meacham, Peter Stansky, and Leslie Hume. Their comments have saved me from many errors of style and substance, and provoked me to more thoughtful analysis. My greatest debt is to R. K. Webb, who directed this study, and who gave me his time, his patient and painstaking criticisms, and the benefit of his great learning. Finally, I would like to thank the

University Research Institute of the University of Texas
at Austin for a grant which provided the funds for the
typing of this manuscript.

P. K.

March, 1981

INTRODUCTION

In 1898 an anonymous Victorian looked back over the years and reminisced, "Were not C. H. Spurgeon in his youth and W. E. Gladstone in his old age the most wonderful phenomena of the nineteenth century?" Some modern historians might consider this pairing an eccentric one, but many Victorians would have found it appropriate. In few other historical periods could the most famous politician and the greatest preacher of the age be so fittingly paired to symbolize the link between the moral and political life of the community as in Victorian England. Gladstone's great career, in youth and old age, has received the scholarly attention his remarkable accomplishments deserve, yet curiously little scholarly work has been done on the career of his contemporary, C. H. Spurgeon, although no history of the religious and intellectual life of the Victorian age can be complete which ignores his influence.

Spurgeon was the most famous preacher in an age of great preachers. He began preaching in London in 1854 when he was only nineteen, and for nearly forty years he continued to attract overflowing congregations. At the time of his death in 1892, his congregation at the Metropolitan Tabernacle in Southwark was the largest independent congregation in the world. His weekly sermons were translated into forty languages and sold an incredible total of one hundred million copies. Spurgeon was the perfect nineteenth-century embodiment of the self-made man: with no formal education beyond the secondary level he became the pastor of a large metropolitan congregation, the founder and president of a college, and director of a large complex of philanthropic institutions. Preacher, teacher, author, philanthropist, and political activist, he played a significant part in the history of Victorian England which has never been fully evaluated.

Spurgeon has not lacked biographers, though none of the biographies of him have done justice to the full range of his activities. He had barely reached his majority when the first biography of him appeared in 1857. George John Stevenson's A Sketch of the Life and Ministry of the Reverend C. H. Spurgeon, which was published in British and American editions, set the tone for most of its successors. Relying heavily upon the autobiographical

material in Spurgeon's early sermons, the work presented
the young preacher as one who had moved from infant pre-
cocity through a troubled adolescence to instant pulpit
stardom. Undaunted by the lack of source material,
Stevenson found suitable parallels in history, and compared
the young preacher to Whitefield, Luther, Washington,
Wellington, and Elijah. Stevenson's pioneering effort was
followed during Spurgeon's lifetime by a number of popular
biographies ranging in form from penny tracts to handsomely
bound gift editions. Lacking in erudition or analysis,
the majority of these early biographies combined platitude
with anecdote in an attempt to appeal to the large market
for cheap religious literature. It was perhaps with some
of these volumes in mind that Spurgeon wrote, "of all
writers, the rarest is a good biographer."

Spurgeon's death in 1892 was followed by the
publication of a number of memorial biographies as well
as the first volume of the inevitable three-volumed Life
and Works, written by Spurgeon's friend, G. Holden Pike,
the author of a previous volume on Spurgeon and the editor
of his collected Speeches. Pike's piously turgid volumes

are rich in source materials, and alone among the
biographies of Spurgeon, hint at his political activity.
In 1897 the first of four volumes of Spurgeon's posthumously
published Autobiography, edited by his wife, Susannah, and
secretary, J. L. Keyes, appeared in an elaborate presen-
tation edition. Much of the material in the Autobiography
had been published previously in Spurgeon's magazine,
Sword and Trowel, which he conceded "had all along been a
kind of biography of its editor." The Autobiography is
the indispensible starting point for any student of Spurgeon,
although every admirer of the great preacher will have to
heartily second the comment of A. C. Underwood that it is
a blessing the volumes never fell into the hands of Lytton
Strachey. Of twentieth century biographies of Spurgeon,
two occasionally rise above hagiography to analysis:
W. Y. Fullerton, C. H. Spurgeon, A Biography (1920), and
John Carlile, C. H. Spurgeon, An Interpretive Biography
(1933). Both biographers were friends and students of
Spurgeon's, and in spite of a strong personal and denominational bias, their works are valuable for the insights
they offer into Spurgeon's personal relationships. The

most recent biography of Spurgeon, Ernest Bacon's Spurgeon: Heir of the Puritans (1967), is an uncritical work based upon secondary sources written by a minister who shares Spurgeon's conservative theological outlook.

None of Spurgeon's many biographers have presented the preacher in the context of his times. There has been little attempt to analyze the basis for Spurgeon's appeal to the solid middle-class citizens who swelled his congregations and supported his philanthropies. Most of Spurgeon's biographers have been ministers, specifically, Baptist ministers. Many were trained at Spurgeon's College. It is understandable that they seek to explain his success and influence as products of his strong religious faith, and yet, inevitably such an explanation leaves the reader with the impression that Spurgeon's success, like the peace of God, passeth all understanding.

This biography of Spurgeon largely ignores the details of his home and family life which have been exhaustively chronicled in his Autobiography. Nor have I attempted to present a full account of the institutions associated with Spurgeon. This is, rather, a study of a

preacher and his audience, and of the techniques he
perfected to sustain its attention through forty years
of preaching. The purpose of this work is to examine the
Spurgeon legend and to attempt to place the man within
the framework of his times. The emphasis is upon Spurgeon
as a representative Victorian who succeeded precisely
because his values were those of the dominant middle class,
who was unique only in his ability to present those values.
Finally, this study of Spurgeon seeks to illuminate the
motives which drove him, time after time, to seek the spot-
light of controversy. Spurgeon began life as an Independent, he ended it as an independent. No ties, no unions,
no party, no organization could hold him. Spurgeon's
innovations were those of style rather than substance, and
he held essentially the same theological views at the age
of fifty that he had maintained at eighteen. He remained
an intellectual captive of the past, and in the end, he
devoted his tremendous energies and talents to sustaining
the religious convictions of another age. "When our
biographies shall come to be written at last," he said,

"God grant that they be not only our <u>sayings</u>, but our sayings and <u>doings</u>." He might not approve of the result, but I have come to admire the Reverend Mr. Spurgeon, and I have attempted in this work to do justice to his sayings <u>and</u> his doings.

C H A P T E R   I

THE EDUCATION OF A PREACHER

Charles Haddon Spurgeon was born in Kelvedon, Essex, on the nineteenth of June, 1834. He was the first child of John and Eliza Spurgeon, members of an old Essex family whose antecedents have been traced by a zealous genealogist all the way back to the Domesday Book.[1] Though the family was an ancient one, it was otherwise undistinguished. For centuries most male Spurgeons had been farmers or artisans, although there was a strong family tradition of preaching. Spurgeon's father was a bookkeeper to a coal merchant during the week, and preached to an Independent congregation at Tollesbury on Sundays. Spurgeon's grandfather, James Spurgeon, was the pastor of an Independent congregation at Stambourne for nearly forty years.

---

[1]W. Miller Higgs, The Spurgeon Family (London, 1906), p. 2.

The history of the Spurgeon family was woven into the fabric of the troubled religious history of Essex. The county history records that from the time of the Reformation, "the religious annals of Essex prove the pre-eminence of that county in determined and earnest Protestant Nonconformity."[2] As the virtual headquarters of Protestant resistance, Essex bore the brunt of the Marian persecutions. During the reign of Elizabeth I, the Protestant tradition was further strengthened by the emigration to Essex of large numbers of Dutch and Flemish exiles. Puritan rule was welcomed in Essex, where residents had a reputation for scrupulously reporting to authorities the sins of any parsons judged leaning toward "popishe doctrine." Following the Restoration and Act of Uniformity of 1662, many families, including the Spurgeons, followed their parson out of the Church of England and into Independency. The Ecclesiastical Survey of 1676 revealed that Essex contained the largest proportion of Protestant Nonconformists in England. One parish even reported

---

[2]J. C. Cox and Horace Round, "Ecclesiastical History," Victoria County History of Essex (London, 1907), II, 34.

Nonconformists in the majority; the parish was Stambourne, where one hundred and sixty years later Charles Spurgeon was to live, enveloped in the shadows of a staunchly Puritan past.[3]

Spurgeon was proud of a family tradition that some of his ancestors were among the Dutch settlers who came to England to escape Catholic persecutions. He also took great pride in the fact that one of his ancestors, Job Spurgeon, had spent fifteen months in the Chelmsford jail for attending a Nonconformist service in defiance of the law. "I would far rather be descended from one who suffered for the faith," he wrote, "than to have the blood of all the emperors in my veins."[4] Spurgeon was from childhood fascinated by stories of religious persecution and martyrdom. In his last years he came to believe that he was a "martyr for truth," and in that belief, was strengthened by the fact that he bore "the same name as

---

[3]_Ibid._, 48.

[4]C. H. Spurgeon, _A Good Start: A Book for Young Men and Women_ (London, 1898), p. 318.

that persecuted Spurgeon of two hundred years ago."[5] The
record of his family was for Spurgeon both a source of
personal inspiration and a constant reminder of the
tyranny of religious establishments.

Spurgeon was born into a rapidly changing society.
William IV sat on England's throne in 1834;
Princess Victoria was still a schoolgirl doing her lessons.
In the year of Spurgeon's birth the first reformed House
of Commons met in temporary quarters because a fire had
destroyed the Houses of Parliament. W. E. Gladstone, whose
great political career was to span the years of Spurgeon's
ministry, was attending that parliament and was amused to
see that some members still sported old-fashioned hair
styles--a pigtail in 1834 was a personal idiosyncrasy, but
symbolic, perhaps, of the resistance of many to change.
Despite the Reform Bill, politics remained largely personal,
a matter of factions and old loyalties. When Spurgeon was
one month old, Lord Grey retired, leaving the leadership

[5]C. H. Spurgeon's Autobiography, compiled from his
diary, letters, and records, by his wife and private secretary, 4 Vols. (London, 1897-1900), I, 8. Hereafter cited
as Autobiography.

to be disputed between Melbourne and Peel. Reform, spurred on by the news of revolution abroad and the threat of revolution at home, was reluctantly accepted by the politicians of both parties; in 1835, Peel pledged in his Tamworth Manifesto that his party would abide by the spirit of the Reform Bill of 1832. In the year before Spurgeon's birth, slavery was abolished in the British Empire and the first effective Factory Act was passed; in 1834 the New Poor Law was adopted; in 1835 the Municipal Corporations Act became law. In 1834 Malthus and Coleridge died; Bentham had been dead for two years. On the day that Spurgeon was born, halfway across the world Macaulay crossed the Mysore; and across the Atlantic President Andrew Jackson brooded over "the monster" Bank and a recent censure voted by the United States Senate. Edward Irving, the popular London preacher whose career in so many ways paralleled Spurgeon's, died that year, as did William Carey, the famous Baptist missionary. The Oxford movement was making important converts, causing many to question the historical foundations of the Church of England, while German scholarship was beginning to cause some to question the scriptural foundations of traditional Christianity.

When Spurgeon was born, a young tutor at the University of Tübingen, David Strauss, was putting the final touches upon his _Life of Jesus_. The year 1834 was one of innovation and transition. Poised on the edge of an industrial expansion that was to revolutionize English society and revitalize the British Empire, the nation still clung to many of the old ways and retained much of the flavor of the eighteenth century.

It is unlikely that much news of the changing world penetrated rural Essex. Spurgeon's boyhood was spent in a society barely touched by the currents of contemporary life. Shortly after his birth, his parents moved from Kelvedon to Colchester. A second child soon followed. The Spurgeons were to have seventeen children, although only eight survived infancy. It was probably the pressure of supporting a growing family which led Spurgeon's parents to decide to send their son to live for a while with his paternal grandparents. He was a year old when he came to live in the village of Stambourne. For the next five years he lived with his grandparents and their spinster daughter, Anne. Thus, his crucial formative years were spent away from his parents and in the company of older

guardians in the quiet setting of a rural parsonage.

Spurgeon's grandfather preached to an Independent

congregation which had been founded following the passage

of the Act of Uniformity of 1662. Henry Havers, the rector

of Stambourne in that year, was one of the more than 1,700

clergymen forced out of the Church of England.[8] Most of his

congregation followed him, and he lived to supervise the

building of a large Independent Meeting House and Manse.

Havers, a former chaplain to the Earl of Warwick, had been

educated at Cambridge, and had accumulated a large library

of theological works which he willed to his successors.

Charles Spurgeon's grandfather was one of those successors,

and Haver's old Puritan editions were the boy's first

textbooks.

The old Meeting House and Manse stood in the center

of the village, and although some of its elegance had faded

with the years, it remained one of the most imposing

---

[8]A. G. Matthews, Calamy Revisited, Being a Revision of Edmund's Calamy's Account of the Ministers and Others Ejected and Silenced, 1660-1662 (Oxford, 1934), p. 252.

buildings in the community. Stambourne had a population of only about five hundred people, who lived in fewer than one hundred cottages. It was an agricultural village, without industry or manufacture of any kind. The Industrial Revolution bypassed the village, and even a forlorn attempt to start a straw-plaiting industry failed. The town had two public houses, but no post office, doctor, chemist, or policeman. Even at the end of the nineteenth century, there was no railroad station in Stambourne. Spurgeon later recalled hearing the natives talking of "the Shires" as if they were foreign parts, and describing anyone who ventured down into "the Hundreds" as an explorer "of a hardier sort." Although Spurgeon's grandfather lived until 1864, Spurgeon was never able to persuade him to visit London. London was indeed remote from this agricultural hamlet, where life went on much as it had done for two hundred years.

It is perhaps inevitable that adults tend to idealize their childhood, forgetting its anxieties and recalling only its protected pleasures. Certainly for Spurgeon, this small village in Essex remained very precious, and in the last month of his life, he felt compelled to make one last pilgrimage to Stambourne. He had preached his last sermon; his body was racked by an incurable disease and his mind tortured by the theological controversy that plagued his last years, and he came to Stambourne seeking to recapture, however briefly, the peace and security of his childhood. The result of his journey was a book, Memories of Stambourne.[7] It was his last book and his last journey to the countryside he loved so well.

Spurgeon found fame and honor in London, but he never shed his countryman's instinctive fear of cities, and he regretted that he had lived to see much of the countryside "sucked into the vortex of London." He viewed the inevitable march of industrialism as a threat to the countryside, and believed that with the passing of the countryside, the character of society itself changed radically, for the destruction of rural society meant the destruction of pastoral virtues as well. Though he felt compelled to go to the city, he never adjusted to the

---

[7]C. H. Spurgeon and Benjamin Beddow, Memories of Stambourne (London, 1892), p. 38.

city's pace. He chose to live on London's fringes in a
country setting, and he left the city each winter for the
sunshine of the French Riviera. He kept to the end of
his days a rural suspicion of "that place where my fellow
creatures love to congregate, and create sewage and
influenza, coal-smoke and yellow fogs." A visit to the
countryside always seem to restore his energy and renew
his faith. But on his final journey to Stambourne he
discovered that even in that beloved setting he could no
longer find peace; another attack of illness destroyed
his holiday. The green pastures he remembered had
vanished, instead, he found them "swampy after rain, the
green lanes are knee-deep in mud, the copses have a chill
blast tearing through them . . . . All is not paradise
even in the parish of Stambourne."[8] His memory had played
tricks upon him, and his "grandfather's country" was no
more.

The Stambourne Spurgeon remembered was above all
else a peaceful place. Only an occasional cow or a stray

---

[8]Ibid., pp. 7-8.

breeze disturbed the stretches of meadowland, or the
groves of fine old trees bordering ponds he described
as being "as brown and foul as stale beer." In the quiet
meadowlands surrounding Stambourne, a person had "a sense
of being out of the world, and having nothing in particular
to do."[8] The central figure in this pastoral childhood
had been his grandfather, an old-fashioned figure in black
silk stockings, knee breeches, and buckled shoes; a man
who dreamed dreams and heard voices and who had once
encountered a devil as real as the one who tempted Luther
to chase him with an ink well. The senior Spurgeon preached
to packed congregations for nearly half a century, and long
after the grandson had made the name of Spurgeon famous,
he was to recall how many in his early congregations had
come to hear him, as one put it, because "I heard your
grandfather and I would run my shoes off my feet any day
to hear a Spurgeon."[10]

Spurgeon's grandfather was a man of importance in
the village. His social position was only slightly lower
than that of the local Anglican rector, Mr. James Hopkins.

_____

[8]Ibid., p. 16.

[10]Autobiography, I, 31.

The Rev. Mr. Hopkins was an Evangelical, and as he preached
much the same gospel as the Independent minister, the two
were close friends. The kindly Mr. Hopkins frequently
supplemented the less-well-endowed Spurgeon pantry with
gifts from his own table. Every Monday, the two ministers,
accompanied by young Charles, paid a call on the local
squire. The weekly tea was a ritual of great importance
for the boy, who never forgot how proud he felt sitting
down every week with the three most important men in the
village to the great treat of sugared bread and butter.
Fifty years later Spurgeon entertained the Archbishop of
Canterbury with an account of these weekly teas.[11]

He was a precocious child, as children who are
reared in the company of older people frequently are. His
earliest lesson was the useful one that a minister's
obligation to prepare his weekly sermons took precedence
over all other household activities. His first playthings
were books, and even before he could read he was put in a

[11]A. C. Benson, Life of Edward White Benson (London,
1899), II, 275.

chair, given a book or a copy of The Evangelical Magazine

to examine, and admonished to remain quiet and not to

disturb his grandfather. He was especially fascinated by

the vivid illustrations in Foxe's Book of Martyrs and

Bunyan's Pilgrim's Progress. "Here I first struck up

acquaintance with the martyrs, and specially with 'Old

Bonner,' who burned them; next, with Bunyan and his 'Pilgrim,'

and further on, with the great masters of Scriptural

theology, with whom no moderns are worthy to be named in

the same day."[12] It is significant that the young Spurgeon's

first books included these two which have influenced so

many generations of Englishmen. While a modern parent

might find Foxe's Book of Martyrs a strange text for a child,

the nineteenth-century parent had no doubt that it was a

suitable choice for a young reader. As E. R. Norman has

pointed out, the Victorian editions of the Book of Martyrs,

complete with graphic illustrations of the St. Bartholomew's

Day Massacre, were nearly as familiar to the Victorians as

the Bible, and served to inflame popular Protestant

----

[12]Autobiography, I, 23.

prejudices against Roman Catholics throughout the nineteenth century.[13] When one of these editions appeared in 1866, Spurgeon commended it as "the Christmas gift-book of the year," and suggested it "should be the Christmas present to his children of every father who can afford it."[14]

The boy who shuddered over "Old Bonner's" iniquities and thrilled to the heroism of the Marian martyrs grew into a man who retained to the end of his days an uncompromising suspicion of Rome. Spurgeon's anti-Catholicism was a vital ingredient in his intellectual and emotional outlook, coloring his attitudes to ecclesiology, politics, and the state Church. He was absolutely incapable of rendering an impartial judgment upon any matter involving Roman Catholicism. For him, as the journalist W. T. Stead observed, "the faggots of Smithfield always began to smoke and sputter whenever he saw a Catholic voter approach the ballot-box or an Irish parliament looming in the distance."[15] Nurtured on stories of martyrdom and opporession, it was

---

[13]E. R. Norman, AntiCatholicism in Victorian England (London, 1968), p. 1.

[14]Sword and Trowel, II (1866), 564.

[15]Review of Reviews, V (March, 1892), 180.

natural that he grew up identifying Rome with religious
tyranny. Nothing that he subsequently read or experienced
eradicated that impression.

If Bishop Bonner and the wily Jesuits were the
villains of Spurgeon's childhood world, his heroes were
found in the pages of Pilgrim's Progress, which he once
claimed to have read over one hundred times.[16] As E. P.
Thompson has written, "many thousands of youths found in
Pilgrim's Progress their first adventure story, and would
have agreed with Thomas Cooper, the Chartist, that it was
their 'book of books.' "[17] For Spurgeon, certainly, the
Pilgrim's Progress was "the book of books." He admired
Bunyan's plain and vigorous prose amd modelled his own
style upon it. The allegory of the Pilgrim captured his
imagination, and references to Christian's struggle toward
the Celestial City appear frequently in the young Spurgeon's
diary, sermons and letters. Walter Besant wrote in 1887
that the Pilgrim's Progress "seems to me the book which has

---

[16]C. H. Spurgeon, Pictures from Pilgrim's Progress
(London, 1903), p.v.

[17]E. P. Thompson, The Making of the English Working
Class (New York, 1963), p. 31.

influenced the minds of Englishmen more than any other
outside the covers of the Bible,"[18] and Spurgeon's example
would certainly seem to substantiate this judgment.

The lessons of books were supplemented in Spurgeon's
childhood experience by lengthy discussions with his grandfather on intricate theological questions. "When I was
but a child," he later recalled, "I could have discussed
many a knotty problem of controversial theology."[19] Even
allowing for the pardonable distortion of time, it is
evident that he showed an interest in theological questions
that was unusual even for a child reared in an evangelical
home. The amusements of the secular world beyond the
rural parsonage were unknown to him. His childhood was
peopled with heroes and villains from another age, his
delight was in unravelling Biblical mysteries (how far
down did the "bottomless pit" actually go, he wondered?),
and he never questioned the limitations imposed upon him.
In Spurgeon's household, novels were anathema and even
nonfiction works were not above suspicion: he was once

---

[18]Walter Besant, _Books Which Have Influenced Me_
(London, 1887), pp. 20-21.

[19]C. H. Spurgeon, _Come Ye Children_ (London, 1897),
p. 99.

punished for reading a book on Spanish bullfights.

Spurgeon's great contemporary, Joseph Parker, the

Congregationalist minister of London's City Temple, came

from a similar background. He later recalled how few

opportunities people of his class had for "worldly"

amusements:

> I sometimes wonder whether all of this early devotion
> to preaching, reading, and debating was not to be
> accounted for by the fact that there was no middle
> course open to youths of my class. Our course lay
> between God and the devil. I seriously believe that
> if I had touched a card or a box of dice there
> would have been murder under our roof . . . . Of
> course the word 'theater' simply meant the devil.
> All actors were hypocrites, all actresses harlots,
> all playhouses led to the pit of perdition. Woe to
> the boy who read a novel! This is the atmosphere
> in which I was brought up.[20]

And this was the atmosphere in which Spurgeon was brought

up; however, unlike Dr. Parker, he never questioned the

restrictions of his youth, but accepted them as the right-

ful guideposts for adulthood as well.

To envision Spurgeon's childhood as one of

unrelenting Sabbatarian piety and hard work would be an

---

[20]Joseph Parker, Autobiography (London, 1899),
pp. 68-69.

error. He was not, like Edmund Gosse, a forced and
unwholesome hothouse flower; nor was he, like John Stuart Mill,
driven by an unreasonable tutor. Though many "worldly"
amusements were forbidden to him, it is unlikely that he
missed the sweets he never tasted, and his childhood was
compensated for its lack of frivolity by its great security.
As the only child in an adult household, Spurgeon was certainly spoiled by his doting grandparents and aunt. In
recalling his childhood, Spurgeon stressed the pleasure of
walking and talking with his grandfather, the delicious
thrill of having his questions and opinions listened to
and discussed seriously, and the frequent treat of animal-
shaped pastries, especially baked for "the child" by his
grandmother and Aunt Anne. If, in common with most children
reared by preachers, he was expected to memorize Bible
verses and hymns, he was petted and rewarded for doing so.
His grandmother paid him a penny for every hymn by Watts
that he learned, a profitable pastime until his grandfather
offered him a shilling for every rat that he killed and he
discovered that "the occupation of rat-catching paid me
better than learning hymns . . . [but] the hymns have

remained with me, while those old rats for years have passed away, and the shillings I earned by killing them have been spent long ago."[21]

Spurgeon had no companions of his own age in Stambourne. He was a secretive child who often disappeared for long stretches of time to hide in one of his favorite secret spaces--an empty tomb in the parish graveyard. His only friend outside his family circle was a neighboring farmer, Will Richardson, whose commonsense philosophy made a great impression upon the boy. Years later he was to use Richardson as a model for his popular fictional character, John Ploughman. It was inevitable that this cloistered life would tend to make him priggish. Reared exclusively in the company of adults, he aped their manners and speech. His Victorian biographers often cited with approval his juvenile peity in rebuking his elders with scripture, and lauded a youthful search through a public house in search of erring members of his grandfather's congregation. A modern biographer is more likely to find

---

[21]_Autobiography_, I, 43-44.

such conduct poisonously unctious. He was a veritable young Samuel for the first six years of his life, petted and admired by approving elders. It was probably very difficult for him to give up this role and return to his parents to be merely one more in a large brood of children.

In August 1841, Spurgeon left Stambourne for Colchester. The town of Colchester had been the capital of Roman Britain, and was something of a tourist resort. It was connected to London by rail, and was an altogether more bustling community than rural Stambourne. Spurgeon was tutored there at a local school, Stockwell House. Schoolwork was always easy for him; he was quick and bright, read rapidly, and possessed a fine verbal memory. His schoolmates later remembered that he usually led the class; apparently he did so without much effort. He had no inclination toward scholarship, but his good memory made learning easy for him, and certainly his quick-study habits greatly aided him in his later sermon-preparation.

He began preaching early in life. His father recalled that his oldest son would force his brother and sisters to be his "congregation" while he preached to them in the barn. Children tend to enact their experience in play, and in the nineteenth century, "playing church" was

common. Henry Liddon, later Canon of St. Paul's, preached

to the children in his neighborhood while wearing a sheet

of The Times as a vestment.[22] Spurgeon, never one for

vestments or ritual, was content with a haystack pulpit.

When he was eleven years old he edited a magazine for the

neighborhood, The Home Juvenile Society, which entertained

the curious with exhaustive accounts of the spiritual

progress and prayer meetings of the Spurgeon children.[23]

As one might expect, its existence was as brief as its

circulation was limited.

Biographers have a natural tendency to discover

portents of the future in the most insignificant episodes

of the past, and neither Spurgeon nor his biographers have

been immune to this weakness. Virtually every episode

of his childhood has been enshrined in his Autobiography

as a clear indication of future greatness. One particular

episode, which he emphasized as a milestone in his devel-

opment, occurred in 1844 when he was visiting his

_____

[22]Rev. Canon Scott-Holland, in DNB, s.v. Liddon,
Henry.

[23]A surviving copy of the magazine is at Spurgeon'
College, London.

grandparents during a school vacation. The Reverend Richard Knill, who was touring Essex on behalf of the London Missionary Society, conducted an appeal in Stambourne. Knill stayed with the Spurgeons and expressed great interest in the visiting grandson, who was no doubt put through all of his precocious paces. On the morning of his departure, Knill took Spurgeon upon his knee, and in the presence of the assembled family predicted, "This child will one day preach the gospel, and he will preach it to great multitudes. I am persuaded that he will preach in the chapel of Rowland Hill."[24] Then he gave the boy a sixpence and made him promise that when he preached in Rowland Hill's chapel, he would ask the congregation to sing "God Moves in a Mysterious Way." This episode of prophecy has been treated as an example of providence by virtually all who have written about Spurgeon, and no one did more to give the story a prominent place in the Spurgeon legend than Spurgeon himself, who spoke of it as a great turning point in his life, "a sort of star to my existence." The prediction came true, the boy grew up to

---

[24]Autobiography, I, 34.

preach to great multitudes, he did preach in Rowland Hill's
chapel, and true to an old promise, he asked the congregation to sing "God Moves in a Mysterious Way." The lives
of few famous men are free from similar episodes, and one
is naturally skeptical. Whatever a skeptic might think,
for Spurgeon the episode assumed all the proportions of
revelation, and he came to believe that Knill's words had
helped to bring their own fulfillment.

In 1848, Spurgeon briefly attended All Saints'
Agricultural School in Maidstone, a Church of England
school. His master, David Walker, was an uncle, a relationship which perhaps explains Spurgeon's habit of correcti
his master's errors before the class. Spurgeon was never
reluctant to correct his elders, but in this case his zeal
earned him a solitary study spot under a tree. Maidstone
was Spurgeon's first contact with young Anglicans, and the
Nonconformist boy was appalled by their ignorance of
scripture and catechism. "I am sure many of the sons of
the gentry in that establishment were more ignorant of
Scripture than the boys in some of our Ragged Schools."
It was during one of the weekly catechism sessions that he
first became disturbed over the question of infant baptism.

A visiting clergyman who was interrogating the boys asked
Spurgeon to justify his baptism, since he had been
baptized as an infant when he was incapable of meeting
the scriptural requirements of faith and repentance. He
was given a week to prepare his defense, a task he accepted
readily, confident that any sacrament practiced by both his
father and his grandfather had to be scriptural. After
diligently searching the scriptures, he was forced to concede that there seemed to be no justification for the
practice of baptizing infants. He remained unconvinced
by the clergyman's explanation that the Church provided
sponsors to speak for the infant. Spurgeon was profoundly
disturbed to discover that his father and grandfather were
acting in a way that he was now convinced was contrary to
the teachings of the scriptures, and he resolved, "that
if ever divine grace should work a change in me, I would
be baptized, since as I afterwards told my friend the
clergyman, 'I never ought to be blamed for improper
baptism, as I had nothing to do with it; the error, if any,
rested with my parents and grandparents.'"[25] He had

---

[25]Ibid., 48, 50.

become intrigued by a subject which never ceased to
interest him, and one which was to lead to his first great
public controversy over Baptismal Regeneration. Characteristically, having become convinced that infant baptism
was unscriptural, he never saw reason to question this
opinion. He was unsuccessful in converting his family to
his views, but he liked to say that the first thing he
would do when he reached heaven would be to look up all
his old friends and say, "You see, you were wrong about
all that infant-sprinkling, weren't you?"

In 1849, Spurgeon became an usher at a school in
Newmarket. The headmaster of the school, John Swindell,
was a Baptist. In return for acting as a junior instructor, Spurgeon was tutored in Greek, a fact suggesting that
his parents expected him to go on to one of the Dissenting
academies. One of his fellow-ushers kept a diary, and
recorded in it his impressions of the new instructor.
He described Spurgeon as "a clever, pleasant little
fellow . . . small and delicate, with pale but plump
face, dark brown eyes and hair, and a bright lively manner,
with a never-failing flow of conversation." After noting

that Spurgeon's knowledge of Greek, geometry, and algebra were inferior to his own, the diarist complained of the new boy's lack of interest in games. He was to recall in later years that young Spurgeon had been "rather deficient in muscle, did not care for cricket or other athletic games, and was timid of meeting cattle on the roads."[26] Spurgeon's father also expressed concern over his son's failure to take any interest in exercise or games. The fact is that Spurgeon was always physically weak. His height at maturity was 5'6", but the fact that he was so frequently described as short in his youth suggests that he was shorter than 5'6" during his adolescence. His head and chest were larger than average (one phrenologist described his head as "massive"), but he was abnormally short from knee to loin, which made if difficult for him to run.[27] His coordination was poor and he was

---

[26]The student was J. D. Everett, later professor at Queen's College, Belfast, and a Fellow of the Royal Society. His remarks are quoted in J. H. Barnes and C. E. Brown, Spurgeon, The People's Preacher (London, 1892), p. 14.

[27]W. Y. Fullerton, C. H. Spurgeon, A Biography (London, 1920), p. 185, and J. C. Carlile, C. H. Spurgeon, An Interpretive Biography (London, 1933), p. 27.

clumsy, as the number of falls he suffered during his life indicates. As a boy he feared chance encounters with cattle; as a man he feared crowds and even hesitated to cross a street alone. His only form of physical exercise was an occasional game of bowls, which he liked because it had been a favorite of the Puritans. He owned a fine pair of horses, but he rarely drove them himself, and on one occasion even had to be rescued from a runaway pair by a female acquaintance. He did try to ride from time to time, but he was forced to concede that on these occasions he felt "such intense love for Mother Earth that before long I embrace her."[28] He said his ideal horse would be quiet, safe, old, and blind. He began to suffer from kidney trouble in his early twenties, which, complicated by rheumatic gout, led finally to chronic Bright's Disease. The truly remarkable thing about Spurgeon was that in the face of chronic illness and natural weakness he managed to give an impression of enormous stamina and energy. As the Bishop of Ripon said of him, "he had what athletes would call 'staying power.'"[29]

---

[28]_Sword and Trowel_, XXII (1886), 398.

[29]_Living Age_, 193 (1892), 312.

While the other boys played cricket or took in
the Newmarket races, Spurgeon stayed at his studies. He
was set apart from his fellows, not only by physical
weakness, but also by his intense spiritual turmoil. He
had reached an age when he knew he should be experiencing
conversion, but though he searched his soul and the scriptures, he could not be assured of his own salvation. He
had been raised in a God-fearing, Bible-reading home, and
he had been taught from childhood that one day he would
experience a definite moment of conversion. Although
impartial observers would think him a singularly blameless
young man, he knew all too well that an apparently blameless life was no substitute for genuine faith and
repentance. He had been "watched with jealous eyes,
scarcely ever permitted to mingle with questionable associates, warned not to listen to anything profane or
licentious, and taught the way of God from my youth up,"[30]
yet he knew parental caution could not ensure grace. His
parents had warned him that salvation would not come from

---

[30]Autobiography, I, 67.

anything that they might do, but only from his own
experience. His mother, in a manner reminiscent of
Susannah Wesley, prayed earnestly and often for her
children. He never forgot hearing his mother pray on one
occasion, "Lord, if my children go on in their sins, it
will not be from ignorance that they perish, and my soul
must bear a swift witness against them at the day of
judgment if they lay not hold of Christ."[31] It never
occurred to Spurgeon to regard this prayer as harsh or
unusual.

All that Spurgeon had been told and all that he
read convinced him of the enormous weight of his sins and
of the implacable judgment of the law. "Was I not an
honest, upright, moral youth? Was all this nothing?
'Nothing,' said law, as it drew its sword of fire."[32] All
the Biblical promises seemed made for others, and nowhere
could he find assurance that he was among the chosen. He
was a bookish boy and he naturally turned to books looking

---

[31]Ibid., 68. Spurgeon referred to the incident in
a sermon, "Heaven and Hell," in 1855. The New Park Street
Pulpit, I, 307.

[32]Autobiography, I, 83.

for the answers to his questions, but nowhere could he
find the answers he was seeking. Though he read again
and again Bunyan's Grace Abounding, Richard Baxter's
Call to the Unconverted, and John Angell James' The Anxious
Enquirer, he found no relief for his spiritual agony.
He felt as though he was permanently mired in the Slough
of Despond. "If you would know a deep, and bitter, and
awful fear of the wrath of God, let me tell you what I
felt as a boy," he later wrote.[33] During those anxious
months his very soul seemed to be set upon "a mad voyage
into the sea of infidelity," and at one point he even
doubted his own existence--"I doubted if there were a
world; I doubted if there were such a thing as myself. I
went to the very verge of the dreary sea of unbelief. I
went to the very bottom of the sea of infidelity."[34]

The history of all major religions records such
stories. There are relatively few figures in the history
of Christianity like St. Paul, who experienced the sudden,
blinding flash of awareness; far more frequent are the

[33]C. H. Spurgeon, Come Ye Children, p. 24.

[34]"The Bible," New Park Street Pulpit, I (1855),
111.

tales of soul-searching agony and indecision experienced
by Luther, Bunyan, Wesley, Whitefield, and Spurgeon. Every
man has a little Thomas in him, and for those like
Spurgeon, warned since childhood that they must undergo a
personal experience of grace, the fear and insecurity of
doubt are all the greater. Such an experience of spiritual turmoil was commonplace among those reared in evangelical circles. Spurgeon's experience had a parallel in
the spiritual struggles of his contemporary, R. W. Dale,
the Birmingham Congregationalist, who also recorded his
youthful agony and search for assurance:

> I read it [James' Anxious Enquirer] on my knees in
> keen distress about my personal salvation. Night
> after night I waited with keen impatience for the
> house to become still, that in undisturbed solitude
> I might agonize over the book that had brought so
> many to God. . . . This set me off on metaphysical
> adventures which yielded no discoveries of the kind
> I wanted. At last--how I cannot tell--all came
> clear. I ceased thinking of myself and of my faith,
> and thought only of Christ; and then I wondered that
> I should have been perplexed for a single hour.[35]

These two famous Victorian preachers came from remarkably
similar backgrounds. Both families came from Essex, both

[35]A. W. W. Dale, The Life of R. W. Dale of
Birmingham (London, 1898), pp. 16-17.

were Independents of middle-class origins, and both were precocious and bookish. Both were preaching at sixteen. When the two experienced spiritual doubts, they turned to books, and quite naturally, they read the very same books. Dale was fourteen-and-a-half when he resolved his problem; Spurgeon was fifteen. For Dale, the answer came gradually; for Spurgeon, the answer became suddenly clear during a sermon.

On the first Sunday in January 1850, Spurgeon was in Colchester during a school holiday, and started out for services at a nearby church. A snow storm came suddenly, turning him away from his original destination into a small Primitive Methodist Chapel. There were only about a dozen worshippers inside, and the boy hesitated for a minute, reluctant to join a sect that had "a reputation for singing so loudly that they made people's heads ache," but he considered the storm and decided to endure the Primitive Methodists. The preacher, "a shoemaker, a tailor, or something of that sort," preached a vivid sermon on Isaiah 45:22, "Look unto Me, and be saved, all the ends of the earth." He directed his appeal to the young stranger. "Young man, you look very miserable.

Young man, look to Jesus Christ. Look! Look! You have
nothing to do but look and live!" Something in this
simple appeal reached the tormented boy, and suddenly he
felt that he had received his answer--"the cloud was gone,
the darkness had rolled away, and at that moment I saw
the sun."[36] Spurgeon had found the answer he had been
seeking, and an unknown Primitive Methodist circuit rider
had made a notable convert.

It seems strange that the sermon of an itinerant
preacher could do for him what all the lessons of books
and the teachings of a pious home could not do. The text
from Isaiah was not new to Spurgeon. It appeared in the
pages of an essay he had written the preceding month.
There could be nothing startling in a message which his
father and grandfather had been preaching for years. Yet,
significantly, his conversion was inspired by a stranger.
In agony, he rejected his father, writing in his
Autobiography that he was "the last person I should have

---

[36]Autobiography, I, 105-118.

elected to speak to upon religion," and instead accepted

the assurances of an unknown preacher.

> I confess to have been tutored in piety, put into
> my cradle by prayerful hands, and lulled to sleep by
> songs concerning Jesus; but after having heard the
> gospel continually, with line upon line, precept upon
> precept, here much and there much, yet, when the Word
> of the Lord came to me with power, it was as new as
> if I had lived among the unvisited tribes of central
> Africa and had never heard the tidings of the cleansing
> fountain filled with blood, drawn from the Saviour's
> veins.[37]

Familiarity had dulled the gospel message for Spurgeon

until he heard the old words from the mouth of a stranger.

It is also distinctly possible that Spurgeon believed that

the true word was more likely to come from a poor and

unlettered spokesman. During Spurgeon's lifetime, many

men appeared claiming to have been the minister present on

that memorable day in his life, but Spurgeon refused to

recognize any of their claims.[38] I believe that he pre-

ferred to let the man who had converted him remain anony-

mous, one whom he could picture as "a poor, uneducated

man, a man who had never received any training for the

---

[37]Ibid., 102.

[38]See W. J. Mayer, Who Led Spurgeon to Christ?
(London, 1927).

ministry, and probably will never be heard of in this
life." Such an image would re-inforce his belief that the
true gospel light is likely to shine most brightly in a
lowly sanctuary, and that the most effective spokesmen for
the gospel are often those whose only virtue is a sincere
faith. Ironically, history repeated itself in the
experience of his own sons, both of whom were converted
by strangers.[39]

In the months immediately following his conversion,
Spurgeon vacillated between moods of ecstacy and despair.
He had lived with doubt too long to be able to banish it
readily. Two surviving records reveal the state of his
emotions during this period. One record is the letters
that he wrote to his family from Newmarket; the other is
a diary that he kept from April to June 1850. He filled
his letters home with the news of his spiritual progress
and his determination to be re-baptized as a believer.
His joy in the "celestial wonders, which now I can in a
measure behold," is tempered by his fear that through neglect or pride he might abuse the spirit. His confidence

[39]A. Cunningham Burley, Spurgeon and His Friendships (London, 1933), p. 33. See also, Sword and Trowel
XXVIII (1892), 208.

concerning "a happy place where we can get rid of sin and this depraved, corrupt nature," is undermined by his periodic falls into "the miry Slough of Despond."[40] No one who reads these schoolboy letters can doubt their sincerity, even though accounts of his spiritual condition are sandwiched between the most mundane comments on his scholarly progress and observations on family business. His momentous decision to break with family tradition and become a Baptist is immediately followed by the droll pronouncement, "You must have been terribly worried when the chimney fell down." His family was not enthusiastic about young Spurgeon's decision to become a Baptist. There is more than a suggestion that the Baptists were not quite the denomination for respectable people. "Charles," said his mother, "I often prayed the Lord to make you a Christian, but I never asked that you might become a Baptist." Was it significant that he chose to leave his family's church and to be baptized on his mother's birthday, May 3, 1850, or was it merely commendable filial behavior? He was fifteen years old. "My timidity was

---

[40]Autobiography, I, 117-118.

washed away; it floated down the river into the sea, and
must have been devoured by the fishes, for I have never
felt anything of the kind since."[41]

In spite of his assertion that baptism washed all
his fears to the sea, the diary that Spurgeon kept in the
spring and summer of 1850 indicates that he continued to
wrestle with the problems of the spirit and the flesh even
after his baptism. This diary is a curious and revealing
document. Bunyan's influence is pronounced. Spurgeon's
experiences are related in Bunyan's metaphors. Troubles
with schoolwork or spiritual difficulties are described as
periods in the Slough of Despond, or wars with the "demons
of the pit," or encounters with Giant Despair. He
describes the city of Newmarket as "a modern day Vanity
Fair," filled with traps for the unwary. He yearns to
be Valiant-for-Truth, serving his captain, Jesus.[42]
Bunyan's metaphors occasionally yield to more contemporary
ones, as Spurgeon's reference to Jesus as the "Great
Conductor." "Lord, give me strength, like the engine, to
go straight on, guided by Thee, my Great Conductor," a

[41]Ibid., 152.   [42]Ibid., 131-134.

reference proving, among other things, that Spurgeon had only a very dim idea of the workings of trains.

The diaries of most adolescents are embarrassing, and Spurgeon's is no exception. The anachronistic flavor of his writing is due, certainly, to his fondness for Puritan prose. The mawkish, frequently erotic tone of the language is familiar to anyone who knows Victorian hymnology. Nevertheless, the choice of such language raises questions in the mind of the reader. Spurgeon's lament that "my soul seems to long after the flesh-pots of Egypt," must be construed as largely rhetorical, for there is absolutely no evidence that the boy had any sexual experience during his adolescence, and one who spurned the races would hardly be likely to seek out New-market's fleshpots. Yet it is possible that one reason for the erotic imagery which pervades the diary is that Spurgeon was changing physically, and although he cer-tainly lacked any sexual experience, he does express his love for Jesus in significantly physical terms. E. P. Thomp-son has written suggestively of the "sanctified emotional onanism" of the Methodist conversion experience, and the manner in which Methodist hymnology was "by turns maternal, Oedipal, sexual and sado-machochistic."[43] Spurgeon's references to Jesus are alternately erotic and sado-machochistic. Jesus is the bridegroom, the beloved, and Spurgeon in his religious fantasies, assumes the sub-missive female role. "I would be ever with Thee, O my spotless, fairest Beloved! Daily meet me, for Thy embrace is heaven," "Desire of my heart, keep me nearer to thy bosom," "I would now come, naked, stript, exhausted, dead. I would cry, 'lash me tighter, firmer, to Thy free-grace raft of life.'" "I am utter weakness, thou must do it all." "My advocate, Brother, Husband, let not my first love chill and grow cold! Keep me and preserve me in Thy hands." "My husband folds me in his arms, I am his, and he is mine."[44] Spurgeon was fifteen years old when he wrote these words.

It was at this time that Spurgeon found a friend in an older woman, Mary King. Mrs. King was the cook-housekeeper of the school, and she became his confidante

[43]Thompson, op. cit., pp. 40, 370-371.

[44]Autobiography, I, 131, 137-141.

and spiritual tutor. The attachment reflected a pattern

of friendship Spurgeon followed throughout his life. As

a young man, he sought the company of older people; as an

older man, he seemed to prefer the company of younger

men. Mrs. King was a strict Calvinist, and she and Spur-

geon had long conversations about election, the covenant

of grace, and the perseverence of the saints. They liked

to read the Gospel Standard together and criticize the

weekly sermons. Spurgeon was later to testify that "I

learnt more from her than I should have learned from any

six doctors of divinity of the sort we have nowadays,"[45]

a comment, while exaggerated, which goes a long way toward

explaining the exasperation his theological views provoked

in his critics. He believed that he had no need to

improve upon the Calvinism he learned in the kitchen at

Newmarket. Again, as in Spurgeon's conversion at the hands

of the Primitive Methodist circuit-rider, his commitment

to the theology of the cook reflects his belief that the

true gospel often is best understood by simple minds. His

[45]Ibid., 53.

friendship with Mrs. King endured after he left Newmarket.
He continued to speak of her fondly and often, and supported her with a pension when she retired from the school.
The relationship was not remarkable in the nineteenth-
century context. Children isolated from their parents
frequently seek companions in those adults available.
Spurgeon was tutored in Calvinism by a cook; Lord Shaftesbury was converted by Maria Millis, his mother's maid.

One of the advantages of Calvinism is that if offers
the believer a comprehensive and systematic creed. Whether
Spurgeon was ever willing to follow that creed to its
logical limits is debatable. Many of his public utterances
on free grace and redemption are at odds with his insistence
that he believed in the Calvininistic doctrine of election,
but as we shall see, Spurgeon refused to admit that a
contradiction existed. He was held a captive intellectually
by the Calvinism he had learned in his youth, but emotionally he rejected the limitations Calvinism imposed
upon his evangelism early in his ministry. By the time
Spurgeon began to preach he had a set of theological views
drawn from three sources: from his grandfather he had
absorbed the teachings of seventeenth-century Independency,

lessons which provided him with an intellectual basis for
most of his convictions concerning church-state relations,
church government and ritual, and public and private
morality; from Mary King and his own reading in Puritan
texts he learned enough of the doctrine of John Calvin to
persuade himself that he was a Calvinist; and from his
searching of the scriptures he became convinced of the
scriptural validity of believer's baptism. He theology
was at times inconsistent, often oversimplified, and never
sophisticated, but it reflected the faith of home, hearth,
and heart.

The manner in which his earliest lessons continued
to shape his attitudes can be demonstrated by an essay
which Spurgeon wrote in the winter of 1850. The essay was
submitted in a national essay contest sponsored by the
well-known Morley family on the subject of the "Papal
Aggression" which had restored the diocesan hierarchy to
England in September. Spurgeon was not alone in viewing
Rome as a menace in 1850. Roman Catholics had gained the
legal right to say Mass in 1791. By 1814, over nine hundred
new chapels had been opened. The Oxford Movement brought
new blood to the Old Cause--in 1845 Newman made his

submission to Rome. Staunch Dissenter that he was, Spurgeon was alarmed and set out to document the evils of "a spirit drunk with the blood of saints."[46] The result was a lengthy essay, "Anti-Christ and Her Brood: Or Popery Unmasked," which contained seventeen documented chapters, each divided into additional topic heads, demonstrating both a formidible amount of reading in anti-Catholic literature and a vivid imagination. The essay was awarded a special cash bonus. He had the essay bound in red leather and kept it on his library shelves until the day he died, tangible evidence that the boy whose first textbook had been Foxe's Book of Martyrs had matured into a man who was not ashamed of the conclusions of his youth.

In June 1850, Spurgeon left Newmarket. A former tutor, Henry Leeding, had opened a school in Cambridge and invited Spurgeon to join him as an unpaid teaching assistant. In August, following a vacation in Colchester, Spurgeon

---

[46]The Ms. copy is the Spurgeon papers, Spurgeon's College, London. In this connection, see G. F. A. Best, "Popular Protestantism in Victorian England," in Ideas and Institutions of Victorian Britain, edited Robert Robson (New York, 1967) for an analysis of the importance of the anti-sacerdotalist element in the literature of popular Protestantism after 1829.

arrived in Cambridge. In October, he joined the local
Baptist church, and accepted an invitation to teach Sunday
School. His weekly lessons attracted some attention, and
there were some who speculated that such a talented teacher
deserved a wider audience. His own ambition was to prepare for advanced study at one of the Dissenting academies,
and the prophecy of Knill, that he would preach the gospel,
if not forgotten, did not appear to concern him. His
letters home were filled with the usual reports of scholarly progress and family gossip. He had written to an
aunt believed to be "somewhat too trusting to works," and
to an uncle whose letters revealed "a tincture of natu-
ralism or reason."[47] Fortunately for good family relations,
Spurgeon was soon able to find a wider field for his good
intentions.

Cambridge was the headquarters of a preaching association, headed by James Vinter, which provided preachers
for villages too poor or too remote to attract a regular
parson. "Bishop Vinter" heard Spurgeon lecturing to a
Sunday School class and decided to recruit him for his

---

[47]Autobiography, I, 191.

association. He realized that the boy, barely sixteen,
would hesitate to preach to a congregation of adults. In
order to get Spurgeon before a congregation, Vinter
resorted to a subterfuge. One day he approached Spurgeon
and asked him to accompany another young man to the village
of Teversham the following Sunday. The young man was
to preach there, and as he had no experience in conducting
services, he would be grateful for the moral support of
Spurgeon's company. Spurgeon readily agreed, and the
following Sunday set off for Teversham. As he walked
along talking to the other young man, it became apparent
that both had been told that the other was to be the morning's preacher. Neither wanted the assignment, but Spurgeon
was slightly less frightened at the prospect than his
companion, and after a short debate, he accepted the
responsibility.

There was no time for him to prepare a formal
sermon. "I walked along quietly, lifting up my soul to
God, and it seemed to me that I could tell a few cottagers
of the sweetness and love of Jesus, for I felt them in my
own soul." In many ways, Spurgeon's whole life had been
leading up to this moment of commitment, and if the choice

came suddenly, he was not without resources. He had listened to sermons all his life, and even in childhood had played at preaching. He had a thorough grounding in the Bible and an acquaintance with the published work of Puritan divines, and, fortunately, he had a fine verbal memory. Even as a schoolboy he could recite whole passages from sermons he had heard, as a friend from his Newmarket days recalled:

> He had a wonderful memory for passages of oratory which he admired, and used to pour forth with great gusto, in our walks, long screeds from open-air addresses of a very rousing description, which he had heard delivered at Colchester Fair by a Congregationalist minister, Mr. Davids. . . . I have heard him recite long passages from Bunyan's Grace Abounding.[48]

Spurgeon delivered his first sermon to a few farm laborers and their wives gathered together under the low-pitched roof of a thatched cottage. "How long, or how short it was, I cannot now remember. It was not half such a task as I feared it would be."[49] The cottagers were not a demanding audience, and their evident pleasure at this sermon encouraged Spurgeon to promise a return visit.

---

[48]Barnes and Brown, op. cit., p. 120.

[49]Autobiography, I, 201.

In this chance fashion Spurgeon commenced his
long preaching career. For three more years he lived in
the Cambridge area, combining the roles of scholar and
preacher. He joined the Preachers' Association and began
to travel to other villages. Word of his preaching
talent began to spread through Cambridgeshire, and people
began to speak of him as "the Boy Wonder of the Fens."
He preached in cottages, in kitchens, even in barns. He
frequently walked long distances to reach an assignment.
"I must have been a singular looking youth on wet evenings,
for I walked three, five, or even eight miles out and back
again on my preaching work; and when it rained, I dressed
myself in waterproof leggings and a mackintosh coat, and a
hat with a waterproof covering, and I carried a dark
lantern to show me the way across fields." Perhaps this
strange figure stalking across the fens frightened an
occasional farmer; Spurgeon admitted he was often frightened himself, although the ghostly apparitions he
encountered proved on closer examination to be nothing
more menacing than whitewashed trees.[50]

---

[50]Ibid., 204, 206.

In October 1851, Spurgeon agreed to accept a
preaching assignment at a small Baptist church in Waterbeach, six miles from Cambridge. The arrangement was to
be a temporary one, but in December he was pressed to stay
another six months. Waterbeach had a preacher at £45 per
year, and Spurgeon had his first congregation. In his
youth and inexperience, he regarded Waterbeach as an
extremely tough town because the usual village vices were
aggravated by the presence of "many an illicit still."
Precisely how many stills flourished in this small hamlet
is unrecorded, but Spurgeon was confident the village was
"one of the worst in England."[51] The decaying chapel he
served could barely afford even the small stipend he
received, as its membership had been steadily declining
for some years. But he looked upon the village and the
small chapel as a challenge, and he brought to the assignment all the natural enthusiasm and energy of a seventeen-
year old soul winner. After he had preached there for a
short while, he became persuaded that the character of
the village had changed, and that Waterbeach was

---

[51]Ibid., 228.

experiencing a real revival. Within a short time of his

arrival, "the little thatched chapel was crammed, the

biggest vagabonds of the village were weeping floods of

tears, and those who had been the curse of the parish

became its blessing."[52] Spurgeon's own testimony upon the

effectiveness of Spurgeon's preaching as a source of moral

regeneration is the fullest evidence on the subject which

exists. It is unlikely he underestimated the impact of

his first ministry. "I am called the 'boy preacher,' or

more commonly 'the lad,' he wrote to an aunt. "I am

eighteen tomorrow and hope Sunday to preach for the 188th

time since I started, which is about one and one-half

years ago. This is the great object of my life. I do not

want to be anything but a preacher of the gospel."[53]

Spurgeon later recalled that he had said many odd

and eccentric things during his Waterbeach days. The

sermon outlines that he preserved reveal that he had a

good sense of organization and a fondness for the expositor

---

[52]Ibid.

[53]Ms. letter to "aunt," June 18, 1852, in
Spurgeon's papers, Spurgeon's College, London.

technique favored by Puritan divines. As he grew more
experienced, the outlines grew shorter. One of the deacons
at Waterbeach, Robert Coe, described some years later
the impact that Spurgeon had made upon the congregation
in his first appearance:

> He looked so white and I thought to myself, he'll
> never be able to preach--what a boy he is! I
> despised him for his youth . . . then, when the
> hymn was over, he jumped up and began to read and
> expound the chapter about the scribes and pharisees
> and lawyers, and as he went on . . . I knew he could
> preach. All along I was fully persuaded in my own
> mind that he would not remain long at Waterbeach. I
> could see that he was something very great, and was
> evidently intended for a larger sphere.[54]

Coe's recollection had the advantage of hindsight, of
course. After Spurgeon achieved fame most of those who
had known him in his youth were sure that they had perceived his qualities of greatness years before the world.
Still, the testimony confirms the fact that Spurgeon made
a remarkable impression upon many who heard him. As he
reported to his father with transparent delight, "my
reputation in Cambridge is rather great."[55]

[54]G. Holden Pike, Seven Portraits of the Reverend
C. H. Spurgeon (London, 1879), p. 8.

[55]Letter to father, December 31, 1851, in The Letters
of C. H. Spurgeon, ed. Charles Spurgeon (London, 1923),
p. 60. Hereafter cited as Letters.

Spurgeon's popularity filled his chapel and
filled his stomach, for his stipend was frequently supplemented by dinner invitations or gifts of food. The
slight young man began to fill out. (By his first year
in London a popular ballad referred to "my plump, rosy
Spurgeon, O.") His growing reputation also brought him
a number of invitations to preach in neighboring chapels,
though his youth rarely failed to astonish the minister
who had extended the invitation: Spurgeon looked even
younger than his years--he was short and pale and had a
round, babyish face. One preacher, meeting the boy preacher
for the first time, was heard to moan, "Oh, dear! What a
pass the world is coming to when we get as preachers a
parcel of boys who have not got their mother's milk out
of their mouths!"[56] One of Spurgeon's favorite stories
concerned a venerable preacher for whom he often preached,
and who invariably announced when Spurgeon was his guest
a hymn beginning,

> Mighty God! While angels bless Thee,
> May an infant lisp thy name?

---

[56]Autobiography, I, 271-272.

When, at age forty, Spurgeon returned to preach again for
the man, he was surprised to hear him announce the same
hymn. "I thought I was a rather largish infant, and felt
I would have preferred to choose my own hymns."[57]

Spurgeon needed a great deal of patience during
his first ministry. Fellow ministers were suspicious of
his youth and ungenerous concerning his abilities. His
congregation was demanding and factious, with all the
doctrinal and social cliques which smallness breeds. At
this time, the Baptist denomination was badly split. The
Particular Baptists were Calvinists, who believed in a
particular redemption, while General Baptists believed
in free will. Many of the General Baptist congregations
were virtually Unitarian in doctrine, and, indeed, some
of the smaller General Baptist congregations survived only
through the support of the Unitarian fellowship funds.
Among the Particular Baptists, some were more particular
than others, and were known as hyper-Calvinists. The
denomination was further split between open-communion
Baptists and closed-communion Baptists. Spurgeon was a

---

[57]Ibid., 274-275.

Calvinist, but rejected hyper-Calvinism. An open-communion Baptist, he allowed the unbaptized to take communion with his congregation, but insisted upon baptism before he would admit a member into his church. He was not entirely insensitive to the charge that _his_ admission standards were higher than his Lord's.[58]

Some of the hyper-Calvinists in Spurgeon's Water-beach congregation were so confident of their election that they claimed to have reached a state of "perfection." He found their attitude distressing. "I like preaching to the vagabonds and vile people for these you can strike at," he confided to an aunt. "But the honest moral people I can never manage. They reject Jesus because they think they are good enough and do not need free grace."[59] The antinomian belief in perfection was always repugnant to Spurgeon, who once remarked that the only "perfect" saint at the Tabernacle pocketed cakes at tea-meetings. He advised his friends that when he reached perfection they

---

[58]Fullerton, _op_. _cit_., p. 290.

[59]Ms. letter to "aunt," June 18, 1852, Spurgeon Papers, Spurgeon's College.

would all know of it from reading the obituary column of
The Times.[60]

The demands of Spurgeon's Waterbeach ministry
finally grew so time-consuming that he was forced to give
up his teaching duties at Cambridge in order to devote
more of his energies to his congregation. His salary was
too small to support him adequately, and he toyed with the
idea of tutoring a few pupils privately. There was also
his own education to consider. A frequent criticism of
the Baptists was that their denomination was untrained in
comparison with other sects, and Spurgeon's parents were
anxious that their son receive a proper training for the
ministry. His father suggested that he consider continuing
his studies at a Baptist school, Stepney College, and an
interview was set up for him with the principal of the
school, Dr. Joseph Angus. The two were to meet at the
Cambridge home of Mr. Macmillan, the publisher. On
February 2, 1852, Spurgeon arrived for the interview and
was shown into a waiting room by the maid. When Dr. Angus

----

[60]A Biographical Appreciation and Sketch of
C. H. Spurgeon by One Who Knew Him Well (London, 1903),
p. 167.

arrived, the maid showed him into another waiting room, and the two sat in separate rooms, each waiting for the other to keep the appointment. Eventually both gave up and left. Neither learned of the maid's mistake until the following day, and by then an interview was impossible.

Once again, the direction of Spurgeon's life was altered by chance. The day after this parlor farce had taken place, he was walking across a Cambridge common, brooding over his disappointment, when he was startled by what "seemed a loud voice," saying, "Seekest thou great things for thyself? Seek them not." The words seemed to come from out of nowhere, and Spurgeon interpreted this strange experience as an indication that he should abandon his plans to leave his pastorate for advanced schooling. Clearly, he was convinced, this was a warning that his responsibility was to his congregation and not to his scholarly ambitions. He came to regard this strange incident, like the prophecy of Richard Knill, as a direct instance of revelation. Spurgeon came from a family with a strong streak of mysticism. Both his father and grandfather had heard "voices" they could not explain, and

accustomed as he was to their recounting their experiences,
he was not altogether surprised when he was addressed
by a similar voice. Perhaps, too, the voice told him what
he wanted to hear, and provided him with a mystical justification for a decision he had already made subconsciously,
to reject his father's plans for his future, and to keep
to the path that he had chosen. In later years he was
reluctant to describe what had occurred as miraculous, and
conceded that what seemed a voice might have been "a
singular illusion," but this was the caution of maturity.
For him, Damascus had come on a Cambridge common, and he
lived to "thank the Lord very heartily for the strange
Providence which forced my steps in another path."[61]

Spurgeon's formal education ended at the secondary
level, and he had no advanced training in theology. He
was certainly not ignorant of theology, but his knowledge
consisted almost entirely of the theology of another
age--Charnock, Owens, Calvin, Knox. His faith was not
uninformed, but it was a simple faith, steeped in the
assumptions of another century's scholarship. Many have

---

[61]Autobiography, I, 242.

speculated that Spurgeon's theological outlook would have
been broader had his formal education not ended so
abruptly. Those who feel that Spurgeon's intellectual
horizons remained frozen by his failure to seek advanced
training point out that he was the outstanding example in
his day of the successful preacher with no formal ministerial training. Although there were of course many
evangelists of little education--men like Billy Bray or
Richard Weaver, former pugilists or colliers turned
preachers--none of them achieved the audience or stature
of C. H. Spurgeon. Although American parallels occur--
notably D. L. Moody--it is virtually impossible to compare
Spurgeon to any other English preacher of his day.
R. W. Dale, like Spurgeon, was preaching at sixteen. But
Dale, unlike Spurgeon, left his first ministry to continue
his theological education. He became a more liberal
theologian than Spurgeon, but it is impossible to conclude
from the example of the Birmingham Congregationalist that
a few years in a Baptist college would have made a
modernist out of Spurgeon. Yet it is notable that even
within his denomination his example was atypical. The
greatest of his Baptist contemporaries--William Landels,

Alexander Macclaren, John Clifford, and Joseph Angus--were all men with advanced theological training. Spurgeon's great strength was his unalterable conviction that his faith was proved by the scriptures, and his uniqueness lay in his ability to present that faith to others. It is possible that formal ministerial training might have polished off some of the rough edges, and in doing so, perhaps have lessened his homely appeal. But this is speculation. Spurgeon's formal education ended when he was eighteen, and because of that circumstance or not, his theological views at fifty were essentially the views he had at eighteen.

Spurgeon had chosen to stay at Waterbeach, but he did not remain in his rural pastorate for long. He determined not "to seek great things for himself," but in rejecting ambition he was to advance it. One Sunday morning in 1853, a letter arrived extending to Spurgeon an invitation to preach at the New Park Street Chapel, London, one of the city's historic Dissenting chapels. Thinking that the letter must be intended for some other, he replied in a note outlining his youth and inexperience.

The answer from the deacons at New Park Street made it clear that he was the very Spurgeon the congregation wished to hear. On December 18, 1853, Spurgeon journeyed to London sporting his best finery, and looking, as he later admitted, "verdant green." There was only a small congregation present for the morning service, but a much larger group came to hear the evening sermon and pressed upon the young preacher an invitation to return and preach during the month of January. On January 25, the invitation was extended for another six months. The Baptists of Waterbeach had lost their pastor, and a Colchester acquaintance was incredulous--"Charlie Spurgeon has been invited to London, and they are actually going to pay him £150 a year!" What prophet has honor in his own country?

C H A P T E R I I

THE PREACHING SENSATION OF LONDON

The first seven years of Spurgeon's London
ministry were hectic, even frantic ones. Within a few
months of his arrival in the metropolis he was drawing
the largest crowds of any preacher in the city, and no
chapel seemed large enough to accommodate the throngs
anxious to hear the young preacher. He moved from chapel
to secular hall, and when even the largest secular halls
filled, he preached outdoors. His reputation spread from
London to the provinces, and he made preaching tours
throughout the country. Wherever he appeared--in London,
in Scotland, in Wales, or some provincial city--he drew
enormous crowds. It was not uncommon for him to preach as
many as three sermons a day. Hailed as a prophet, derided
as a comet, his like had not been seen in London since
the days of Edward Irving, or in the kingdom since Wesley
and Whitefield.

The period of Spurgeon's early ministry, 1854-
1861, was one of economic and political distress, and in

67

part his ministry can be seen as a response to the unease

of the times. His arrival at New Park Street coincided

with the beginning of the Crimean War and an outbreak of

cholera in London which reached epidemic proportions. In

1857, Spurgeon addressed nearly 27,000 people on the

occasion of a day of "National Humiliation" which commeno-

rated the victims of the Indian Mutiny. His Metropolitan

Tabernacle opened its doors in the month in which the

American Civil War began. While the connection between

Spurgeon's popularity and the distress of the period is

apparent, his success cannot be explained solely in terms

of the need for religious solace in times of trouble.

Spurgeon's early ministry must be viewed in terms of a

larger social and intellectual context. His ministry

was both an expression of the "Great Revival" which swept

through England in the eighteen-fifties, and an example

of what Dr. Kitson Clark has described as the "popular

romanticism" of the mid-Victorian years.[1]

---

[1]G. S. R. Kitson Clark, "The Romantic Element, 1830-1850," in Studies in Social History, ed. J. H. Plumb (London, 1955), pp. 221-223.

Spurgeon's popularity was exceptional, but his ministry was also an indication of the growth in membership of the free churches in the nineteenth century, and of the Baptists in particular. The Baptists experienced a great growth in membership and churches in the period which followed the establishment, in 1784, of the Baptist Case Committee, a central organization of the denomination which provided funds for the construction of new chapels. In 1811, there were 257 Baptist chapels in Britain. In 1812, sixty Baptist churches joined together to form the Baptist Union. The Baptist Union was a voluntary organization; independent Baptist congregations were free to join or not, and the Union had no power to force its members to accept as binding decisions reached by a majority of Union members. By 1827, the number of Baptist chapels had tripled, and by the time of the religious census of 1851, the number of Baptist chapels had reached 2,789. The census figures indicated 587,978 Baptists were attending services. When Spurgeon came to New Park Street, he found the congregation "a mere handful." At the time of his death in 1892, his congregation was the largest in Britain, and he preached to 10,000 every Sunday.[2]

---

[2]Horton Davies, Worship and Theology in Great Britain From Newman to Martineau, 1850--1900 (Princeton, 1962), pp. 71-72.

Only five members of the congregation had voted
against extending an invitation to Spurgeon. Plainly
there was a strong sentiment in the congregation for doing something about the chapel's dwindling congregation,
and Spurgeon's youth and vigor had made a very favorable
impression. Two of his famous predecessors, John Gill
and John Rippon, had also been only nineteen when called
to preach to the congregation, so Spurgeon's youth was
not a great deterrent, and may have tempted some to hope
that history would repeat itself. Spurgeon confided to
his father that many had "expressed their belief that my
originality, or even eccentricity, was the very thing to
draw a London audience."[3] It seems likely that the congregation at the New Park Street Chapel decided to gamble
on Spurgeon, hoping that his fresh manner and unconventional sermons might revive their sagging fortunes.

If so, the gamble paid off, and the congregation
did not regret the decision. In only a few weeks, Spurgeon attracted enough people to fill the once empty chapel.
"My chapel, though large, is crowded; the aisles are

---

[3] Autobiography, I, 342.

blocked up, and every niche is as full as possible," he wrote to friends in March 1854.[4] Old members returned and visitors became new members as news of the preaching prodigy spread through London. Weeks before the original probationary period of six months had expired, Spurgeon was offered permanent tenure. Something of the impact that he made when he first began to preach can be gathered from the enthusiastic comments of the playwright and actor Sheridan Knowles, who heard Spurgeon preach and described his impressions to his students in elocution at Stepney College:

> Boys, have you heard the Cambridgeshire lad? Then
> boys, go and hear him at once. His name is Charles
> Spurgeon. He is only a boy, but he is the most
> wonderful preacher in the world. He is absolutely
> perfect in his oratory; and besides that, he is a
> master in the art of acting. He has nothing to learn
> from me or anyone else. . . . I was once a lessee of
> the Drury Lane Theater; and were I still in that
> position, I would offer him a fortune to play for one
> season upon the boards of that house. . . . Mark my
> words, boys, that young man will live to be the
> greatest preacher of this or any age.[5]

---

[4] Ibid.

[5] Ibid., 354. Dr. Kitson Clark describes Knowles as "perhaps the best tragic dramatist of his day." Knowles left the stage to become a Baptist preacher and teacher. Op. cit., p. 223.

Knowles' comments on the young Spurgeon are of
great interest, for he pinpoints with an actor's peculiar
sense the quality so striking in Spurgeon's early ser-
mons--their dramatic content. As Dr. Kitson Clark has
noted, the oratory of the mid-Victorian years ought to be
compared to what was going on in the theater of the time.
People accustomed to the romantic rhetoric of the stage
enjoyed dramatic preachers, and even those strict evangelicals who never ventured inside a theater savored the
dramatic elements encountered in the respectable confines
of chapels and meeting houses. Spurgeon's sermons clearly
catered to the popular taste for melodrama. "Spurgeon,"
wrote his friend John Carlile, "was dramatic to his finger-
tips."[6] In his first years in London Spurgeon preached
as often from platforms as pulpits, and the freedom of
the platform allowed him abundant opportunities for indulging
his dramatic talents. "The most striking feature of
Mr. Spurgeon's preaching," wrote a reporter in 1856, "is
the strong dramatic element which is so prominent. . . . He
walks up and down the platform, throws himself into various

---

[6]Carlile, op. cit., p. 110.

73

attitudes, gesticulates, varies his voice, and roars,
bellows, or whines. . . . He has not the slightest hesi-
tation in putting a long speech in the mouth of the Saviour.
He does not scruple at all to report conversations between
other persons whom he introduces into his dramatic
scenes."[7] Spurgeon's early sermons are filled with
pathetic stories of homeless waifs, dying mothers,
repentant harlots, and prodigal sons. They are punctu-
ated by personal appeals to the experience of the audience.
Biblical characters appear speaking the language of the
nineteenth-century marketplace. Jacob is "a broken-
hearted old man" who had "to go all his life with his
thigh out of joint."[8] The Devil, Job, and God engage in
a debate; Spurgeon acted out all the roles. Spurgeon's
Devil was properly fiendish, his God suitably anthro-
pomorphic: "Our God [is] pre-eminently ancient. His head
and his hair are white like wool, as white as snow."[9]
Biblical episodes are vividly re-created:

[7]The Popular Preachers: The Rev. C. H. Spurgeon,
his Extraordinary 'Sayings and Doings' (London, 1856),
pp. 6-7.

[8]The New Park Street Pulpit, I (1855), 7.

[9]Ibid., II (1856), 209.

Let me take you where Moses and Aaron dwelt--to the
vast and howling wilderness. We will walk about it
for a time; sons of the weary foot, we will become
like the wandering Bedouins, we will tread the desert
for a while. There lies a carcass whitened in the sun;
there another, and there another. What means these
bleached bones? What are these bodies--there a man,
and there a woman? What are all these? How came these
corpses here? Surely some grand encampment must have
been here cut off in a single night by a blast, or by
bloodshed? Ah, no, no. These bones are the bones of
Israel, those skeletons are the old tribes of Jacob.
They could not enter because of unbelief.[10]

And here, in Spurgeon's words, Jesus before Pilate:

I will lead you into Pilate's hall, and let you see
Him endure the mockeries of cruel soldiers: the
smitings of nailed gloves; the blows of clenched
fists; the sname; the spitting; the plucking of the
hair; the cruel buffetings. Oh! Can you not picture
the King of Martyrs, stript of his garments; exposed
to the gaze of the fiend-like men? See you not the
crown about his temples, each thorn acting as a lancet
to pierce his head? Mark you not his lacerated
shoulders, the white bones starting out from the
bleeding flesh? Oh, Son of Man! I see Thee scourged
and flagellated with rods and whips, how can I
henceforward cease to remember Thee?[11]

The imagery of death, flagellation, and blood is recurrent.

Many passages in his sermons sound as though they might

have been taken from the pages of a gothic novel:

---

[10]Ibid., I, 22.   [11]Ibid., 12.

> We have a worm in the heart, a pest-house, a charnel-
> house within, lusts, vile imaginations; and strong
> evil passions, which like wells of poisonous water,
> send out continually streams of impurity. I have a
> heart, which God knoweth, I wish I could wring from
> my body and hurl to an infinite distance; a soul
> which is a cage of unclean birds, a den of loathsome
> creatures, where dragons haunt and owls do congre-
> gate, where every evil beast of evil-omen dwells.[12]

Delivering these sermons was a physical and emotional drain

upon the preacher. Spurgeon said later that in his youth,

faintness "was the usual forerunner of every sermon," and

several times he was so exhausted by his efforts that he

had to be assisted from the platform.[13]

The energy, earnestness, and eloquence of the young

preacher inspired prophecies from the very beginning. But

if many perceived qualities of greatness in Spurgeon,

others saw only a loutish and vulgar country boy. Even in

his own congregation there was an occasional complaint

about the preacher's unorthodox pulpit style. One young

visitor to the New Park Street Chapel, Miss Susannah Thomp-

son, recorded her first impressions of Spurgeon as

distinctly disappointing:

---

[12] Ibid., 10.

[13] Autobiography, II, 201.

I was not at all fascinated by the young orator's
eloquence, while his countrified manner and speech
excited more regret than reverence . . . the huge
black satin stock, the long, badly-trimmed hair, and
the blue pocket-handkerchief with white spots . . .
these attracted most of my attention, and I fear,
awakened some feelings of amusement. There was only
one sentence of the whole sermon which I carried
away with me, and that solely on account of its
quaintness, for it seemed to me an extraordinary thing
for the preacher to speak of the "living stones in the
Heavenly Temple perfectly joined together with the
vermillion cement of Christ's blood."[14]

The sentence was in character, and so was the dress

described by Miss Thompson. Spurgeon's appearance was

never his strong point. At best he looked négligé,

at worst ridiculous, and his country "best" might well have

provoked amusement in a city-bred young lady. His deacons

tactfully presented him with a dozen white handkerchiefs

and the blue-polka-dotted one which so amused Miss Thomp-

son was retired. Whatever her first impressions of

Spurgeon, Miss Thompson was to soon change her earlier

verdict, and not long after, changed her name as well--

to Spurgeon.

For a young man with very limited pastoral

experience, Spurgeon had very decided opinions on matters

---

[14]Ibid., 5.

of church government and ritual. He objected to the ceremony of ordination (commonly practiced by the Baptists as well as most other Dissenting sects), arguing that the Divine Call is the only real ordination of a minister, and any ceremony is superfluous. When his deacons, following custom, planned an ordination service, he objected strenuously, declaring that he would endure it only as a form of self-mortification. The matter was not pressed, and Spurgeon was never ordained. When he discovered that his church had deacons, but not elders, he suggested that elders be elected at once, for he was convinced that the scriptures called for both. Elders were elected. In the beginning of his ministry, he accepted the courtesy title of "reverend," but abandoned it in 1864, arguing that "reverend and sinner make a very curious combination; and as I know I am the second, I repudiate the first."[15] Henceforth he signed his correspondence simply, "C. H. Spurgeon," and was called "Pastor," a form of address also used by the graduates of his Pastors' College. R. W. Dale

---

[15]C. H. Spurgeon, Only a Prayermeeting (London, 1901), p. 35.

also rejected the title, "reverend," but he did accept

an honorary degree, and with it, the title of "doctor."

Spurgeon steadfastly rejected all donated dignity, stating

that in his opinion, D. D. frequently stood for "doubly

destitute." Virtually alone among the distinguished

clergy of his day, Spurgeon was neither reverend nor

doctor.

This same independence and aversion to formality

was reflected in Spurgeon's refusal to wear any special

clerical garments. "Except a duck in pattens," he said,

"no creature looks more stupid than a Dissenting preacher

in a gown."[16] Only once in his life did he wear full

canonicals, when he was invited to preach in Calvin's

pulpit in Geneva in 1860; and though he admitted that in

order to preach in Calvin's pulpit he would have worn the

Pope's tiara, he complained that he felt like "a man

running in a sack."[17] In his very early days in London

he dressed in a typical Dissenting preacher's costume of

---

[16]C. H. Spurgeon, John Ploughman's Talk (London, 1868), p. 27.

[17]G. Holden Pike, ed., Speeches by C. H. Spurgeon at Home and Abroad (London, 1878), p. 112.

black frock coat, white stock, and stovepipe hat.   The
photographs of Spurgeon taken during the fifties show
him in this garb, generally awkwardly posed by some
photographer determined to capture a suitable ministerial
stance.   By the 'sixties he had abandoned his parson's
attire and simply wore conservative business suits.
Except for his distinctive wide-brimmed "wideawake" hat,
he looked exactly like a prosperous shopkeeper.   At the
age of thirty-five, he grew a beard.   A beard, he declared,
was a custom both "manly and scriptural," whereas a clean-
shaven chin was "a woman's chin."   This sentiment was not
limited to Spurgeon.   Charles Kingsley shared the opinion
that there was a connection between manliness and a full
growth of hair.   Roman Catholic priests, in his view, were
"effeminate shavelings."[18]

Since much of Spurgeon's preaching in his early
days in London was done in secular buildings, he had
abundant opportunities to compare the advantages of
preaching from a platform with the limitations imposed

------

[18]R. B. Martin, The Dust of Combat, A Life of
Charles Kingsley (New York, 1960), p. 107.

upon a preacher confined in a pulpit. The box-like

proportions of the nineteenth-century pulpit drew pro-

tests from many of the great preachers of the day. Henry

Ward Beecher, in a series of lectures on preaching, warned

against "those churns called pulpits," declaring that

"they teach a man bad habits; he is heedless of posture,

and learns bad tricks behind these bulwarks."[19] As a

short man, Spurgeon often had to stand on hassocks or

stools to see over the pulpit, and endured, in conse-

quence, several humiliating spills. As he later told

his students, he could well sympathize with Sydney Smith

who fell down in the pulpit after announcing as a text,

"We are cast down but not destroyed."[20] When the

Metropolitan Tabernacle was built, it had no pulpit. The

Tabernacle was designed in such a way that Spurgeon,

standing on a platform, could be seen and heard by every-

one in the audience. In later years Spurgeon was not so

prone to roam across the platform as he preached. Gout

---

[19]Henry Ward Beecher, Yale Lectures on Preaching
(New York, 1872), I, 136.

[20]C. H. Spurgeon, Lectures to My Students, 3 vols.
(London, 1875, 1893, 1894), II, 105. Hereafter cited
as Lectures.

slowed him down, and it was often necessary for him to preach with his knee resting on a chair to ease his pain.

The young Spurgeon had no such physical limitations, and his lively and dramatic sermons soon brought him more hearers than the New Park Street Chapel could comfortably accommodate. Within a few months of arriving in London he declared "the harvest is too rich for the barn." His chapel was often so crowded that people were forced to stand in the aisles. On warm Sunday nights the air in the chapel was so stifling that Spurgeon later compared it to the black hole of Calcutta. To make matters worse, the upper windows in the chapel had not been designed to open, and Spurgeon's repeated requests to the deacons to replace them were ignored. He finally resorted to more direct action, and one night smashed all the upper windows with his walking stick.

Spurgeon had a true countryman's passion for fresh air, ranking it second only to the grace of God as a preacher's best tool. Perhaps his love of fresh air and sunlight dated back to his childhood. His grandfather's house, in common with many older buildings, had many of its windows blacked out and plastered over to avoid the payment of the curious tax upon windows, and the interior, in consequence, was stuffy and dark. It may also have simply occurred to him that fresh air helps keep a congregation alert. Whatever his reasons, he believed in opening windows in chapels as well as windows in souls. He frequently declared that he preferred preaching in the open to "some horrible hole called a chapel." He had few peers at preaching in the open, and he analyzed the topic in some depth in a series of lectures on open-air preaching. He offered advice on matters ranging from choosing a good site (one free of swamps or rustling trees) to methods of conserving the voice. His mania for fresh air did have some limits, however. Preaching one day in an especially breezy chapel, his shoulder-length hair became such a problem that he was forced to interrupt his sermon with a plea to close the windows, since "I am not like Burton's beer, best on draught."[21]

At the end of Spurgeon's first year in London, his congregation voted to enlarge the chapel. A momentous

---

[21]R. H. Barnes and C. E. Brown, Spurgeon, the People's Preacher (London, 1892), p. 92.

decision was reached to lease Exeter Hall in the Strand during the period of renovations. From February 11 to May 27, 1855, Spurgeon preached at Exeter Hall. The hall had been frequently used for religious services. Since 1851, a committee of Nonconformists and Evangelical Churchmen had leased the hall each May in order to hold special services for London's churchless.[22] Spurgeon's innovation was in leasing the hall for a period of months in order to hold regular services.

Exeter Hall was ninety feet broad, one hundred and thirty eight feet long, and could hold four thousand people. It was common to sell more tickets than there were seats available, and crowds of five thousand were not unusual.[23] Other religious services held there had attracted capacity crowds, and few doubted that Spurgeon would be able to draw enough pious or merely curious people to fill the hall again. The real challenge would be to fill the hall for months, week after week. Spurgeon

---

[22]K. S. Inglis, Churches and the Working Classes in Victorian England (London, 1963), p. 64.

[23]Leonard W. Cowie, "Exeter Hall," in History Today, XVIII (June 1968, p 391).

did not conduct a single sensational meeting or revival;
he made Exeter Hall his chapel. His success dispelled
the idea that a couple of Sundays would end his novelty
and leave him with an empty building. Every Sunday
through the Spring of 1855, enormous crowds filled the
Strand, and thousands were turned away from the doors of
Exeter Hall. No other preacher in Britain could duplicate
this feat, and the young preacher's astounding success
forced the Church of England to reappraise its whole
program for attracting the poor and churchless. If this
young man, barely twenty and lacking degree or ordination, could attract vast throngs by preaching simple
gospel sermons, plainly the Church was failing to meet
its responsibilities.

The Church's response to Spurgeon's Exeter Hall
campaign can be measured by the zeal of the Evangelicals
to follow his example. The Earl of Shaftesbury proposed
that the laws which prevented the Church from holding
worship services in secular buildings should be modified,
the Archbishop of Canterbury spoke publicly of the need
to change to meet the necessities of the age, the House
of Lords debated the merits of mass services, and the

Evangelical clergy rushed to preach to gypsies and costermongers.[24] Punch observed that this must all be "very cheering; very delightful, and Mr. Spurgeon complacently rubs the hands of his soul, and his soul meekly whispers, 'I have done this.'"[25] Dr. John Campbell, the editor of the Nonconformist paper, the British Banner, summed up Spurgeon's influence when he wrote:

> There was no preaching . . . in great public edifices till Mr. Spurgeon went to Exeter Hall; but now people, both Churchmen and Dissenters, are eager to imitate him. Deans and chapters and bishops and clergy are all imitating him; and as if the great Cathedral were not enough, they actually go to Exeter Hall, nay, they rush to the very theater. All this, whether for good or ill, undoubtedly originated with C. H. Spurgeon.[26]

Soon even Exeter Hall proved too small for Spurgeon's audience. Dissatisfied with the renovations at New Park Street, Spurgeon announced plans to build a "monster" chapel that would hold his expanding congregation.

---

[24]G. S. R. Kitson Clark, The Making of Victorian England (London, 1962), pp. 187-191.

[25]Punch, XXXII (June 6, 1857), 231.

[26]G. Holden Pike, The Life and Work of Charles Haddon Spurgeon, 3 vols. (London, 1892), II, 47.

Rumors circulated that the new chapel would hold 15,000, and that Spurgeon had threatened to resign and become an itinerant evangelist if it were not built. A great subscription drive began, and Spurgeon preached all over the country to raise funds for the new building. In October, 1856, he announced that he had leased the new Music Hall in Surrey Gardens for £15 a Sunday. The Music Hall was capable of holding almost twice as many as Exeter Hall. It stood in the middle of the Surrey Gardens, an amusement park and zoo. The park was linked in the public mind with elaborate fireworks shows and with a giant tortoise that children rode about on.[27] Compared to the sedate and respectable Exeter Hall, the Surrey Gardens seemed garish indeed, and one of Spurgeon's deacons pleaded with him not to go there and preach in "the devil's house."[28]

The reservations that some had expressed privately to Spurgeon concerning the wisdom of conducting religious

---

[27]G. M. Young, ed., Early Victorian England (Oxford, 1951), p. 153. The proprietors sold the animals shortly before Spurgeon began to preach at Surrey Gardens.

[28]Autobiography, II, 199.

services at Surrey Gardens appeared valid, when, during

Spurgeon's first service there, an event occurred which

he termed "the most memorable crisis of my life." His

opening service there on October 19 had been well publi-

cized, and quite early in the evening a large crowd began

to gather at the gates of the hall. Although the hall

could hold 10,000, by most accounts fully 12,000 managed

to squeeze inside, while several thousand others crowded

the exits and entrances.[29]   The general mood of the large

congregation was not reverent, but when Spurgeon appeared

on the platform, the noise subsided. The service pro-

ceeded in the usual way, when suddenly in the middle of

the pastoral prayer which preceded the sermon, a noise

was heard in the crowd. Eye-witness accounts disagreed

on what prompted the disturbance--some heard a general

rumble, others cries of "fire," still others heard voices

crying out that the roof was falling in. The voices

seemed to come from several directions.[30]   People

panicked and struggled to get out of the building.

---

[29]The Times, October 20, 1856, reported 12-14,000
inside the Music Hall and 5-6,000 outisde the doors.

[30]Autobiography, II, 204.

Spurgeon, looking up and seeing that there was no sign of
fire or structural collapse, shouted out for the crowd to
remain in their seats and watch out for pick-pockets.
His words failed to halt the confusion, and in the
struggle and chaos, many people were trampled under foot.
A reporter for The Times wrote that the scene was one of
"indescribable agony and confusion."[31] Seven people were
killed in the stampede and a number of others injured.

Spurgeon, unaware of the casualties, attempted to
subdue the frenzied crowd by suggesting that they sing a
hymn and then file out in an orderly manner. People
seated near the front began to shout out for him to go on
and preach, and he made an attempt to do so. Scrapping his
planned sermon, he announced as a text, Proverbs 3:33,
"The curse of the Lord is in the house of the wicked."
This impromptu choice was a blunder, for many took panic
anew at this judgment and swelled the mob still fighting
in the rear. After a brief, confused address, Spurgeon
dismissed what was left of the audience and fainted. He

---

[31]The Times, October 20, 1856.

was carried out of the building by friends who kept the news of the casualties from him until the next day.[32]

The press accounts of the tragedy varied as widely as the reports of the eye-witnesses. It was never established what triggered the panic, though it was probably cries of "fire!" If the deed was the act of a group of conspirators determined to discredit Spurgeon—as he firmly believed—then who they were or how many were involved was never substantiated. A subsequent inquest ruled that the seven deaths had been accidental. The press joined in censuring Spurgeon for tempting fate by daring to preach in such an enormous hall. The Times editorialized that "there are limits to all things, even hearers," and cautioned Spurgeon to be "content with as many as the Surrey Gardens Music Hall was intended to hold sitting in comfort and with sufficient means of exit."[33] Spurgeon's attempt to carry on with his service after the crowd panicked was widely criticized, and many accounts reported that his deacons continued to pass

[32]Autobiography, II, 207.

[33]The Times, October 21, 1856.

the collection plates throughout the service. "The
deacons, with an eye to business and the new conventicle,
in the midst of agonies and fractured limbls, the death
groans and shrieks of women, and the sobs of children,
handed round the begging box," the Saturday Review assured
its readers. The staunchly conservative periodical took
a very dim view of Dissenters generally, and Spurgeon
particularly. The editors predicted that Spurgeon would
go right on and "preach another crowd into a frenzy of
terror--kill and smash a dozen or two more," in order to
pay for the proposed new chapel.[34]

Spurgeon was deeply affected by the tragedy. "I
refused to be comforted; tears were my meat by day, and
dreams my terror at night," he recalled.[35] In an excess
of romantic grief, he declared that even "the sight of
the Bible, brought from me a flood of tears, and utter
distraction of mind."[36] He maintained at first that he
would never preach again, and his friends feared for his

---

[34] Saturday Review, II (October 23, 1856), 563-564.

[35] Autobiography, II, 195.

[36] Ibid., 207.

physical and mental health. He continued to be haunted by that night of terror--the screams, the panic, the deaths--the sheer horror of the experience threatened to overwhelm him. But in spite of his grief and his remorse, he was young enough and resilient enough to recover his spirits. "I am all right now," he wrote to his mother a few weeks after the tragedy. "I am almost restored to spirits, but I shall never forget this burning furnace."[37] And although he recovered, he never did quite forget the "burning furnace."

Eighteen months after the Surrey Gardens disaster, Spurgeon preached in Halifax in a wooden building hastily constructed for his services. As the service ended and the congregation was leaving, one of the galleries collapsed and two people were injured. The following morning, the entire structure, burdened by the accumulation of the previous night's snow, caved in. Another tragedy was narrowly averted, and Spurgeon vowed that had there been a second loss of life, he would never have preached

---

[37]Letter to his mother, n.d., facsimile reproduction in Spurgeon, the Early Years (London, 1962), Figure 22.

again.[38] With these memories in mind, it was always
difficult for him to feel comfortable in the presence of
large crowds. As late as 1881 he was unnerved in the
presence of a large congregation in Portsmouth and wondered aloud if the building was structurally sound. It
is understandable that he feared crowds, for he knew how
a frenzied crowd could behave. To the end of his life he
suffered periodic attacks of acute depression brought on
by the recollection of the Surrey Gardens disaster.
"There are dungeons underneath the Castle of Despair as
dreary as the abodes of the lost, and some of us have been
in them,"[39] he confided to a friend. The friend observed,
"I learned from the mere mention of it how permanent was
the effect upon his mind of that night's awful disaster,"
and speculated that Spurgeon's early death was in part the
result of "the furnace of mental sufferings he endured on
and after that fearful night."[40] Mrs. Spurgeon wrote that

---

[38]Autobiography, II, 219.

[39]William Williams, Personal Reminiscences of
Charles Haddon Spurgeon (London, 1895), p. 166.

[40]Ibid., p. 46.

on one occasion, when they were mountain-climbing in the
Alps, a packing mule slipped and Spurgeon, startled by
the accident, collapsed in the snow. He sat there for
some time, expressionless, seemingly in shock, refusing
to move. His wife explained his strage behavior (and
suggested that it was not an isolated case) with the comment that the Surrey Gardens disaster had "injured the
delicate organism of his wonderful brain" so that "any
sudden fright, such as the swift descent of the mule down
the mountain, would have the power, for a moment or two,
to disturb its balance."[41] This may or may not have been
the correct diagnosis of his strange behavior on this
occasion. He was a man whose emotions were always very
close to the surface; he was easily moved to tears or
laughter, prone to fainting spells, and subject to periodic
bouts of depression. Referring to these "fits of
despondency," he said that "they render me very bad company," and that during these periods, "in the lone watches
of the night I sometimes find myself in such anguish that

_____

[41]Autobiography, III, 101.

I need someone near to speak to me."[42] "And as to mental
maladies," he once wrote, "is any man altogether sane?
Are we not all a little off balance?"[43] Spurgeon never
completely recovered from the emotional disturbance suffered as a result of the Surrey Gardens disaster, but he
did, somehow, find the courage to go before a crowd again,
and at the very scene of the disaster. On November 23,
Spurgeon returned to preach again at the Music Hall. He
continued to preach there until December 1859, when he
cancelled his services in protest against the decision of
the proprietors to open the amusement park on Sundays.
He returned to Exeter Hall, where his congregation held
services until the new Metropolitan Tabernacle was opened
in March 1861.

In Spurgeon's time, a preacher's most valuable
asset was his voice, because his congregation's size was
limited by his ability to be heard. Spurgeon was able to
preach to enormous crowds because he possessed one of the

[42]Ms. letter to the Rev. E. A. Chichester from
Paris, January 18, n.d. (possibly 1880), Spurgeon's College.

[43]Sword and Trowel, III (1868), 270.

great speaking voices of the age. Englishmen compared his

voice to Bright's, Americans to Beecher's or Blaine's.

Spurgeon died before the age of effective recording and a

record of his voice was never made.[44] Before the age of

recording, as Alexander Maclaren observed, a preacher had

to be content with an ephemeral reputation which died with

the last survivor who had heard him. Of those who recorded

their impressions of Spurgeon's voice, virtually all,

whether sympathetic or hostile to the preacher, testified

to the great power of his voice. In 1863, a reporter

described his voice as "beyond question, the most valuable

voice for pulpit purposes to which we have ever listened.

. . . It possesses marvelous compass, flexibility, and

power. It has to be an extent we never heard before, a

property which may be termed lashing."[45] It was, said

Joseph Parker, "the mightiest voice I ever heard--a voice

that could give orders in a tempest, and find its way across

---

[44]However, in 1905, Spurgeon's son, Thomas, whose voice was said to closely resemble his father's, made an Edison-Bell recording of one of Spurgeon's sermons. Those people who have told me that they have heard recordings of Spurgeon doubtless have this recording in mind.

[45]John Campbell, The Modern Whitefield (London, 1863), p. 8.

a torrent as across a silent aisle."[46] Although Spurgeon

had difficulty carrying a tune, his voice was musical.

"That voice! It is like a flute, like a silver bell,

like a trumpet, like an organ. The pathos in it wins you,

the roundness in it satisfies you, the music of it

enchants you, the power of it subdues you, overwhelms,

enthralls."[47] Elizabeth Haldane, recalling the Victorian

years, wrote, "For beauty and timber of voice, the finest

orator was not a politician at all, but a minister, Charles

Haddon Spurgeon."[48] "He had a glorious voice," wrote

John Morley.[49] "He had the finest voice I ever heard,"

declared H. H. Asquith, "all the resources of an accomplished

actor, and could move his hearers at will to laughter and

tears."[50]

---

[46]The Times, February 3, 1892.

[47]William Wilkinson, Modern Masters of Pulpit Discourse (New York, 1905), p. 104.

[48]Elizabeth Haldane, From One Century to Another (London, 1937), p. 104.

[49]John Morley, Recollections (New York, 1917), I, 4.

[50]The Earl of Oxford and Asquith, Memories and Reflections (London, 1928), I, 20.

Preachers today are able to speak to much larger audiences than Spurgeon ever addressed. Yet one wonders how many modern preachers could be heard easily by nearly 24,000, as Spurgeon was in the Crystal Palace, without benefit of amplification? Reform lecturers abandoned the vast Agricultural Hall because they had difficulty being heard there; Spurgeon preached there to 15,000 people. He was told that he could be heard as far away as a mile (he said he very much doubted it), and he frequently tested his voice by speaking in the open--to some 9,000 in Scotland and to 10,000 at Hackney. All the evidence supports the view that he had a truly remarkable voice, although one can doubt whether it owed much to the two precautions he took to protect it--growing a beard and drinking chili vinegar.

Like Wesley and Whitefield before him, Spurgeon attracted a great deal of attention to his ministry by preaching in unlikely places. He had a real publicist's flair for selecting unusual places to deliver a sermon. He also had quite a knack for choosing appropriate texts. Speaking at Epsom Downs, his text was, "So run that ye may obtain." Preaching once in an open field, he announced as a text, "He shall come down like rain upon mown grass, as showers that water the earth," and was probably as startled as the crowd when a violent rain storm ensued. His eye for news enlivened his sermons and enabled him to capitalize on current events. Following an explosion in a colliery in Wales, Spurgeon spoke near the spot to an enthusiastic audience that kept him preaching three sermons, one right after the other, until midnight.[51] When a tree on Clapham Common was struck by lightning, killing a man who had taken shelter under its branches, Spurgeon preached under the tree to 10,000 people and took up a collection for the widow. He preached in halls, streets, fields, even skating rinks and theaters--and before the "Great Revival" of 1859 had made such practices commonplace.

In 1855, Spurgeon began to issue weekly "penny sermons." To publicize their sale as well as his own activities, Spurgeon borrowed many techniques of mass advertising. He was not the most flamboyant figure in the history of nineteenth-century popular religion, but he introduced many methods later employed by more sensational

---

[51]Autobiography, II, 93.

figures. Years before the Salvation Army appeared on the
scene with its banjos, drums, and hallelujah lassies,
Spurgeon had showed the way advertising can gather an
audience. Like the Army preachers, he was willing to
preach anywhere, and if he had no tambourine, it was only
because he doubted it would do any good. Long before
General Booth offered to stand on his head for Jesus,
Spurgeon had made a similar suggestion to a group of
Scots: "I am not very scrupulous about the means I use
for doing good. . . . I would preach standing on my head,
if I thought I could convert your souls."[52] Before the
Salvation Army formulated the "orders and regulations"
for designing eye-catching posters, multi-colored posters
had appeared all over London advertising Spurgeon's
meetings, sermons, and views. His promotional activities
led the Sunday Times to protest against "the 'starring' of
his name in every chapel bill . . . on every available
nook about the dead walls."[53] Punch observed, "Mr. Spurgeon

---

[52]The Reverend C. H. Spurgeon, His Friends and Foes
(London, 1855), p. 4.

[53]An Apology for Spurgeon (London, n.d.), p. 6.

is becoming as familiar to the readers of posting bills on the Surrey side of the Thames as 'Tom Barry' the ex-clown at Astleys' formerly used to be,"[54] and speculated whether if "Mr. Spurgeon's name is thus bruited about much longer," there would not soon be "a race horse named Spurgeon," or advertisements that "Spurgeon will, for a certain sum or number of postage stamps, in a given time destroy a quantity of rats."[55]

It was considered highly unorthodox for a preacher to advertise his sermons and meetings. The public associated posters with the circus and the theater; preachers who borrowed the techniques of the circus were open to the charge of being sensational. When the Church of England's Young Men's Society handed out 20,000 handbills promoting a sermon by Bishop Carlile in Exeter Hall, critics accused the Church of trying to "out-Spurgeon Spurgeon." The critics were forced to concede that Spurgeon's advertising campaigns were effective. One journalist admitted that Spurgeon was a master "pamphleteer, preacher, and puffist.

---

[54] Punch, XXXI (December 6, 1856), 228.

[55] Punch, XXXI (July 19, 1856), 30.

Than he, none has higher appreciation of the efficacy of bold advertisement. He is the very BARNUM of the pulpit."[56] Certainly some of the hostility toward the use of advertising was based upon a general suspicion of the advertising business itself. A word used interchangeably with "advertising" was "puffery." An advertising man was a professional "puffist," one who would, for a given sum, make false, flattering claims. A jingle in _Punch_ suggests this feeling:

> My son, each rogue eschew
> Of the advertising pack.
> He's generally a Jew,
> Invariably a Quack.[57]

Despite the prejudice against advertising, advertising by religious bodies was in general use by the end of the century. Moody drew freely from the rhetoric of circus posters to promote his campaigns, and the Salvation Army refined the production of eye-catching posters into a fine art.[58]

---

[56]_The Universe_, August 19, 1882.

[57]_Punch_, XXXIII (December 12, 1857), 246.

[58]On the Salvation Army, see, "The Methods of the Salvation Army," _Contemporary Review_, XXXXII (August 1882), pp. 189-199. General Booth put signs advertising his meetings on umbrellas, top hats, and donkey carts.

As Spurgeon's reputation grew, the desire to know more about him became insatiable. "So intense was the desire for information respecting Mr. Spurgeon," declared an early biographer, "that whosoever would risk a few pages of biographical anecdotes, historical incidents, or doctrinal peculiarities at the price of a penny, was sure to sell the work by thousands."[59] An epidemic of badly-written biographical pamphlets appeared, comparing the young hero to Whitefield, Wellington, Washington, and Julius Caesar.[60] Stationers sold photographs of the preaching sensation and advertisements appeared in the papers offering his likeness in life-size and full color. Small plaster busts of Spurgeon competed for a place on the whatnot with flower vases shaped like Spurgeon in a pulpit. A manufacturer of stereoscopic slides offered the young preacher in a variety of suitable poses, and Spurgeon's unauthorized endorsement appeared in advertisements for items ranging from cough-syrup to lady's wear.

------

[59]George Stevenson, Sketch of the Life and Ministry of the Rev. C. H. Spurgeon (London, 1857), p. 6.

[60]See, for example, ibid.

Cartoonists found his plump face a good subject—he was drawn as "Catch 'Em Alive-O" (a popular brand of fly paper), pictured as a young lion to a Churchman's old woman, sketched as "brimstone" in opposition to another popular preacher's "treacle." The most famous of the early cartoons showed Spurgeon astride a steaming locomotive rapidly passing an Anglican parson who was poking along on a stagecoach.

Virtually the only appeal of popular religion which Spurgeon never appears to have used fully was popular hymnology. He never lost his taste for the more sedate hymns of Watts, and thought very little of most modern compositions. For a popular preacher, he had very curious ideas about what constituted suitable religious music. His musical abilities were slight, but he did not hesitate to force his musical prejudices upon his congregation. Spurgeon followed the Puritans in objecting to musical accompaniment in churches. He refused to allow an organ to be installed in the Tabernacle, even though many in his congregation wanted one. He believed that singing should be unaccompanied, so the singing was unaccompanied. Spurgeon had little interest in choirs or soloists--he could never have shared the stage with a

Sankey. After listening to one of the famous "sweet

singers" of his day he remarked to a friend that he

finally understood why Saul threw a javelin at David.[61]

When Ira Sankey's Sacred Songs and Solos swept through

Britain, Spurgeon welcomed it without enthusiasm,

observing that although Sankey's hymns might be all right

for enlivening weekly prayer meetings, they were not

suitable for Sunday services.[62] Sankey did sing at

Spurgeon's funeral; but that, of course, was one service

over which the great preacher had no control.

Popular preachers, especially when they are young

bachelors, face a multitude of temptations. The young

Spurgeon had more than his share of female admirers. It

was widely reported that he had been deluged by handmade

slippers, lovingly stitched by anonymous well-wishers.

One journal credited him with enough to start a shoe

shop.[63] Punch announced in 1856 that the time had come

---

[61]A Biographical Sketch and Appreciation of Charles
Haddon Spurgeon by One Who Knew Him Well (London, 1903),
p. 110.

[62]Sword and Trowel, XVIII (1882), 495.

[63]The Lambeth Gazette, September 1, 1855.

for "the pet of the pulpit" to be enshrined in wax at
Madame Tussaud's, though warned that "it would be necessary to surround the reverend figure by a rail; and
further to guard it by a policeman-visitor in plain
clothes," lest the preacher's image "be picked to pieces
by female worshippers. His locks would daily disappear
from his caput sacrum to be enshrined in lockets, warmed
by the pious warmth of fair idolators."[64] Spurgeon
possessed an abundant head of hair, but he was far too
sensible to pass his locks around to admiring females. He
could do nothing to prevent them from wearing his miniature, however, and he observed to his mother in 1855 that
lockets containing his miniature were being offered in
the shops for 7'6.[65]

Spurgeon, in common with all newsworthy figures,
was often slandered during his lifetime, yet even his most
vituperative critics rarely dared hint of any personal
scandal, for his private life was above reproach. Certainly one reason for the lack of scandal was his early

[64]Punch, XXXI (November 1, 1856), 179.
[65]Ms. letter to his mother, May 10, 1855,
Spurgeon's College.

marriage, which helped to insulate him from rumors.
Spurgeon's courtship and marriage have all of the quaint
charm of a Victorian valentine. Shortly after his arrival
in London he was introduced to Miss Susannah Thompson,
the only daughter of a prosperous ribbon manufacturer.
Miss Thompson's initial impressions of the young preaching
sensation were unfavorable, but she soon revised her
first judgment and became a frequent visitor at the New
Park Street Chapel. Spurgeon guided her spiritual
development until, satisfied with her Christian experience,
he baptized her. His interest in her was more than professional, but never removed from a Christian context.
His first gift to her was predictable--a copy of his own
favorite book, Pilgrim's Progress. He first revealed his
feelings for her as the two sat with friends in the stands
waiting for the ceremonies opening the Crystal Palace at
Sydenham to begin. Spurgeon, as unorthodox in courtship
as in the pulpit, announced his intentions in the middle
of a crowd under the great dome of the Crystal Palace.
That Victorian landmark became their trysting place. They
both purchased season passes and met there frequently
during the next few months, talking of their future as

they strolled through the exhibits and gardens. She was
two years older than he, small and pretty in a quiet way,
with a mass of brown curls and a singularly sweet smile.
He was a great figure in her eyes, which love blinded to
his physical faults, for he was short, plump, and care-
lessly dressed, with protruding teeth and eyes that did not
quite match. The two were married before an overflowing
congregation on January 8, 1856, and spent a brief honeymoon in Paris before the busy preacher had to return to
his duties. Mrs. Spurgeon had made "many previous visits
to that fair city," prior to their honeymoon, and now had
"the intense gratification of introducing my husband to
all of the sights and places which were worthy of arousing
his interest and admiration." Paris was then "in the
days of her luxury and prosperity; no Communistic fires
had scorched and blackened her streets, no turbulent mobs
had despoiled her temples and palaces, and laid her glories
in the dust," so that it was possible for the young
couple to go "to every place where Christian people might
go, and yet bring away with them a clear conscience."[66]

---

[66]Spurgeon, The Early Years, pp. 411-412.

In September, twin sons, Charles and Thomas, were born to

the Spurgeons, and the proud father sent the tidings to

his family in an envelope covered with the figure "2."

The constancy of the Spurgeons' affections

remained undiminished through a series of crises. Early

in the marriage, Mrs. Spurgeon became seriously ill. She

remained an invalid for the rest of her life, a victim of

what has been described as "that morbid realm of Victorian

illness which is likely to escape modern understanding

entirely."[67] Susannah Spurgeon was still another of

those remarkable Victorians who "stayed in bed," and like

---

[67]R. K. Webb, Harriet Martineau, A Radical Victorian
(London, 1960), p. 193. The exact nature of Mrs. Spurgeon's
illness remains shrouded in those twin phrases dear to the
prose of Victorian chroniclers, "delicacy forbids," and
"there are some things too sacred to discuss." She was
operated on in 1869 by Sir James Y. Simpson, a man described
by his biographer as "a religious crank," yet nonetheless
regarded as one of the founders of modern gynecology. Sir
James, who was professor of obstetrics and gynecology at
Edinburgh, normally received 1,000 quineas for an operation,
but he sent the Spurgeons no bill. He told Spurgeon he
would send the bill when Spurgeon became Archbishop of
Canterbury. The fact of this operation, the failure of the
Spurgeons to have more children, and the presence in the
Spurgeon library of a book entitled A Practical Treatise on
the Inflammation of the Uterus, the Cervix, and on its
Connections with Other Uterine Diseases--rather glaringly
out of place amid the scriptural commentaries--suggests
the nature of her problem.

many other chronic invalids she did a great deal of work
from the sanctuary of her couch. She organized a book
fund for needy ministers, aided her husband's editorial
tasks, and conducted a large correspondence.[68] Her
invalidism kept her from the scenes of her husband's
greatest triumphs, and even prevented her from accompanying him
on his vacation retreats. It was not until the last months
of his life that she was able to leave her bed and join
him at his holiday villa in Mentone, France. The burden
of her chronic illness was complicated by her husband's
increasingly frequent bouts with disease, but through
these periodic crises they maintained a very deep affection. In spite of his demanding schedule, he was never
too busy to enliven "wifey's" invalidism with amusing
letters, sketches, and acrostic postcards. (A postcard
from Pompeii bore the message, "I send tons of love to
you, hot as fresh lava.") Even her random wishes were his
commands. Did she sigh and say she wished for an opal

[68]Mrs. Spurgeon is another case for Mrs. Woodham-
Smith. See, "They Stayed in Bed," Listener, February 16,
1956. Spurgeon had a table specially designed for his wife's
use. It was designed to fit over the bed, had flaps to hold
pages, and screwed up and down to various positions.

ring and a bullfinch? He found them for her.[69] In spite
of her long illness, she survived him by ten years,
spending the years alone in a vast labor of love organ-
izing and editing his autobiography. To the end of their
lives, they were lovers; and what could be more touching
than these two old invalids, she grown plump and looking
slightly absurd wearing the girlish curls, he prematurely
tired and aged, yet writing each other love poems as though
they were still twenty and courting under the dome of
the Crystal Palace.

Spurgeon's marriage helped sustain him through
some very rugged experiences during his early years in
London. Though crowds thronged his services, public reaction to his ministry was largely hostile. As might be
expected, the most virulent attacks came from other ministers.[70] It would have taken more charity and grace than
most of them possessed to welcome an unordained country
boy who promptly drew the largest congregation in the city

---

[69]Autobiography, III, 183-185.

[70]"Scarcely a Baptist minister of standing will
own me," letter to J. S. Watts of Cambridge, April 1855,
in Autobiography, II, 101.

and who had announced plans to build the largest chapel
in the world. The first hostile notice of his ministry
came in The Earthen Vessel, a Baptist paper published by
a hyper-Calvinist splinter group. An extremely caustic
review of his sermons was signed, "Job," a pseudonym used
by the Reverend James Wells of the Surrey Tabernacle.
Wells was so incensed by Spurgeon's sermons that he even
devoted a portion of each of his Sunday services to
attacking the sermon published by Spurgeon the previous
Thursday. On one occasion he refused to preach in a pulpit
which had been lent to Spurgeon. Wells, as a strict
Calvinist, felt that Spurgeon had diluted Calvinism in
order to appeal to both "the intellectually High Calvinists
of easy virtue," and "the Low Calvinists who make him
their dear Brother."[71] It was ironic that the first attacks
upon Spurgeon were led by members of his own denomination
representing the very theological position he claimed as
his own.

Even at Waterbeach Spurgeon had been criticized
for being "too Methodistical," and "preaching too many

---

[71]Ibid., 40.

invitation sermons," and he quickly discovered that many at New Park Street inclined toward hyper-Calvinism. "The London people are rather higher in Calvinism than I am," he confided to his father, "but I have succeeded in bringing one church to my own views, and will trust, with divine guidance, to do the same for another. I am a Calvinist; I love what is called 'glorious Calvinism,' but 'hyperism' is too hot-spiced for my palate."[72] Because Spurgeon announced to the world that he was a Calvinist, he was often criticized for preaching a hard, reactionary gospel, yet the manner in which he defined Calvinism led strict Calvinists to label him an Arminian. A passage from a sermon preached by Spurgeon in 1855 makes apparent the dilution of the doctrine of election which strict Calvinists found objectionable:

> He that believeth and is baptized shall be saved, and
> he that believeth not shall be damned. Weary sinner,
> hellish sinner, thou who art the devil's castaway,
> reprobate, prolifigate, harlot, robber, thief,
> adulterer, fornicator, drunkard, swearer, Sabbath-
> breaker--list! I speak to thee as well as the rest.
> I exempt no man. God hath said there is no exemption

---

[72]Ibid., I, 342.

here. "Whosoever believeth in the name of Jesus Christ
shall be saved." Sin is no barrier. Thy guilt is no
obstacle. Whosoever--though he were as black as Satan,
though he were as filthy as a fiend--whosoever this
night believes, shall have every sin forgiven, shall
have every crime effaced, shall have every iniquity
blotted out, shall be saved in the Lord Jesus Christ,
and shall stand in heaven safe and secure.[73]

Spurgeon often said that John Calvin stood on the
shoulders of every other divine, and to the end of his
life he identified his theology as Calvinistic Christianity. His influence was frequently cited as the major
reason a large segment of the Baptist denomination remained
Calvinist in doctrine. Yet Spurgeon's definition of his
creed was at best hazy: "Calvinism is neither more nor
less than the good old gospel of the Puritans, the Martyrs,
the Apostles, and our Lord Jesus Christ."[74] This definition
put him in good company but did little to clarify his
beliefs. Pressed by critics to be more specific, he
replied, "I believe both free agency and predestination to
be facts, how they may be made to agree I do not know or
care to know; I am satisfied with anything which God

[73]The New Park Street Pulpit, I (1855), 40.

[74]Ibid., preface.

chooses to reveal to me, and equally content not to know

what He does not reveal."[75] Spurgeon refused to be

pinned down to a more specific definition of his creed

because, as modern critics have noted, he was caught in

a fundamental conflict between the theological demands of

his Calvinism, and the emotional demands of his evan-

gelism.[76] A narrow interpretation of election would ser-

iously undermine his effectiveness as a soul-winner. He

never escaped the rhetoric of Calvinism, but he managed

to extricate himself from most of Calvinism's rigors. To

a man who feared that he might not be among the elect,

Spurgeon said, "I can tell you, if you are willing to be

a Christian, you are elected,"[77] echoing a definition of

---

[75]C. H. Spurgeon, A Good Start (London, 1898),
p. 101.

[76]A. C. Underwood, A History of the English
Baptists (London, 1947), pp. 203-204, and Willis Glover,
Evangelical Nonconformists and Higher Criticism in the
Nineteenth Century (London, 1954), p. 163. I am unconvinced by Ernest Bacon's attempt in Spurgeon, Heir of the
Puritans (London, 1967), pp. 84-86, to refute Underwood's
interpretation of Spurgeons' Calvinism. My own reading of
Spurgeon's sermons substantiates Underwood's contention
that "the old Calvinistic phrases were often on Spurgeon's
lips, but the genuine Calvinistic meaning had gone out of
them."

[77]New York Watchtower, January 8, 1880, scrapbook
clipping, Spurgeon's College.

election he had announced in a sermon in 1855: "he that believes is elect."[78] He once prayed, "Lord hasten to bring in all thine elect and then elect some more," and he confessed to the Archbishop of Canterbury, "I am a very bad Calvinist. . . . I look on to the time when the elect will be all the world."[79]

Considering the equivocal nature of Spurgeon's Calvinism, it is hardly surprising that hyper-Calvinists were numbered among his persistent critics. Unfortunately, since he continued to maintain that he was a Calvinist, he was the target of the other side as well. George Eliot criticized him for preaching "a most superficial grocer's back-parlour view of Calvinistic Christianity,"[80] and Henry Ward Beecher, in a series of lectures on preaching delivered at Yale, compared Spurgeon's Calvinism to a camel's hump--an awkward and unnecessary appendage.[81]

---

[78]The New Park Street Pulpit, I (1855), 320.

[79]Benson, op. cit., II, 276.

[80]J. W. Cross, ed., George Eliot's Life (London, 1885), III, 122.

[81]Beecher, Lectures, I, 102. The analogy was an unfortunate one. Spurgeon responded with a lengthy defense of the utility of the camel's hump.

One of the ironies of the pamphlet warfare which raged about Spurgeon was that almost every attack labeling him a reactionary Calvinist was matched by one accusing him of being a rank Arminian. Perhaps in every Calvinist there is an Arminian struggling to become free; it was certainly true of Spurgeon.

The early critics of Spurgeon were as much offended by his preaching style as by his theological views. High Churchmen and ritualists were appalled by his lack of learning and his racy, colloquial manner. To them he was a vulgar ranter--an unlettered boy who dared to tell jokes in the pulpit and to pray as though he were on intimate terms with his Creator. To these critics, Spurgeon's popularity was merely confirmation of his sensationalism, and they feared that his success would bring all religion into contempt. The charges were familiar ones--they had been employed against Wesley and Whitefield, and would be warmed up again for Moody and Booth long after Spurgeon had been accepted as respectable. It was not merely the Anglican and Roman Catholic ritualists who were offended by Spurgeon's style, but conservatives of all denominations,

including his own. Many were simply opposed to all
clerical innovation on principle. Finally, Spurgeon was
criticized by free-thinking and intellectual journals for
what they believed to be his over-simplification of the
gospel. Given Spurgeon's views, attacks by atheists were
predictable enough, but not a source of real concern to
him, for he recognized that their opinions were
unrepresentative.

The first reaction of the popular press was to
dismiss Spurgeon as a nine days' wonder, a comet destined
to shoot briefly across the horizon and then to disappear
forever. Many journalists enlivened their reporting of
the popular preacher with implausible fabrications--he was
accused of preaching on Palm Sunday wearing a crown and
waving palm branches, and eyewitnesses swore that he slid
down the bannisters into his pulpit to illustrate the
dangers of backsliding. So many false stories were spread
about him that he found it impossible to refute them, and
decided early in his career to ignore most press errors
and fabrications. In general he kept to his resolution,
though he did sometimes correct a major error of fact. On
these occasions he did so in a letter to the editor of

The Times, his daily paper, or in a note to the readership
of the Sword and Trowel, a periodical he founded in 1865.
He once said that he rarely read any story in print about
himself which had a shade of truth in it, and he cautioned
that "no man's speeches or lectures should be judged by
an ordinary newspaper summary, which in any case is a mere
sketch, and in many instances a vile caricature."[82]

Spurgeon's suspicions concerning the press were
founded upon bitter experience. Few Victorian public figures were more libelled than C. H. Spurgeon. Considering
the nastiness of some of the early reviews of his ministry,
it seems surprising that he even read them, much less that
he would wish to preserve them; yet he carefully clipped
and saved all reviews, hostile or favorable. He began a
series of scrapbooks of his press clippings; he eventually
collected over fifty volumes. The first volume, which
contained largely unfavorable criticisms, he entitled,
"Facts, Fiction, and Facetiae." The scrapbooks have been
preserved at Spurgeon's College, London, and it is possible
to gather from them as well as the pages of his Autobiography

---

[82]C. H. Spurgeon, Eccentric Preachers (London,
1879), Preface.

an indication of the treatment he received in the press.
An early review in The Ipswich Express called him "a
clerical poltroon," and dismissed his ministry with the
observation that there was "enough foolishness in London
to keep up in flourishing style, Tom Thumb, Charles Kean,
the Living Skeleton, C. H. Spurgeon and many other delusions
all at once." The Essex Standard reported that "this
ranting fellow" profaned "all the most solemn mysteries
of our holy religion," and The Sheffield and Rotheram
Independent said "the Exeter Hall demagogue" had "gone
up like a rocket and ere long will come down like a stick."
The London press--with the notable exception of The Times--
was largely hostile. The Daily News accused him of "pulpit
buffoonery," and "utter ignorance of theology."[83] In
Belfast, he was termed "a rank mountebank," by the Northern
Whig,[84] and in Glasgow, a newspaper predicted that the
preacher, "like an early gooseberry or an overgrown
cucumber, will go back to the nihility from whence he
sprang."[85]

---

[83]Autobiography, II, 46, 49, 55, 60.

[84]The Times, August 28, 1859.

[85]The Popularity of the Rev. C. H. Spurgeon
(London, 1858), p. 3.

As the years passed, the personal attacks grew
fewer. Most of the papers which had criticized his youthful sermons were eventually to eulogize him. As
Mrs. Spurgeon pointed out, the paper which had once called
him "the Exeter Hall demagogue," later described him as
"this noble Puritan preacher and saintly Christian."[86] In
preaching, as in most things, nothing succeeded like
success. Even the free-thinking journals, while remaining
critical of Spurgeon's message, were forced to concede to
him the grudging respect due a worthy foe. There was one
notable holdout, however. Spurgeon's most consistently
unrelenting critics wrote for the Saturday Review, and the
"superior sarcasm" of their comments cut him very deeply.
The editorial board of the Saturday Review ranged from
ritualists to agnostics, but the periodical generally
supported the Tory party and the Established Church. It
was always contemptuous of the religion and politics of
Nonconformity. Merle Mowbray Bevington, in a study of the
Saturday Review, wrote, "The Saturday was the organ of
moderation and tolerance, of decorum and decency, and the

---

[86]Autobiography, II, 55.

unsparing critic of the bigotry, vulgarity, sensationalism, obscurantism, and puritanism of the extremists of the dominant middle class."[87] As Bevington has documented, in the period 1856-1868, the Saturday devoted nearly as much space to Spurgeon as to Gladstone and Disraeli.

The Saturday Review's editors, led by Fitzjames Stephen, took an almost fiendish delight in pinpointing the foibles of "the Anabaptist Caliban," Stephen's term for Spurgeon. The editors lamented that they lived in "the age of spirit-rapping and Mr. Spurgeon," confessing sorrowfully that a society which tolerated Spurgeon could not afford to sneer at the Dark Ages. "The crowds who flock to the various Spurgeon conventicles are only of the class who would follow the bottle conjurer, or anyone who chose to advertise that he would fly from the Monument to St. Paul's."[88] For years the editors protested that they would certainly prefer to write about something other than Spurgeon, but they apparently could not resist the

---

[87]Merle Mowbray Bevington, The Saturday Review, 1855-1868 (New York, 1941), p. 77.

[88]Saturday Review, II (October 25, 1856), 563-564.

temptation to snipe at "the comic Christianity of which the Tabernacle is the fountainhead."[89] Spurgeon's associates bitterly resented the "Satanic Review," or "Saturday Reviler," as they alternately termed the publication, and even Spurgeon was once stung to the point that he declared a man could be confident that he was in the right if he had the love of God and the hatred of the Saturday Review. The comment elicited from the Saturday editors the resigned observation, "What the Pharisees and Sadducees, Herod and Pontius Pilate were to the Savior of the World, that the Saturday Review is to Mr. C. H. Spurgeon."[90] He tried hard to turn the other cheek, but it was difficult: a note in his handwriting opposite a clipping from the Saturday entitled "Spurgeon on Shrews," reads, "God forgive the wretched man who wrote this. 'He knew not what he did.'"[91] Spurgeon and the editors of the Saturday Review were

---

[89]Saturday Review, XVIII (December 3, 1864), 690.

[90]Saturday Review, XI (March 23, 1861), 294.

[91]Scrapbook clipping, Spurgeon's College.

irreconcilable, each a representative of an important
segment of Victorian intellectual life, but separated by
a gulf which could not be breached.

The frequent jibes of the press depressed Spurgeon,
and plunged him, as he expressed it, "down in the valley."[92]
He assured his parents that the beating he was taking in
the press would not shake his faith: "I have had some
serious smashings in the papers but by God's grace I am
not scarred by all their arrows. The Lord is on my side,
whom shall I fear?"[93] He knew that every Pilgrim must
bear his cross and spend some time in the Dungeon of
Despair. He also had enough instinct about the value of
publicity to realize that even the exaggerated and critical
reports of his ministry would bring in people curious to
hear the sensational preacher. "You have, of course,
seen the Express," he wrote to his father in September 1855.
"What a capital advertisement! The enemy is more of a fool

---

[92]Autobiography, II, 19.

[93]Ms. letter to mother, May 10, 1855, Spurgeon's
College.

every day."[94] He realized that many in his audience had
come only out of curiousity, but he was willing to have
them on any terms as long as he had a chance to tell them
about the gospel. "While the whole of London is talking
of me, and thousands are unable to get near the door, the
opinion of a penny-a-liner is of little consequence,"[95]
he maintained. When at last a favorable review did appear,
he was unimpressed. "The press has _kicked_ me quite long
enough, now they are beginning to _lick_ me; but one is as
good as another so long as it helps fill a place of worship.
I believe I could secure a crowded audience at dead of
night in deep snow."[96]

Spurgeon's continued popularity was the most effective rebuttal to his critic's contention that he would
cease to draw an audience once the novelty had worn off.
Not all who came to scoff stayed to pray, certainly; George
Eliot was lured by the press reports and had her worst
suspicions confirmed:

[94]Ms. letter to father, September 24, 1855,
Spurgeon's College.

[95]_Autobiography_, II, 44.

[96]_Ibid._, 99.

My impressions fell below the worst judgment I have
ever heard passed upon him. He has the gift of a fine
voice, very flexible and various; he is admirably
fluent and clear in his language, and every now and
then his enunciation is effective. But I have never
heard any pulpit reading and speaking which, in its
level tone, was more utterly common and empty of
guiding intelligence. . . . I was shocked to find how
low the mental pitch of our society must be, judged
by the standards of this man's celebrity.[97]

Spurgeon would have replied to her verdict that he had

not been sent to edify intellectuals, but to preach the

gospel to common people. George Eliot was herself enor-

mously popular, yet Spurgeon had the surer sense of what

gospel was appropriate for a mass audience.

It is curious to reflect upon the fact that if

George Eliot found Spurgeon's preaching without a "guiding

intelligence," John Ruskin thought Spurgeon's sermons

"very wonderful,"[98] and he confided to a reporter that

"there is always in Spurgeon's sermons at least one passage

which no other man in London could have given."[99] During

_____

[97]Cross, op. cit., pp. 121-122.

[98]Joan Evans and John Howard Whitehouse, eds., The
Diaries of John Ruskin, 1848-1873 (Oxford, 1958), I, 256.

[99]The Weekly Post (Manchester), November 3, 1879,
scrapbook clipping, Spurgeon's College.

the 'fifties, Ruskin frequently attended Spurgeon's services, and visited the preacher at home as well. His admiration for Spurgeon can be measured in part by the fact that he contributed £115 to the Tabernacle building fund. Mrs. Spurgeon recorded that Ruskin called upon her husband in 1858 when the preacher was ill, and "threw himself on his knees by the patient's side, and embraced him with tender affection and tears. 'My brother, my dear brother, how grieved I am to see you thus,'" he lamented.[100] In spite of such outbursts, Ruskin did not really understand Spurgeon, and on one occasion greatly offended him by telling him he was destined for greater things than "preaching to that herd at Newington."[101]

Spurgeon's services at Exeter Hall and the Surrey Gardens attracted many people who were willing to attend a Nonconformist meeting held in a secular building, but who would have balked at going to a chapel. Lord John Russell, Lady Peel, Lord Shaftesbury, Lord Campbell, and Florence Nightingale were numbered among his audience.

---

[100]Autobiography, II, 289.

[101]Williams, op. cit., p. 69.

On one occasion over thirty members of parliament were

present, and it was rumored that only an attack of gout

had prevented Palmerston from joining them. "Hearing

Spurgeon" was a fashionable thing to do, at least once.

One who followed the fad, Charles Greville, recorded his

impressions of the preacher in his diary:

> February 8, 1857--I have just come from hearing the
> celebrated Mr. Spurgeon preach in the Music Hall of
> the Surrey Gardens. . . . He is certainly very
> remarkable, and, undeniably a fine character; not
> remarkable in person, in face, rather resembling a
> smaller Macaulay, a very clear and powerful voice,
> which was heard through the whole hall; a manner
> natural, impassioned, and without affectation or
> extravagance; wonderful fluency and command of
> language, abounding in illustration, and very often
> of a familiar kind, but without anything either
> ridiculous or irreverent. He gave me an impression
> of his earnestness and sincerity; speaking without
> books or notes, yet the discourse was evidently
> very carefully prepared.[102]

There were 9,000 people present on the day that Greville

heard Spurgeon preach in the Surrey Gardens on the text,

"Cleanse me from my Secret Sins." Among the 9,000 was

John Ruskin, who also described the sermon in his diary.[103]

---

[102]Charles C. F. Greville, Memoirs (London, 1887),
II, 83-84.

[103]Evans and Whitehouse, op. cit., I, 256.

This coincidence suggests one of the problems encountered
in attempting to analyze the social composition of Spurgeon's audience. When an articulate diarist or famous
novelist recorded their impressions of a visit to hear
Spurgeon, the evidence survives, while the impression of
an unknown visitor does not. One must be cautious in
weighing the evidence presented by the diaries and memoirs
of notable individuals lest it lead one to conclude that
Spurgeon's audiences were heavily populated with witty
and intelligent people. The opposite is more likely.
The Victorians, like their descendants, were name-droppers,
and when Ruskin, Gladstone, or Livingstone went to hear
Spurgeon, the visit was prominently featured in the press,
while the average hearer is lost in a statistic of total
attendance. And yet it is these "average" people who
accounted for the great bulk of Spurgeon's congregations
and support. Though Spurgeon attracted celebrities throughout his career, the mass of his followers were unknown and
undistinguished. He was a famous preacher, but his congregation was not a fashionable one. As an observer noticed,

"the character of mediocrity wrote itself legibly,
unmistakably over the aspect of a Tabernacle congregation."[104]

Who were the people who came in such numbers to
hear Spurgeon preach? Were they merely curious, lured by
the preacher's sensational reputation, or were they con-
ventionally pious churchgoers? How many of the people
attending a popular service came, as the Saturday Review
suggested, "to bolster their smug, self-satisfied middle
class respectability, smirkingly confident of its own
spiritual security, well up in hymns, and anxious to take
part in a ceremony which is flattering to its own vanity
and self-sufficiency."[105] Spurgeon aimed to bring the
gospel message to the unregenerate masses, but did he
really succeed? There is little evidence that he reached
many of the really desperate urban poor. His greatest
appeal was to the small shopkeeper, the clerk, the trades-
man--the solid, decent citizens of the metropolis. One
would not look in Spurgeon's congregation for the lost
dregs of London society.

[104]Wilkinson, op. cit., p. 69.

[105]Saturday Review, XXXIX (March 20, 1875), 374.

When Spurgeon arrived in London, "popular services" were already a part of the religious life of the Metropolis. The use of gaslights in churches made it possible for congregations to gather mornings and evenings, and allowed those with a taste for sermons to attend two or even three services on a single Sunday. At the time Spurgeon preached at New Park Street, the Congregationalist Thomas Binney preached at King's Weigh House, Newman Hall was at Black-friar's Road, F. D. Maurice was at the Great Portland Street Chapel, Dean Stanley was at Westminster Abbey, and Canon Liddon was at St. Paul's. Santayana once observed that oratory is a republican art, and the same enthusiasm for oratory that sustained the Chautaqua circuit in the United States filled the great public halls in Britain with audiences eager to hear religious lecturers like J. B. Gough, Samuel Booth, or Morley Punshon. Celebrated orators and famous preachers rarely had trouble securing an audience in Victorian England, and it seems fair to conclude that there were always present in any Spurgeon congregation a certain number of sermon devotees who regarded an opportunity to hear him preach as a form of recreation.

A sermon is rarely reported in today's press, and it is sometimes difficult for a modern observer to realize that in the last century, the news media devoted a great deal of attention to the activities of the major preachers of the day. Many newspapers carried in their Monday editions a full text of a notable sermon preached the preceding day. Anyone reviewing the files of nineteenth-century periodicals will be struck by the number of features concerned with the pulpit. Sermons were dissected endlessly, and the popularity of certain preachers relentlessly explored. Within these pages are some clues for determining the social composition of Victorian congregations.

A number of periodicals cited pew rents as a factor limiting the size of congregations. Since many preachers supplemented their income from pew rentals, they were understandably anxious to perpetuate the system. When Spurgeon came to the New Park Street Chapel, he was given the income from pew rents, and he volunteered to pay the cost of church maintenance from the surplus. When his congregation moved to Exeter Hall and Surrey Gardens,

tickets of admission were substituted for pew rents. The
tickets were sold at a variety of prices, with the
highest prices naturally commanding the best seats, a
fact that did not escape Spurgeon's critics. The income
from the sale of tickets was used to defray the cost of
renting the hall, with the surplus going to the Tabernacle
building fund. There were always free places, but those
wishing free admission had to wait in long lines on the
day of the service. After the Tabernacle was built, guests
could secure tickets allowing them to enter before the
general crowd was admitted. However one might justify pew
rents and admission tickets, the system obviously limited
the character of the congregation. People too poor to pay
for a ticket or lacking the time to wait in line for a
free one did not attend Spurgeon's services.

Spurgeon attempted to reach a different type of
hearer by directing the regular members of his congregation
to stay away from one evening service a month so that non-
members could attend and find seats. These "open nights"
at the Tabernacle were well-promoted and well-attended,
but even Spurgeon had to concede that he was not reaching
the audience he hoped to see. He frequently commented on

the zeal with which these "open night" crowds sang hymns, a sure indication that they were not unfamiliar with church worship. The same standard could be applied to other "mass" services. Lord Shaftesbury made a revealing note in his diary concerning one of the Church's special services in Exeter Hall in 1857: "An attendance of more than 3,000--order, decency, attention, and even devotion. They sang well and lustily, and repeated the responses to the Litany (the only part of the Liturgy used) with regularity and earnestness."[106] During one of his London campaigns D. L. Moody complained that he was tired of seeing the same faces night after night, and that it was "time for the Christians to stop coming here and crowding into the best seats."[107] It was a common problem for evangelists--who were the people they were reaching with their mass services and popular campaigns? Who were the people who read the tracts and sermons and posters? The success of the Salvation Army in the urban slums later in

[106]Edwin Hodder, The Life and Work of the Seventh Earl of Shaftesbury (London, 1892), p. 542.

[107]William Moody, D. L. Moody (New York, 1930), p. 24.

the century suggests that there were many people who had
not been reached by the mass services of the popular
preachers. Spurgeon's Tabernacle stood in one of the
poorest working-class districts in London, but his congregation came from all parts of the city. Charles Booth, in
his pioneering study of Life and Labor in London, observed
after studying the religious life of South London that
great as Spurgeon's success had been, his ministry "left
practically untouched the great mass of the population
whether poor or the working class."[108]

K. S. Inglis, in discussing the general subject of
Victorian church attendance, notes that more women than
men attended church services.[109] If so, Spurgeon's congregation is the exception proving the rule. Many observers
were struck by the fact that more men than women were seen
in most of Spurgeon's audiences. A biographer remarked in
1855 that a large proportion of Spurgeon's congregation
was male,[110] and Spurgeon was surprised himself to find

[108]Charles Booth, Life and Labor in London, series 3,
"Religious Influences in South London" (London, 1902), p. 76.

[109]Inglis, op. cit., p. 333.

[110]Edmund Fry, Life and Labors of the Reverend
C. H. Spurgeon (London, 1855), p. 311.

that "nine-tenths of my hearers are men." He felt that
one reason this might be so was that women were reluctant
to face the pressure and crush necessary to attend one of
his services. "Women cannot endure this awful pressure,
the rending of clothes, etc."[111] This explanation, if
valid for the early years of his ministry, would not
explain the reasons for the continued popularity Spurgeon
enjoyed among male hearers long after the days of crowding
into Exeter Hall or the Surrey Gardens had ended. Yet,
twenty years later, a visitor to the Tabernacle described
the congregation as predominantly male--"men of solid
sense and intelligence."[112] Others described the congregation as evenly divided, but there were few services
numbering significantly more women than men (excepting,
of course, those intended primarily for women--Bible
classes, bazaar meetings, etc.). Spurgeon was one of the
most aggressively masculine of the popular preachers, and
those looking for "treacle" had to search elsewhere. This

[111]Letters, p. 107.

[112]Andrew Steinmetz, A Chance Visitor to the
Tabernacle on Easter Sunday With the Reverend C. H. Spurgeon
(London, 1873), p. 4.

does not mean that Spurgeon failed to attract women; he obviously did, but his language, his image, and his style made his gospel as palatable to men as to women.

Spurgeon's congregations were frequently described as being middle-class bodies. While this term was often used by the Victorians, a modern historian, duly cautious of its ambiguities, is reluctant to employ it. The Saturday Review felt that Spurgeon's chief appeal was to "that Philistine of Philistines, the middle-class, prosperous, Nonconformist tradesman,"[113] while the Anglican paper, The Hornet, described Spurgeon's congregation as "in the social zone between the mechanic and the successful but not fashionable tradesman."[114] There were a few wealthy individuals in Spurgeon's congregation--William Higgs, a prosperous building contractor, and Joseph Passmore, Spurgeon's publisher--and perhaps significantly, the more prosperous members of the congregation held the most important lay posts. Spurgeon's brother, James, married

_____

[113]Saturday Review, LV (February 3, 1883), 159.

[114]The Hornet, August 14, 1878, p. 918. Scrapbook clipping, Spurgeon's College.

the daughter of Lord John Burgoyne, Constable of the
Tower, but the fact that Spurgeon mentions the Burgoynes
so often suggests that there were few other titled members
of his congregation.

Perhaps more applicable than "prosperous" is
another adjective used to describe Spurgeon's followers,
the word "respectable." The typical member of Spurgeon's
audience was "respectable"--the respectable servant, the
struggling clerk, the thrifty artisan, the small shop-
keeper--people who were not wealthy, or even "prosperous,"
yet people able to afford a tithe, a pew, and Sunday
clothes. Charles Booth wrote, "The congregation consists
of middle-class, chiefly lower-middle-class people--for
the most part comfortable, successful, Godly folk. It is
not to any considerable extent a working-class body."[115]
Consider the victims of the Surrey Gardens disaster. They
were all, according to The Times, "respectably dressed."[116]
One was described as "a respectable boy of thirteen,"

[115]Booth, op. cit., p. 82.

[116]The Times, October 19, 20, 1856.

another a twenty-six year old workman, another a maid-
servant. A couple of housewives, a boy, a maid, a working-
man--long forgotten statistics in a remote tragedy, they
tell us something about the sort of person who would
attend a popular service. For every famous person who
dropped in to hear Spurgeon, there were thousands like the
"respectable" victims of the disaster. Spurgeon was once
visiting Dr. Benson, the Archbishop of Canterbury, when
the Archbishop pointed to his butler and footman and said,
"There are two members of your congregation. . . . When
your coachman gets round to the stables he will recognize
another Tabernacle attendant."[117] Dr. Benson was not suggesting that Spurgeon's appeal was chiefly to servants,
but he was not far from the truth about the composition of
Spurgeon's congregation. For it was such people--decent,
respectable, and now forgotten--who were the real basis
for Spurgeon's popularity. They were the ones who came to
hear him in undiminishing numbers for nearly forty years.

The young Spurgeon was an extraordinarily confident
man, who projected confidence in himself, his abilities,

---

[117]Autobiography, IV, 85.

and his mission to all he came in contact with. His
self-confidence was taken by many to be egotism, and perhaps it was; but it was the innocent egotism of youth,
confident in its own powers to change the old order.
W. C. Wilkinson, who heard Spurgeon preach first when the
preacher was twenty-four, wrote that he took a "boyish
delight" in his power over an audience and in his sudden
fame, and it was only the chastening of years which led
Spurgeon to view his power as an awesome responsibility,
one he found sobering, and almost solemn. [118] From the
vantage point of maturity, Spurgeon denied the apparent
confidence of his youth:

> When I first became a pastor in London my success
> appalled me; and the thought of the career which
> seemed to open up, so far from elating me, cast me
> into the lowest depths. . . . Who was I that I should
> continue to lead such a great multitude? I would
> betake me to my village obscurity, or emigrate to
> America and find a solitary nest in the backwoods,
> where I might be sufficient for the things which
> might be demanded of me. [119]

---

[118]Wilkinson, op. cit., p. 181.

[119]Lectures, I, 173.

Escape was impossible, and it is doubtful that Spurgeon would have been able to evade the public eye even if he had indulged his romantic fancy to flee to the American backwoods. His ministry flourished in spite of the hostility of the popular press, and he learned to live with criticism, and even to welcome it as a sign of his successful witness. Over his desk hung a text his wife had framed for him "in large old English type, and enclosed in a pretty Oxford frame": Matthew 5:11, "Blessed are ye, when men shall revile you, and persecute you, and shall say all manner of evil against you falsely; for so persecuted they the prophets which were before you." When the abuse began to taper off, and his ministry attracted favorable reviews, he expressed some fear at the change. "My name is somewhat esteemed," he wrote in 1857, "but this makes me fear lest God should forsake me while the world esteems me. I would rather be despised and slandered than aught else."[120] The sojourn in the Dungeon of Despair had ended; but ahead were the temptations of Vanity Fair.

------

[120]Autobiography, IV, 85.

The secular press led the denominational press in the reassessment of Spurgeon's ministry. His success led the Globe to compare him to Whitefield, while the Morning Advertiser, edited by James Grant, a prominent Noncon- formist, became his consistent champion. The Times, which had remained aloof from the early baiting, announced, "We are delighted that there is one man in the metropolis who can get people to hear his sermons from any motive other than the fulfillment of religious obligation."[121] On March 16, 1857, The Times printed a letter to the editor from "Habitans in Sicco, Broad Phylactery," which described a visit to hear Spurgeon. The writer, evidently an edu- cated Anglican layman, wrote frequent letters to the editor on religious topics.[122] He wrote that he had gone to hear Spurgeon reluctantly, expecting the boorish ranter pilloried in the popular press. Instead he heard an articulate and sincere young man whose obvious gifts led the writer to suggest that the Church lend Spurgeon the

[121]The Times, October 21, 1856.

[122]See also his letters to The Times of March 23, 27, 1856, and December 8, 1857.

Abbey or St. Paul's.[123] The letter was widely discussed
and provoked a lively exchange of letters in The Times.
Spurgeon and his friends felt that its publication marked
the turn in the tide in the press battle against his ministry. After five years in London, Spurgeon continued to
draw enormous crowds in all weather, and the press, bowing
to his success, concluded that whatever else this young
man might be, he was no nine days' wonder.

On August 16, 1859, Spurgeon presided over a ceremony which offered tangible evidence of his determination
to remain a permanent part of the religious life of London.
On that day the foundation stone of the Metropolitan
Tabernacle was laid by Sir Samuel Morton Peto, M.P. This
personal milestone in Spurgeon's career occurred in a year
which has been often celebrated for its remarkable intellectual record. It is perhaps worth recalling that 1859
marked not only the publication of The Origin of the Species,
but was also the year in which the so-called "Great Revival"
swept through Ireland and Scotland into England, igniting

---

[123]The Times, March 16, 1857.

fires of religious enthusiasm which had not been witnessed in Britain since the days of John Wesley. Spurgeon's London ministry antedated the Great Revival by five years, and he could not be labeled a revivalist; however, it was not entirely coincidental that plans for his Tabernacle were laid in 1859, for certainly his ministry benefited from the religious enthusiasms engendered during that year. This "Second Evangelical Awakening" recalled the camp meetings of the American frontier more than the carefully managed revivals of the second half of the century. "Those who know a revival only as seen in the quiet stepping over the line of the Moody and Sankey season of grace," reminisced one preacher, "can little understand the strong, often wild emotions of the earlier time."[124] The "Great Revival of '59" spawned a host of revivalists such as Richard Weaver, a former collier, and Robert Cunningham, "the Briggate Butcher,"--both were former prizefighters and both were capable of reducing an audience to "one molten mass of humiliation" with their fervent sermons.

---

[124]Simeon McPhail, quoted in <u>Reminiscences of the Revival of '59 and the Sixties</u> (Abderdeen, 1910), p. 12.

The revival reached its greatest peak in Wales, where
groups of fishermen, "drunk with the spirit," performed
wild, trance-like dances.

Reports of revivalistic excesses offended conservatives, and even Spurgeon felt constrained to remark
in 1859, "I have at all times been peculiarly jealous and
suspicious of revivals. Whenever I see a man who is called
a revivalist, I always set him down for a cipher. I would
scorn the taking of such a title to myself."[125] In a year
of revival, Spurgeon distinguished between revivals of
religion, which he regarded as genuine outpourings of the
spirit, and the stage-managed revivals of professional
revivalists. He regarded his own ministry as the product
of a genuine revival of religion. In 1855 he spoke of
his Exeter Hall experiences as climaxing "a year of
miracles," and in a sermon the same year he said, "Unbelief
makes you sit here in times of revival and of outpourings
of God's grace, unmoved, uncalled, unsaved."[126] There was

---

[125]Sermons, Fifth Series (New York, 1859), p. 337.

[126]Spurgeon, The Early Years, p. 329, f.n.

no inconsistency for him in praising a <u>genuine revival</u>

while expressing scepticism for a professional revival-

istic "campaign." He saw himself as God's tool in a time

of genuine revival, but he denied that he was a "revival-

ist." His lectures to his students frequently warned

against the more common lapses of professional soul-

winners. He had only contempt for the statistical conver-

sions of many revivalists--"this counting of unhatched

chickens, this exhibition of doubtful spoils."[127]   "Do

not aim at sensation and effect," he warned. "Flowing

tears and streaming eyes, sobs and outcries, crowded

after-meetings and all kinds of confusions may occur, and

may be borne with as concomitants of genuine feeling;

but pray do not plan their production." "Remembering the

vagaries of certain wild revivalists," he felt compelled

to add:

> I delight not in the religion which needs or creates
> a hot head. Give me the Godliness which flourishes
> upon Calvary rather than upon Vesuvius. The utmost
> zeal for Christ is consistent with common-sense and
> reason: raving, ranting, and fanaticism are products
> of another zeal which is not according to knowledge.

---

[127]The Soul-Winner, p. 19.

> We would prepare men for the chamber of communion,
> and not for the padded room at Bedlam.[128]

It is certain that these were the reflections of maturity.

Spurgeon's early ministry was one expression of the

"Second Evangelical Awakening." If his sermons appear

sedate compared to those of some of the "hallelujah coal-

heavers" of 1859, they were not viewed as sedate by many

of Spurgeon's critics. The methods of many of the revival-

ists of 1859 were not his methods, yet he did baptize

Richard Weaver, which indicates that he was not unsympa-

thetic to Weaver's approach to the gospel. By 1861, the

revival had faded, and Spurgeon had moved into the

Tabernacle. He lasted longer than the other major figures

of the revival because he had a home base and pastoral

responsibilities. He may have toyed with the idea of

becoming an itinerant evangelist, but it was a fleeting

fancy. His followers gave him his Tabernacle, and he put

down roots. A new phase in his career had commenced.

C H A P T E R   I I I

THE PASTOR OF THE TABERNACLE

In March 1861, Spurgeon moved his flock into the
new Metropolitan Tabernacle, soon to become, in W. T. Stead's
words, "one of the pilgrim shrines of the nineteenth century, one of the unifying nerve-centers of our race."[1]
"Spurgeon's Tabernacle," as it was immediately known, was
a monument to an extraordinary personal accomplishment
and a physical symbol of the staying power of evangelical
doctrine. The Tabernacle, with its congregation of nearly
five thousand, was the base around which a complex of
educational and philanthropic institutions arose, all presided over by Spurgeon, who revealed in his new setting a
talent for painstaking administration that few would have
suspected of the preaching sensation of Exeter Hall. His
success as a preacher and an administrator was noteworthy,
but not unique in a century which celebrated the saga of

---

[1]Review of Reviews, V (February 1892), 117.

the self-made man. Spurgeon thought of himself as cast
in the Puritan mold, but he was far more a child of his
century than he realized. He succeeded in a variety of
roles--pastor, teacher, author, administrator--precisely
because he was an accurate reflection of the virtues of
his times, a man who perfectly embodied the shrewd,
pragmatic qualities of the dominant middle class.

Spurgeon's energy, determination, and vision were
responsible for the Metropolitan Tabernacle, and the
building bore the firm impression of his personality. He
personally supervised every aspect of the project. He
chose the site over the objections of his deacons, he
selected the name, he even dictated the architectural
style of the building. His innate shrewdness is certainly
revealed in his choice of a site. In spite of the reservations of many members of his congregation, he selected a
section of land in Newington Butts, Southwark, opposite a
famous old public house, The Elephant and Castle. The
area seemed unpromising; it was neither centrally located
nor in a fashionable suburb, but six major roads converged
at the spot, and Spurgeon predicted that the area would
be likely to grow rapidly. He also insisted from the

beginning that the building be erected on a freehold,
which required an act of Parliament. In the end he prevailed, and the land was purchased from the Fishmongers'
Company for ₺5,000.

Spurgeon invited architects to submit designs for
the projected new building, but stipulated in advance that
only Grecian designs would be considered. In this he
deliberately flouted the current vogue for Gothic architecture, and his chapel was built in a style which was
rapidly becoming dated. The Baptists, as Horton Davies
has pointed out, were the architectural conservatives of
the day, for by mid-century much Dissenting architecture
reflected the growing popularity of the Gothic.[2] As the
largest and most important of Baptist buildings, Spurgeon's
Tabernacle was a significant model for "Baptist classical
style," and an important influence upon architectural style
within the denomination. Spurgeon rejected Ruskin's
argument that the Gothic style was the best expression
of Christian architecture, and instead saw in the Gothic

---

[2]Horton Davies, Worship and Theology in England,
Newman to Martineau (Princeton, 1962), p. 54.

revival a return to the superstitions of the middle ages.
Greek, he argued, was the Christian tongue and the language
of the New Testament, and therefore should be "the Baptist
tongue." Latin was "Rome's mongrel tongue," and it followed from this that "every Baptist place of worship should
be Grecian--never Gothic. We owe nothing to the Goths as
religionists."[3] Spurgeon had his way, and there were no
"hobgoblins and monsters" on his church. The completed
Tabernacle resembled a Victorian Parthenon, a pristine contrast to the Elephant and Castle across the way. While
it is possible to question Spurgeon on aesthetic grounds,
time has proved him correct in his choice of a site. The
Tabernacle--"the Tab" to its neighbors--still stands on
its freehold facing one of the busiest intersections in
London. The original Tabernacle burned in 1898, and was
rebuilt according to the original plans. (Significantly,
the total seating capacity was reduced, for after Spurgeon's
death no one else could fill such a large building.)
During World War II the whole Elephant and Castle area

---

[3]_Autobiography_, II, 327-328.

was heavily bombed, and the Tabernacle was once again destroyed. After the war the Tabernacle was rebuilt again, but this time only the old facade was retained. The present structure preserves Spurgeon's original exterior design of six Grecian pillars supporting a triangular arch, but the interior has been completely remodelled. The old Elephant and Castle public house which gave the area its name has disappeared, replaced by a modern shopping complex. The only reminder of the Victorian past which still remains in this modern center is the outline of that venerable antique, Spurgeon's Tabernacle.

According to a report in The Times, Spurgeon announced that the land had "been as much given to them by the Lord as if an angel had come down from heaven and cleared it." The hyperbole is obvious, but certainly Spurgeon might well have said, as the reporter claimed, that he would consider himself a "guilty sneaking sinner" if the Tabernacle were opened with any debts unpaid.[4] Spurgeon insisted from the beginning that the building

---

[4]The Times, August 22, 1860.

would be opened without any debt or not at all. He refused

to allow the congregation to worship in the new structure

until all the costs of the building were completely paid

for. In order to raise money for the new building, Spurgeon

preached for three years all over the kingdom, sometimes

delivering as many as ten sermons a week. He regarded the

Tabernacle as a crucial test case of the Nonconformist

belief in religious voluntaryism. If his people could not

raise the funds to pay for their building, how could they

argue that the Church of England, if disestablished, would

be supported by voluntary contributions? His insistence

on opening the Tabernacle without debt also reflected an

almost morbid fear of insolvency. He once confessed that

since childhood he had "hated debt as Luther hated the

Pope,"[5] a sentiment he attributed to parental instruction.

As a child he had once purchased a slate on credit from

a local merchant, and had been severely chastised by his

father, who made him return the slate and explain that he

had taken it under false pretenses. Honesty and thrift

were commonplace teachings in most evangelical households,

---

[5]Autobiography, I, 40.

but the early lessons made a deeper impression upon
Spurgeon than upon most. During his lifetime he earned a
great deal of money, but he put most of it back into his
institutions. Despite his obvious earning power, he never
felt financially secure, and was plagued throughout his
lifetime by anxieties about money, which he admitted were
largely unfounded. His homely wisdom and teachings on
the virtue of solvency--"Better to go to bed without
supper than to get up in debt"--masked a strange and per-
plexing anxiety about his financial resources that he did
not hide and was unable to explain. In any event, he was
a splendid fund-raiser, personally raising £11, 253, 15s.
6d. of the total cost (£31, 332, 4s. 10d.) of the Tabernacle. He was not only a generous man; he had the ability
to inspire generosity in others.

Spurgeon was a man of fixed opinions and prejudices, many reflecting his background and some his
experience. Most of his ideas concerning worship were
grounded in the teachings of the Puritans. He had the
Puritan's horror of graven images and stained glass. He
said of stained glass windows that Cromwell's hammer was

the best way to deal with them and the Romish superstition they represented.[6] He was also in the Puritan tradition in his refusal to describe any Dissenting house of worship as a "church"--as Richard Mather said, "There is no just ground from scripture to apply such a trope as church to a house for public assembly."[7] Spurgeon quoted with approval the remark of the Quaker George Fox, that churches were "steeple houses," and he insisted that his congregation, like the children of Israel, were still wanderers in the wilderness, and therefore still in the "tabernacle stage." Since they had not reached the promised land, there could be no temple. In the great wilderness of Victorian London, they would erect a Tabernacle.

Spurgeon's Tabernacle could hold as many as six thousand worshippers, slightly more than Exeter Hall. The interior was semi-circular, with two tiers of balconies facing a raised platform and baptismal pool. The design was intended to allow as many people as possible to see the preacher, for this was a preacher's church. Only a few

---

[6]C. H. Spurgeon, What the Stones Say, or Sermons in Stones (London, 1894), pp. 29-30.

[7]Quoted in Daniel Boorstin, The Americans: The Colonial Experience (New York, 1964), p. 17.

seats had an obstructed view, and the accoustics were
excellent, as another seasoned speaker, John Bright, testified.[8] In building such a large church, Spurgeon's congregation gambled that his popularity would not fade.
There were no lack of competitors, spiritual and secular,
to lure the London populace, but for those who had argued
that "Spurgeonism" was a passing fad, on an intellectual
par with spirit-rapping, his continuing power to attract
an audience was a tribute both to his abilities and the
drawing power of the Victorian pulpit.

When the Tabernacle was opened in 1861, Spurgeon
was twenty-seven years old. Though he was young, he
managed his huge congregation with a sure hand. The control that he exercised was all the more remarkable considering his real lack of pastoral experience--a couple of
years in rural Waterbeach followed by the frenzied years
of his early London ministry. If he experienced any doubts
about his ability to manage a large congregation, he did

---

[8]R. A. J. Walling, ed., The John Bright Diaries
(London, 1930), p. 319.

not reveal them. He once likened the management of a
congregation to the navigation of a large boat:

> I confess I never had the ability to manage a small
> church. They are like those canoes on the Thames--
> you must not sit this way, or the other, or do this
> thing or that thing lest you should be upset. I
> happen to have a big church like a big steamboat,
> and whether I walk here or there my weight will not
> upset it. If a big fellow thinks himself to be some-
> body, his importance vanishes when he joins a church
> like mine.[9]

There was little doubt that Spurgeon was the master of his
congregation. At the end of his life he confided to
W. T. Stead that in the forty years of his ministry he had
never known any appeal from his decisions, a boast that
must be virtually unique in the history of congregational
government. His was a Protestant community, but there were
some who detected Papal authority in the manner in which
Spurgeon wielded power. In later years, younger Baptist
ministers were known to grumble about "the modern Vatican
in Newington Butts,"[10] and the Westminster Review, in a
perceptive analysis of the denomination, termed Spurgeon

---

[9]Pike, Speeches, p. 92.

[10]Christian World, September 8, 1887.

"a regular Pope."[11] A Church of England publication, The
Hornet, maintained that the power of patriarchs, Bedouin
sheiks, or heads of Scots clans dimmed beside that exercised by Spurgeon,[12] an exaggeration certainly, but how
much of an exaggeration? Spurgeon himself saw some truth
in the charge that he was "a regular Pope," but he denied
infallibility, claiming that he maintained "a democracy
with a very large infusion of constitutional monarchy in
it."[13] He elaborated on this curious metaphor to Dr. Benson,
the Archbishop of Canterbury, telling him, "Mine is a
benevolent autocracy based upon absolute democracy. It
has taken no little tact and trouble to keep a democracy
straight thirty-eight years."[14] Perhaps a more exact idea
of the sort of power Spurgeon fancied is revealed in the
comment of his friend and biographer, G. Holden Pike, who

---

[11]Westminster Review, XL (October 1871), 437.

[12]The Hornet, September 4, 1878, p. 952. Scrapbook
clipping.

[13]C. Maurice Davies, Unorthodox London (London,
1873), p. 64.

[14]Benson, op. cit., I, 276.

denied the charge that Spurgeon was a Pope, maintaining that his "benevolent rule" was similar to that exercised by Cromwell.[15]

Spurgeon's congregation was a closed community in which membership was subject to the absolute veto of the pastor. Every applicant for Tabernacle membership had personally to satisfy the pastor of the sincerity of his conversion, for as he frequently warned his students, even if only a few unconverted souls slipped into the church, those few could change the whole tone of the congregation.[16] Once admitted into Spurgeon's congregation, members were expected to maintain a very rigorous standard of public and private morality. He told one visitor to the Tabernacle that he had over 4,000 members on his roll-books, and "if one of them got tipsy I should probably hear of it before the week was out." "Mr. Spurgeon," mused the visitor, "speaks as lightly of his thousands as the Shah of Persia."[17]

---

[15]Pike, Life, III, 23.

[16]C. H. Spurgeon, An All-Round Ministry (London, 1900), p. 318.

[17]Maurice Davies, op. cit., pp. 64-65.

Any member of his flock who ventured past the portals of
a theater "would cease to be a part of my fellowship."[18]
This was a moral dictatorship. Those who protested Spurgeon's autocracy were free to go elsewhere, but few protested. During his ministry, 14,691 new members were added
to the Tabernacle membership rolls.[19] "People come to me
for one thing, and it is no use my pretending to give them
the opposite as well," he said. "I preach to them a
Calvinistic creed and a Puritanic morality. That is what
they want and that is what they get. If they want anything
else they must go elsewhere."[20] Spurgeon knew his congregation. They idolized him, accepted his dictates, and
followed him cheerfully. One of his deacons, William Olney,
once told the Tabernacle congregation: "Our minister has
hitherto led us forward and we have followed heartily. . . .
If our pastor has brought us to a ditch which looks as if
it could not be passed, let us fill it up with our bodies,

[18]Review of Reviews, V (March 1892), 249.

[19]Autobiography, IV, 336.

[20]Pall Mall Gazette, XXXIX (July 19, 1884), 12.

and carry him across." "This," said Spurgeon, "was grand talk!"[21]

Because he was a natural leader and a determined man, Spurgeon usually had his own way; and in common with many other natural leaders he was faintly contemptuous of what often appeared the vacillation of leaderless groups. He was always faintly uneasy when forced to share responsibility. As a famous man, he frequently found himself upon committees, but he did not relish the opportunity to pool ideas and responsibility. He said, "Lord, lead me not into temptation," meant "lead me not into a committee meeting," and he once defined an ideal committee as being composed of three members, two of whom stayed in bed.[22] Spurgeon was a star of the pulpit, and had a star's prima-donna tendencies. He did not share the stage willingly.

The autocratic element in Spurgeon's personality contrasted stragely with his trusting, even gullible behavior on many occasions. He was an open, seemingly guileless man. He told a would-be biographer, "You may

---

[21]The Soul-Winner, p. 176.

[22]Pike, Speeches, p. 183.

write my life across the sky; I have nothing to conceal."[23]
The labels, "child-like" and "trusting" appear over and
over in the descriptions of those who knew him. Lord
Shaftesbury, who knew him well, recorded in his diary that
Spurgeon was "a wonderful man, full of zeal, affection,
faith, abounding in reputation and authority, and yet
perfectly humble, with the openness and simplicity of a
child."[24] "He looked upon the world with a child-like
eye," wrote W. T. Stead.[25] "That which often impressed
me was his child-likeness," said Newman Hall.[26] R. W. Dale
sensed the same quality: "There is about him a rare
sweetness and brightness so that he creates a sunny atmosphere wherever he goes. . . . With the strength of the man
is blended the gentleness of a spirit wonderfully child-
like."[27] Gullible, unsophisticated, too trusting, Spurgeon

---

[23]Williams, op. cit., p. 13.

[24]Edwin Hodder, The Life and Works of the Seventh
Earl of Shaftesbury (London, 1892), p. 708.

[25]Review of Reviews, V (March 1892), 248.

[26]Good Words, XXXIII (1892), 236.

[27]The Congregationalist, XIII (1884), 579.

was an easy target for the unscrupulous. A close

associate, W. Y. Fullerton, said, "Spurgeon was not a

good judge of men and could be easily deceived by them,

except in spiritual matters, where his own spiritual genius

gave him great power. He believed in men, was loyal to

them, and trusted in them."[28] The Metropolitan Police

once discovered a professional beggar's handbook listing

the names of potential donors. The list of those counted

easy marks was labeled the "Soft Tommies," and heading the

list was the name, "C. H. Spurgeon."[29] Informed by the

police of this dubious distinction, Spurgeon consoled him-

self with the reflection that it was preferable to be

known as a "Soft Tommy" than a "Hard Jack." The beggars

knew their man--a curious combination of autocracy and

gullibility. Inside the Autocrat of the Tabernacle was a

"Soft Tommy."

When the Tabernacle opened, Spurgeon declared

that he looked upon its opening as a mere preamble to a

---

[28]Quoted in Seymour Price, The Spurgeon Centenary, Gleanings from the Minute Books (London, 1934), p. 12.

[29]James Ellis, Spurgeon Anecdotes (London, 1892), p. 142.

a great missionary enterprise with the Tabernacle as its
fountainhead. Within a few years, his prophecy was fulfilled. In 1857, he had begun to tutor a street-preacher,
T. W. Medhurst, one of his first converts.[30] In this
informal manner, the institution known as the Pastors'
College had its beginning. Facilities for the college
were located in the Tabernacle basement, and as Spurgeon's
reputation grew, applications poured in from all over the
kingdom and even from abroad. One student walked all the
way from the highlands of Scotland to enroll in Spurgeon's
college. The admission standards of the college were
academically lax. Because he had not taken a degree, he
was suspicious of the quality of most higher education and
considered it a very mixed blessing when the universities
were opened to Dissenters. There was little emphasis in
the college on "mere" academic learning. The course of
study was for two years, and the aim of the college was
to graduate preachers rather than scholars. He emphasized

----

[30]Ironically, Spurgeon's first pastoral protégé
"crossed over to America and became head of some strange
sect, and appeared arrayed in gorgeous robes," Bacon,
op. cit., p. 91.

that it was not the intention of his college to turn "a rough and ready evangelist into a sapless essayist."[31] His concern was with a candidate's ability to preach the gospel, and if satisfied with that potential, he was not scrupulous about his academic background.

He did insist that applicants for his college have some preaching experience, and he absolutely refused to consider anyone who had failed at another occupation. "Jesus Christ deserves the best men to preach his gospel, and not the empty-headed and shiftless," he declared.[32] He defended this standard by unconsciously invoking the logic of social Darwinism: "Men of inferior abilities, who mistake their calling, will always be in want in the ministry, as they would have been anywhere else. This is not a failure of any system, but a law of nature."[33] As a successful man, Spurgeon tended too often to apply the lessons of his own life to the experience of others. Believing that he would have been successful in another

---

[31] Sword and Trowel, XIII (1887), 206.

[32] Autobiography, III, 145.

[33] Sword and Trowel, IV (1868), 327.

occupation had he not been called to the ministry, he was
intolerant of failure in others. Spurgeon began his
preaching career as a boy, and unlike that successful
shoe-salesman, D. L. Moody, had no actual experience in
any occupation except preaching. But he was firmly wedded
to the Calvinist myth that given certain virtues--honesty,
diligence, and thrift--failure was impossible. Spurgeon
had great compassion for the poor, writing that "if there
are any people who love the cause of God better than
others, I believe it is the poor,"[34] yet he occasionally
allowed himself to equate poverty with vice--"very much of
the poverty about us is the result of idleness, intemperance,
improvidence, and sin," and his remedy for "laziness" was
to the point--"give me a long whip."[35] On both sides of
the Atlantic nineteenth-century evangelicals displayed an
awesome smugness concerning the origins and remedies of
poverty. D. L. Moody said, "I never knew a lazy man to
become a Christian. . . . It is the devil whose workers
are idlers," and he urged workers to be content with

[34]Autobiography, III, 2.

[35]Spectator, LXVIII (1892), 188.

twenty-five cents a day if that was all they were offered.[36] Beecher believed a man could support a family on a dollar a day, if he did not smoke or drink. His own income was in excess of $20,000 a year and he had two summer homes, yet he counseled workers to be content with subsistence wages.[37]

The eighteen-sixties and 'seventies were years in which the vogue of the self-made man enjoyed enormous popularity in the English-speaking world. The American Baptist Russell Conwell thrilled audiences for years with his famous lecture, "Acres of Diamonds," which he delivered over 6,000 times. Preaching that opportunity was "waiting in your own backyard," Conwell urged his listeners to honor God my making money and using it wisely. The Unitarian clergyman Horatio Alger found millions of readers for his simple tales of poor-but-honest lads who won wealth by fortuitous good deeds. Alger's English counterpart, Samuel Smiles, preached the gospel of work in a series

[36]James Findlay, Dwight L. Moody: American Evangelist (Chicago, 1969), p. 224.

[37]Constance Rourke, Trumpets of Jubilee (New York, 1927), p. 234.

of best-selling books bearing such titles as <u>Thrift</u>,

<u>Character</u>, and <u>Duty</u>. His most famous work, <u>Self-Help</u>,

sold over a quarter of a million copies by 1905. Smiles

taught that success was the result of practicing the "old-

fashioned but wholesome lessons" of thrift, hard work,

and self-reliance. He illustrated his popular works with

the true stories of engineers, inventors, politicians,

and other successful men who had, through hard work and

perseverance, achieved wealth and fame.[38] Spurgeon

declared Smiles "one of the ablest authors of our time,"[39]

and the basis of his admiration is clear, for his own life

was perfectly tailored to the pattern of success eulogized

by Smiles. He was the poor country boy who had made good

in the city. Though lacking the advantages of birth, edu-

cation, or wealth, he had gone, as an early biography pro-

claimed, <u>From the Usher's Desk to the Tabernacle</u>. Spurgeon's

advice to aspiring preachers, while filled with good sense

and presented with good humor, was heavily weighted by his

---

[38]Asa Briggs, <u>Victorian People</u> (Chicago, 1955), pp. 116-139.

[39]<u>Autobiography</u>, I, 7.

own success story, and the moral, all too frequently, was the obvious one--"Go thou, and do likewise."

The Pastors' College remained Spurgeon's favorite institution and private philanthropy, his "first-born and most-beloved." He enjoyed being with his students, and they, in turn, admired "the Guv'nor" to the point of slavish imitation. What wits termed "the Royal College of Spurgeons" tended to produce preachers cast in the stylistic and theological mold of the founder. He was teacher, mentor, and father to many of his students, and did not limit his advice to affairs of the classroom. He was not reluctant to undertake the management of the financial or even the romantic problems of his students. He had a certain flair for playing Solomon. On one occasion, hearing that a student had managed to become engaged to two young women at the same time, he called him into his office, produced the two young women, and ordered him to make a choice at once.[40]

----

[40]Carlile tells the story with two young women, Williams has Spurgeon parading three females before the startled student. I think two is probably correct although three makes a better story.

The Pastors' College was the nucleus of an Evangelical Association which sent out lay-preachers to twenty-two street missions located throughout London. Some of the livlier passages in Spurgeon's Lectures to My Students are concerned with the hazards and rewards of street preaching. He was practical enough to caution against falling flower-pots, but idealistic enough to believe that persecution created martyrs, and martyrs were effective witnesses to faith. "I am somewhat pleased when I occasionally hear of a brother's being locked up by the police, for it does him good, and it does the people good also. It is a fine sight to see the minister of the gospel marched off by the servant of the law! It excites sympathy for him, and the next step is sympathy for his message."[41] The Pastors' College graduated over nine hundred preachers during Spurgeon's lifetime, and he personally found each graduate a chapel or helped him to build a new one. The increasing number of "Spurgeon's men" led to speculation that he might be thinking of founding a new denomination.

[41]Helmut Thielicke, Encounter With Spurgeon (Philadelphia, 1963), pp. 172-173.

This speculation was especially rife at the time of his break with the Baptist Union, and there is some evidence that he toyed with the idea, but in the end decided against it.

In 1867, a clergyman's widow, Mrs. Anne Hillyard, bequeathed to Spurgeon a sum of £10,000 to start an orphanage for boys at Stockwell. Shortly thereafter, another gift provided quarters for girls. Spurgeon's orphanages were enormously popular with the public. They were progressive, healthy institutions for their day. Destitute fatherless children from "Evangelical churches dissenting from the Church of England and not holding Unitarian or Socinian opinions,"[42] were housed in family-styled "house units." Those who know Victorian orphanages only from novels would find Spurgeon's orphanages a pleasant contrast to the dreary and oppressive institutions so often chronicled in fiction. Spurgeon knew each child by name, and always found the time to speak to one with a problem or to write to one who was ill. He was at his best

---

[42]Kathleen Heasman, _Evangelicals in Action_ (London, 1962), p. 92.

with children, and he enjoyed taking a break from his
other duties and driving out to Stockwell to visit with
"his" orphans. His Christmas days were always spent with
the orphans, distributing oranges and shillings, and pre-
siding over a full Victorian Christmas table. His visits
were eagerly anticipated by the children, who quickly
learned what professional beggars already knew, that this
particular "Soft Tommy" was always susceptible to an
appeal to the heart. Now known as "Spurgeon's Homes,"
the orphanages continue to provide a home for two hundred
children at Birchington in Kent.[43]

Among Spurgeon's other institutions were a Col-
portage Society which employed nearly one hundred
colporteurs who distributed over 20,000 Bibles and religious tracts through thirty-three counties; twenty-seven
Sunday schools and ragged schools; and an almshouse with
quarters for seventeen poor women. To publicize their
activities, he began publication in 1865 of a monthly
magazine, the Sword and Trowel. The cover of the first

[43]Bacon, op. cit., p. 100.

issue showed Nehemiah--the Tirshatha, or "Governor"--
standing on a wall exhorting the children of Israel to
build with their trowels, but to stand ready with their
swords. Under his editorship, the magazine reached a
circulation of 15,000. The success of Spurgeon's institutions was in large part due to his personal popularity.
He had personal contacts and financial resources that few
other dissenting ministers had, and his personal appeals
guaranteed the solvency of the Tabernacle philanthropic
agencies. His reputation was such that he could request
Lord Shaftesbury or Gladstone to preside over a fund-
raising ceremony and be sure that they would give his
request serious consideration. His example was on the
whole exceptional; the trend in the second half of the
nineteenth century was away from single-congregation
agencies toward the interdenominational or community
approach to social problems.[44]

Many of the Victorians were prodigious workers
and writers who frequently overwhelm the students of their

_____

[44]Heasman, op. cit., p. 52.

work by the sheer volume of their production. Spurgeon's accomplishments compare favorably with those of his contemporaries. He preached twice on Sunday and once on Thursday, addressed a prayer meeting on Wednesday, and was in great demand for lectures and sermons on his "free days." He revised and published a weekly sermon, and prepared and delivered a weekly college lecture. He supervised the growing enterprise of Tabernacle philanthropies and somehow always found the funds to keep them solvent. He edited a monthly magazine, contributed to denominational periodicals, and maintained a large correspondence. He was politically active, working behind-the-scenes on behalf of the Liberal party. The total number of his published works, including his sermons, was over one hundred and fifty volumes.

Spurgeon's brother, James Archer Spurgeon, became his co-pastor in 1868. The title of co-pastor was more honorary than descriptive, for the deacons made it clear in an invitation of startling bluntness that his position was to be subservient to his brother's in every way. James Spurgeon accepted the limitations of such a position with good grace, and served his brother faithfully until the

elder Spurgeon's death. He was an important factor in
his brother's record of accomplishments, for he freed him
from the humdrum and time-consuming pastoral responsibilities of conducting weddings and funerals, chairing
meetings, and attending teas and bazaars. He worked
quietly in the background and allowed his more talented
brother to monopolize the center of the stage. Spurgeon
was grateful, but there was never any question of sharing
the limelight. In a candid moment, his father had once
remarked to the assembled family: "My dears, we are a
family of nonentities. I am his father; you, James, are
his brother; you, dear girls, are his sisters. Mother over
there, is his mother. We are a bunch of nobodies and make
no mistake. We live in the light of your brother Charles'
glory."[45]

Spurgeon was frequently accused of egotism, and
anyone who spends much time with his printed works can
readily appreciate the charge. All of his writing is autobiographical, and consequently, not only his _Autobiography_,

---

[45]A. Cunningham Burley, _Spurgeon and his Friendships_
(London, 1933), p. 40.

but also his magazine, his lectures, his sermons, and his
books are permeated by _his_ own experience, _his_ advice,
his testimony, _his_ character. When his own experience is
not invoked, then the reader must endure the wisdom of
his wife, _his_ sons, _his_ father, _his_ grandfather. Nepotism
reigned at Newington Butts, and the Tabernacle enterprises
were swarming with Spurgeons. He missed few opportunities
to promote his family or himself. "The _Antiquus Ego_ was
ever before his eye," mused the Archbishop of Canterbury
after a visit with Spurgeon, "but he made us all like him
very much, and respect the Ego which he respected."[46]
Spurgeon, in common with most successful men, did not
underestimate his own abilities. He was a firm believer
in the thesis that great men made history. In 1866 he
wrote: "All great movements need the entire self-sacrifice
of some one man who, careless of consequences, will throw
himself upon the spears of the enemy." He then went on to
describe such a man:

> He must be simple-minded, outspoken, bold and fearless
> of consequences. To him courage must be instead of

---

[46]Benson, _op. cit._, 276.

prudence, and faith instead of policy. He must be
prepared to be apparently despised and really hated,
because intensely dreaded. He must reckon upon
having every sentence he utters distorted, and every
action misrepresented, but in this he must rejoice so
long as his blows tell and his utterances win a
hearing. Ease, reputation, comfort, he must renounce,
and be content so long as he lives to dwell in the
world's camp. [47]

In 1884, on the occasion of his fiftieth birthday, he
reiterated the same theme: "Whenever anything is done,
either in the Church or in the world, you may depend upon
it, it is done by one man. The whole history of the Church
from the earliest ages teaches the same lesson. A Moses,
a Gideon, an Isaiah, and a Paul are from time to time
raised up to do an appointed work; and when they pass away
their work appears to cease."[48] Spurgeon clearly had
faith in himself as one who could meet these rigorous
standards. His egotism was balanced by his conviction
that he was a mere instrument, a frail tool, useful only
because his Lord willed his success; but even so, in a
lesser man his confidence would be labeled conceit, and
even in a sincere and good man it can be disturbing.

---

[47]Sword and Trowel, II (1866), 341.

[48]Pall Mall Gazette, XXXIX (June 19, 1884), 11.

Spurgeon was central to the successful operation of the Tabernacle enterprises, and as nearly irreplaceable as one man could be. At his death, his heirs began feuding, and his pastoral empire nearly collapsed. His family split over choosing a successor, the college took sides, the congregation dwindled, the Tabernacle burned, and the rumor even spread that "the college had burned the Tabernacle."[49] His institutions survive, though not, perhaps, in a form of which he would completely approve. But he was sensible enough to realize that some modification was inevitable; though for this reason he refused to endow his college, arguing in a wholly characteristic way, "Why should I gather money which would remain after I am gone to uphold teachings which I might entirely disapprove? No! Let each generation provide for its own wants."[50]

Amidst a host of duties, preaching remained the principal obligation of the Pastor of the Tabernacle, and

---

[49]See Chapter IX, "The Tabernacle Tempest," in W. Y. Fullerton, Thomas Spurgeon (London, 1919), pp. 144-163.

[50]Pall Mall Gazette, XXXIX (June 19, 1884), 11.

as a preacher, the Spurgeon of the Tabernacle proved a
different Spurgeon from the preaching sensation of Exeter
Hall and the Surrey Gardens. Perhaps he matured; certainly he was more confident; he was no longer bothered
by the necessity of filling a great secular hall--whatever
his reasons, it was evident to those who followed his
career that both the substance and style of his sermons
altered in the years which followed the opening of the
Tabernacle. The "Boy Wonder" was a boy no longer, and the
wonders were less obvious. His sermons were mellower, and
his delivery less dramatically sensational. A few,
nostalgic for the exciting days of the past, regretted
the changes. One acquaintance told Spurgeon that he
thought the sermons Spurgeon preached in the first ten
years of his Tabernacle ministry were not up to the level
of either the years preceding or following, and Spurgeon
conceded that this was probably true. His friend explained
the change as resulting from a change in emphasis--Spurgeon
was no longer trying to gather a congregation, but rather
to lead one. As his sermons became more pastoral and
didactic in character, "in the place of the dashing cataract

and leaping torrent of eloquence there was an ever-deepening,
ever-widening flow of a refreshing river of instruction."[51]

Stylistic changes were inevitable. Although he
was not yet thirty when the Tabernacle opened, Spurgeon
had been preaching for nearly a decade in all parts of the
country. Physically, the strain of those hectic, fund-
raising years was beginning to leave its mark. Never
strong, he had taxed his physical resources to their limits,
and he was forced to slow his pace. His gestures became
less theatrical, his movements across the platform less
startling, the "Spurgeonisms" less frequent. He could not
resist pathos, but his emotional appeals were less
blatantly maudlin. Those who had likened the young Spurgeon
to an actor were correct, but just as a good actor mellows
over the years, depending less upon surface ranting and
and more upon the quiet authority of experience, so
Spurgeon's pulpit style altered and mellowed as the years
passed. For those who remembered the preaching sensation
of the 'fifties, the Spurgeon of the Tabernacle was a

---

[51]Williams, op. cit., p. 237.

revelation. One visitor's account of the mature Spurgeon describes the changes in the preacher's manner:

> It was a sound, practical discourse, of upwards of an hour in length, delivered without a note of any kind, with all the preacher's old earnestness, but without a single trace of his former eccentricity. There was not a single "Spurgeonism" from beginning to end. . . . Remembering what Mr. Spurgeon was when he came to London seventeen years ago, a boy of nineteen, one cannot but congratulate him on the change; while the vast building, with all its varied works-- happily compared by himself to the cathedral of ancient times--bears witness to the sterling stuff there was in the man below all his eccentricity.[52]

W. C. Wilkinson, reporting for the _Independent_, contrasted the Spurgeon he had heard first when the preacher was twenty-four with Spurgeon at fifty-three, and concluded: "Apparent ease on his part in preaching was a very marked trait of the youthful Spurgeon; apparent ease is equally the trait of the older man. But twenty-nine years ago the ease seemed, in great part, the buoyant exultation of youth and health; the present ease is that of mastery assured through much experience."[53]

---

[52] Maurice Davies, _op_. _cit_., p. 68.

[53] Wilkinson, _op_. _cit_., p. 181.

The substance of Spurgeon's sermons also changed over the years. In the early years of his ministry his sermons were frequently topical, drawing upon contemporary events for vividness. As he grew older, he preached fewer topical sermons, preferring instead to emphasize the unchanging character of the gospel promises. The young Spurgeon's "Turn or Burn" sermons had earned him the sobriquet of "Brimstone." Punch noted in 1856 that "on the average the reverend teacher uses in every sermon no less than three tons of coals, and all red hot. Last winter poor people were known to warm their hands at his periods."[54] As he matured, Spurgeon discarded some of the vivid descriptions of the torments of hell, and his sermons were more likely to welll upon the joy of salvation rather than the threat of damnation. His basic theology remained unaltered; he believed in a literal hell and the eternal damnation of the wicked; but he ceased to paint the horrors of hell in such graphic detail. A comparison of two selections from Spurgeon's sermons will suggest this

----

[54]Punch, XXI (November 8, 1856), 190.

shift in emphasis. The first selection is from a sermon

delivered at the New Park Street Chapel in 1856:

> When thou diest thy soul will be tormented alone--
> that will be a hell for it--but at the day of judgment
> thy body will join thy soul, and then thou wilt have
> twin hells, body and soul shall be together, each
> brimfull of pain, thy soul sweating in its inmost pore
> drops of blood, and thy body from head to foot suf-
> fused with agony; conscience, judgment, memory, all
> tortured, but more--thy head tormented with racking
> pains, thine eyes starting from their sockets with
> sights of blood and woe; thine ears tormented with
> "sullen moans and hollow groans, and shrieks of tor-
> tured ghosts." Thine heart beating high with fever;
> thy pulse rattling at an enormous rate in agony;
> thy limbs cracking like the martyrs in the fire; and
> yet unburnt; thyself, put in a vessel of hot oil,
> pained, yet coming out undestroyed; all thy veins
> becoming a road for the hot feet of pain to travel on;
> every nerve a string on which the devil shall ever
> play his diabolical tune of Hell's Unutterable Lament;
> thy soul forever and ever aching, and thy body pal-
> pitating in unison with thy soul. Fictions, sir!
> Again, I say, they are no fictions, and as God liveth,
> but solid, stern truth. . . . Ah! fine lady, thou who
> takest care of thy goodly fashioned face, remember
> what was said by one of old when he held up the skull!
> "Tell her though she paint herself an inch thick, to
> this complexion she must come at last." And something
> more than that: thy fair face shall be scarred with
> the claws of fiends, and that fine body shall be only
> the medium of torment. Ah! dress thyself proud gentle-
> man for the worm; anoint thyself for the crawling
> creatures of the grave; and worse, come thou to hell
> with powdered hair--a gentleman in hell; come though
> down to the pit in goodly apparel; my lord, come there,

to find yourself no higher than others, except it be higher in torture and plunged deeper in flames.[55]

Compare this passage to a sermon on the resurrection preached by a mature preacher who chose to stress the message of redemption rather than damnation:

I do not know why we always sing dirges at the funerals of the saints, and drape ourselves in black. I would desire, if I might have my way, to be drawn to my grave by white horses, or to be carried on the shoulders of men who would express joy as well as sorrow in their habiliments, for why should we sorrow over those who have gone to glory, and inherited immortality? I like the old Puritan plan of carrying the coffin on the shoulders of the saints, and singing a psalm as they walked to the grave. Why not? What is there, after all, to weep about concerning the glorified? Sound the gladsome trumpet! Let the shrill clarion peal out the joyous note of victory! The conqueror has won the battle; the king has climbed to His throne. "Rejoice," say our brethren from above, "rejoice with us, for we have entered into our rest." Blessed are the dead which die in the Lord. . . . Let us, in the next place, cheer our hearts in the prospect of our own departure. We shall soon pass away. My brethren, we too must die; there is no discharge in this war. There is an arrow and there is an archer; the arrow is meant for my heart, and the archer will take deadly aim. There is a place where you shall sleep, perhaps in a lone grave in a foreign land; or perhaps in a niche where your bones shall lie side by side with those of your ancestors; but to the dust return you must. Well, let us not repine, it is but for a little,

---

[55]New Park Street Pulpit, II (1856), 105.

it is but a rest on the way to immortality. Death
is a passing incident between this life and the
next--let us meet it not only with equanimity, but
with expectation, since it is not death now but
resurrection to which we aspire.[56]

It is undeniable that maturity also brought to

Spurgeon a diminishing of physical energy and freshness,

and he was human enough to lament the limitations which

advancing age imposed upon him. "For my own part, I would

have remained a young man if I could, for I fear I am by

no means improved by keeping. Oh, that I could again

possess the elasticity of spirit, the dash, the courage,

the hopefulness of days gone by! My days of flying are

changed to running, and my running is slowing down to a

yet steadier pace."[57] The next two decades would be

satisfying and rewarding years for the Pastor of the

Tabernacle, but in truth his days of flying were over, and

the days of walking were not without regrets.

Anyone who seeks to explain the reasons for

Spurgeon's popularity by analyzing his published sermons

_____

[56]Twelve Sermons on the Resurrection (Grand
Rapids, 1968), pp. 77-78.

[57]An All-Round Ministry, p. 139.

will encounter certain problems. Much--perhaps the greatest part--of his unique appeal cannot be resurrected, for these fragments provide only hints of his persuasive abilities. What is left is a part of the record, a part shorn of the physical power of his presence, and even the part must be studied cautiously. What is read as a sermon delivered by Spurgeon on a given occasion may not be an entirely accurate record of what he did in fact say. His sermons were carefully revised for publication, and all grammatical errors as well as most of the colloquialisms and "Spurgeonisms" were struck from the printer's proof. In the early editions, the sermons were published quickly without much revision, but in later years the revisions became more rigorous.[58] Spurgeon did not preach from a manuscript, and the text he revised was a stenographer's account of his sermon. (According to his stenographer, he spoke, on average, one hundred and forty words per minute.) The stenographer's account was lengthened or cut to meet

---

[58]"The earlier sermons . . . owing to my constant wanderings abroad, received scarcely any revision, and consequently they abound in colloquialisms and other offenses," Autobiography, II, 158.

publishers' requirements, and in the last years of his life he passed the job of revision on to W. Y. Fullerton, who frequently expanded the seven pages of notes to twelve pages of text for publication.[59] Thus, a printed record of a sermon by Spurgeon is quite possibly a stenographer's account of what Spurgeon said, shorn of all its spontaneity and roughness, and expanded several pages by Fullerton. In addition, the American editions of Spurgeon's sermons were frequently censored or abridged to meet the requirements of the American market.

Spurgeon prepared his Sunday sermon on Saturday evening, a period when he could not be disturbed. Even an invitation to dine with the Prime Minister could not tempt Spurgeon out on a Saturday evening.[60] Rather curiously, his greatest problem in preparing a sermon was in finding a suitable text to expound. Moody told Spurgeon he had a book full of texts, but found trouble putting a sermon

----

[59]W. Y. Fullerton, C. H. Spurgeon, A Biography (London, 1920), p. 218.

[60]Ms. letter, Spurgeon to W. E. Gladstone, October 24, 1882, "I cannot be out on a Saturday night for it is the only time I have to get my sermons." British Museaum, Gladstone Papers, Vol. CCCXCII, No. 44477, f. 150.

around them; Spurgeon replied, "My difficulty is to find a text, for when a text grips me I have found the sermon."[61] When the text materialized, he began his preparation. "I like to lie and soak in my text," he said.[62] After sufficient soaking, Spurgeon jotted down an outline on any handy scrap of paper and his sermon was ready for delivery. Only rarely did he experience diffi- culty in treating texts, though on a few occasions he had to wrestle with a particularly stubborn text for hours. Once, early in his ministry, having exhausted himself trying to understand the meaning of a text, he yielded to his wife's plea that he rest briefly. Worn out by his efforts, he fell into a deep sleep, and then began to deliver a sermon. According to the not entirely disinter- ested testimony of his wife, the result was "a clear and distinct exposition of its [the text's] meaning, with much force and freshness."[63] With great presence of mind, Mrs. Spurgeon proceeded to take notes during the

---

[61]Fullerton, op. cit., p. 196.

[62]Williams, op. cit., p. 174.

[63]Autobiography, II, 188.

somnambulistic sermon and was able to present her waking

spouse with a fully prepared sermon outline. The story

strains credibility, but both were fond of repeating it as

a factual instance of a wonder-working providence. Indeed,

Providence did seem to have a special eye out for

Spurgeon, as still another episode he related suggests:

> Once . . . I intended to preach on a certain text,
> but during the hymn felt I <u>must</u> take another. So I
> began, not seeing how to go beyond my first topic,
> hoping "secondly" would come when called for. Just
> when I got into difficulty, the lights went out and
> I had to stop. When the place was relighted I said I
> would take another text relating to light after
> darkness. One person was converted by each discourse.[64]

The Victorians were delighted by such stories, and Spurgeon

delighted in telling them, but in general he relied upon

preparation rather than providence in composing his sermons.

Spurgeon spoke extemporaneously from a brief out-

line. Many of the famous preachers of the day preferred

speaking from written texts, and a few even delivered their

sermons from memory. Spurgeon rejected both of these

methods, saying that to memorize a sermon was "a wearisome

exercise of an inferior power of the mind and an indolent

------

[64]<u>Good Words</u>, XXXIII (1892), 236.

neglect of other and superior faculties,"[65] while "the
best reading I have ever heard has tasted of paper, and
has stuck in my throat. I have not relished it, for my
digestion is not good enough to dissolve foolscap."[66]
Spurgeon's sermon outlines, although brief, were so well-
organized that he needed no other prop. A modern scholar
has commented on the great ingenuity which made his sermons
easily memorable, "by their orderly sequence, and their
headings, each of which was the summary of a lesson."[67]
He had learned the lesson of concise organization and
structured subdivision from Puritan divines, and it was
the secret not only of his own extemporaneous skill, but
also the reason his audience found it so easy to follow
his reasoning and to remember what he said. The following
introduction to one of his sermons is an example of his
closely structured organization:

> The narrative before us seems to me to suggest three
> points, and these three points each of them triplets.

---

[65]Lectures, I, 153.

[66]Thielicke, op. cit., pp. 238-239.

[67]Horton Davies, op. cit., p. 338.

I shall notice in this narrative, first, <u>the three stages of faith</u>; in the second place, <u>the three diseases to which faith is subject</u>; and in the third place to ask <u>three questions about your faith</u>.[68]

Spurgeon aimed to make each of his sermons simple enough for a child to understand; he usually succeeded. "If I am understood by poor people, by servant-girls, by children, I am sure I can be understood by others," he maintained.[69] He urged his students to always include a portion in each sermon that would appeal especially to the children in the congregation. "Can you not put in a little story or parable on purpose for the little ones?"[70] He was not trying to preach sermons which would satisfy theologians, and modern critics are frequently appalled by his explication of texts. As Horton Davies points out, "his exegesis could be capricious, idiosyncractic, and even grotesque."[71] He tended to play too much upon the meanings of words in the English text without a really

---

[68]Thielicke, <u>op</u>. <u>cit</u>., p. 248.

[69]<u>Come Ye Children</u>, p. 11.

[70]<u>Lectures</u>, III, 137.

[71]Horton Davies, <u>op</u>. <u>cit</u>., p. 337.

thorough grounding in the original language of the text.
The error was a common failure of Victorian homiletics--
Macaulay once heard a sermon preached on the single word,
"therefore," and E. E. Kellett recalled hearing one
preached on the word, "how."[72]

Spurgeon was often compared to Whitefield, which
was natural enough since he admitted that he sought to
model himself after the great preacher's example. He
urged his students to combine the zeal of the Methodists
with the doctrine of the Puritans, to "seek the fire of
Wesley, and the fuel of Whitefield."[73] Spurgeon was both
more successful and less effective than his chosen model.
Both were fiery, emotional preachers who burned perhaps
too brightly--both died at the same age. But Whitefield
was an evangelist who preached on two continents, constantly on the move, seeking to awaken new audiences;
Spurgeon, though an evangelist, was also an administrator
and pastor, who announced after he moved into the Tabernacle
that his traveling days were over. Perhaps Whitefield's

---

[72]E. E. Kellett, Religion and Life in the Early
Victorian Age (London, 1938), p. 111.

[73]Lectures, I, 83.

sermons had greater emotional impact, but Spurgeon's were
more reasoned and better-organized.

Spurgeon's greatest contribution to nineteenth-
century pulpit style was his emphasis upon naturalness.
"The best, surest, and most permanent way to fill a place
of worship is to preach the gospel, and to preach it in a
natural, simple, interesting, earnest way," he declared.[74]
He detested artificial rules of oratory and constantly
stressed the advantages of a natural speaking style. He
cautioned his students against imitation and affectation,
suggesting that most teachers of oratory and elocution
created more problems than they corrected. "Artificial
rules are an abomination," he insisted. "Give us the
vulgarities of the wildest backwoods' itinerant rather
than the perfumed prettiness of effeminate gentility."[75]
In voice and gesture, he argued, the best practice was
unstudied naturalness. He professed to be flattered when
visitors to the Tabernacle grumbled that there was nothing
so special about his preaching, for he believed that "the

---

[74]Sword and Trowel, XIX (1883), 421.

[75]Lectures, III, 132.

best style of preaching in the world, like the best style
of dressing, is that which nobody notices."[76] He lived
in the heyday of studied elocution and flamboyant oratory, so his success was an effective argument for the
persuasiveness of unaffected, natural speech. Spurgeon's
preaching, observed a reporter, was without a trace of
"pulpitation." "He speaks to the people, not in the
language of books, but in their own language."[77] The
mature Spurgeon seemed to "talk" his sermons, presenting
his points in a deceptively casual, conversational manner.
On his fiftieth birthday, a periodical commented, "If we
merely tabulate the causes that have contributed to the
simplification of pulpit style in the last fifty years the
index will read thus--Reform Bill, anti-slavery agitation,
Penny Magazine, cheap postage, Corn Law League, telegraphs,
Charles Haddon Spurgeon."[78] The point was well made. In

---

[76]The Soul-Winner, p. 101. Spurgeon's own pro-
nunciation was not quite pure. He had the countryman's
habit of pronouncing "ah" and "or" endings as "re." Thus,
Noah was "Nore," and poor was "pore." Fullerton, op. cit.,
p. 190.

[77]Living Age, LV (December 5, 1857), 620-621.

[78]The Freeman, June 20, 1884.

the age of the telegraph, an artificial pulpit manner was
as dated as the three-hour sermons of Edward Irving.

Spurgeon's lectures to his students on preaching
were printed in three volumes and continue to attract a
wide readership in modern editions. Most of the advice
that Spurgeon passed out to aspiring preachers was eminently practical. He urged his students to avoid cant,
long prayers, and studied poses. Though he cautioned
them against dropping their "h's" or speaking through their
noses (an indication of the social class of the students
at Pastors' College), he devoted relatively little attention to the mechanics of delivery. The emphasis in his
teaching as in his ministry was on the substance, not the
style of the sermon. Any style which did not detract from
the message was satisfactory. As D. L. Moody pungently
observed, "Samson slew his enemies with what? the jawbone
of an ass. Be always ready to grab up the first jawbone
of an ass you come to, and let the world laugh as much as
it likes."[79] The purpose of the sermon was to present the
gospel to the people in the language that they could

---

[79]Maurice Davies, op. cit., p. 78.

understand. "<u>Suit yourselves to your audiences</u>," Spurgeon urged. "He who goes down amongst miners and colliers with technical theological terms and drawing-room phrases acts like an idiot."[80] Spurgeon believed that the secret of his own success was that he preached the old doctrines of the Puritans in the language of the nineteenth-century marketplace. He reserved his greatest scorn for those preachers who attempted to improve the gospel message with embellishments drawn from contemporary philosophy, or science, or quotations from obscure texts. "It has become fashionable to allow the title of 'intellectual preachers' to a class of men whose passionless essays are combinations of metaphysical quibbles and heretical doctrines; who are shocked at the man who excites his hearers beyond the freezing point of insensibility, and are quite elated if they hear that their homily could only be understood by a few."[81] Many a "deep preacher," according to Spurgeon, was deep only because "they are like dry wells with nothing

---

[80]<u>Lectures</u>, III, 86.

[81]C. H. Spurgeon, <u>Complete in Christ and Love's Logic</u> (London, 1892), p. 138.

whatever in them, excepting decaying leaves, a few stones,
and a dead cat or two."[82] He often boasted that no one
needed to bring a dictionary to the Tabernacle, and he
admonished his students to stick to plain, Saxon speech
if they wished to be understood. "Crumble down the bread
when you serve it out to the children. Break down the
loaves and fishes for the multitude. Our common people
like to hear that which their mind can grasp, but they shun
the jargon of the schools."[83] Spurgeon believed that
preachers who paraded their learning in the pulpit displayed an effeminate affectation which repulsed honest
working people. "I am persuaded that one reason why our
workingmen so universally keep clear of ministers is
because they abhor their artificial and unmanly ways."[84]
"We must talk like men if we would win men," he said.
"Manliness must never be sacrificed to elegance. Our
working classes will never be brought even to consider
the truth of Christianity by teachers who are starched

[82]Lectures, II, 281.

[83]Sword and Trowel, XIX (1883), 423.

[84]Thielicke, op. cit., p. 226.

and fine. The British artisan admires manliness, and prefers to lend his ear to one who speaks in a hearty and natural style."[85] As for himself,

> I speak for the English people and I demand English preaching. If there is a mystery, let it be in the truth itself, and not in the obscurity of the preacher. . . . Now the Devil does not care for your dialectics, and eclectic homiletics, or Germanic objectives and subjectives; but pelt him with Anglo-Saxon in the name of God, and he will shift his quarters.[86]

This was advice with which most of the great popular preachers of the day would concur. Beecher too urged preachers to "use homely words,--those which people are used to, and which suggest things to them. . . . Words borrowed from foreign languages, and words that belong especially to science, learning, and literature, have very little suggestion in them to the common people."[87] Dr. Parker once observed that "the preacher who tells his audience that he is about to point out the difference between intuitive and empirical morality does not speak

---

[85]Ibid., pp. 126, 158.

[86]Sword and Trowel, VII (1871), 218.

[87]Yale Lectures on Preaching (New York, 1872), I, 230.

the language of the race, but the jargon of a class. He

may be a philosopher, but he is no preacher."[88] Spurgeon

was well aware that words have a class bias: "the language

of one class of Englishmen is a dead language to another

class; and many a word which is very plain to many of us,

is as hard and difficult a word to the multitude as if it

had been culled from Hindostani or Bengali."[89]

Spurgeon's faith in plain speech was reinforced

by his conviction that plain people were often the most

effective ministers of the gospel. "He who talks plain

gospel themes in a farmer's kitchen, and is able to inter-

est the carter's boy and the dairymaid," he said, "has

more of the minister in him than the prim little man who

keeps prating on about being cultured--and means by that

being taught to use words nobody can understand."[90]

> Scattered all over England and Scotland are self-
> educated men who have been called of God to be soul-
> winners, who care not a jot what Darwin or Colenso

---

[88]Joseph Parker, Pulpit Notes (London, 1873),
p. 112.

[89]New Park Street Pulpit, III (1857), 59.

[90]Autobiography, I, 202.

or even the great Scotch Latitudinarians may have to say for themselves, who are doing their work all the better because they have eschewed the refinements of modern scepticism, and have not looked into the secrets of the new liberalism.[91]

The fear that too much learning could serve to separate a

preacher from his audience was frequently expressed by

nineteenth-century evangelicals. R. W. Dale, who

championed higher education, nonetheless lamented,

Some ministers seem to think that churches are founded in order to provide salaries for men who wish to master speculation on the Origin of the Species and the Descent of Man, or to study at their leisure Auguste Comte or Herbert Spencer, or to make themselves familiar with Germanic literature and to form a judgment on the movement of Germanic philosophical thought from Kant to Schopenauer.[92]

Lecturing to a group of Oxford undergraduates, Canon Liddon

described the pitfalls of "philosophical preaching,"

and suggested a ministerial model to avoid:

His thought will drift naturally away from the central and most solemn truths to the literary embellishments which surround the faith; he will toy with questions of geography, or history, or custom, or scene, or dress; he will reproduce, with vivid power, the

----

[91]Sword and Trowel, IV (1868), 175.

[92]R. W. Dale, Nine Lectures on Preaching (London, 1877), p. 221.

personages and events of long past ages, and this, it
may be, with the talent of a master artist; he will
give to the human side of religion the best of his
time and toil, and in doing this, he may, after the
world's measure, be doing good work. But let us not
deceive ourselves; he will not be saving souls. Souls
are saved by men who count all things but dung, that
they may win Christ, and be found in Him; and who,
even if they be men of refined taste, and of cultivated
intellect, know well how to subordinate the embellishments of truth to its vital and soul-subduing
certainties.[83]

These comments from three of the great preachers of the

Victorian age suggest a great deal about the state of

nineteenth-century homiletics. As traditional Biblical

scholarship came under increasing attack by higher critics

and scientists, preachers were divided as to the most

effective way to meet the new challenges to scriptural

authority. Many chose the way of accommodation, and

struggled to master at least the superficial vocabulary of

science and criticism in order to demonstrate that there

was no inherent inconsistency between Christianity and

the new learning. For others, there could be--and needed

to be--no accommodation to the new heresies, no dilution

[83]Wilkinson, op. cit., pp. 234-235.

of the old message. As a leading spokesman for this group, Spurgeon was sure that "God revealeth himself rather to babes than to the wise and prudent, and we are fully assured that our own English version of the scriptures is sufficient for plain men for all purposes of life, salvation, and godliness. We do not despise learning, but we will never say of culture or criticism, 'These be thy Gods, O Israel.'"[94]

In suggesting, as he once did, that diplomas should be transferred from scholars to ploughmen, Spurgeon underlined his suspicion of higher education and his preference for practical knowledge over abstract theory. In elevating intuitive wisdom over reason Spurgeon illustrated the anti-intellectualism so common to the romantic mind. In one of his earliest sermons he had proclaimed:

> For my own part, I desire to be somewhat a student of the heart; and I think I have learned far more from conversation with my fellow-men than I ever did from

---

[94]C. H. Spurgeon, The Greatest Fight in the World (London, 1896), p. 29.

reading; and the examination of my own experience, and the working of my own heart, have taught me far more of humanity than all the metaphysical books I have ever perused.[95]

Spurgeon's anti-intellectualism was also expressed in his emphasis upon practicality and common sense, and in his frequently voiced opinion that these qualities were more likely to be found in ordinary people than in "refined intellects." In this attitude he was typically Victorian; the appeal to common sense and indifference to abstract speculation fed the anti-intellectualism which Walter Houghton has described as one of the most conspicuous features of the Victorian mind.[96] Spurgeon did not despise learning, but he did not understand the life of the mind, and learning for him was a means to an end. Knowing that "an ignoramus is not likely to be much of a soul-winner," he continually urged his students to "get all the education you can, drink in everything your tutors can possibly impart to you." He was aware that a national system of education would mean better-educated congregations

[95]New Park Street Pulpit, I(1855), 277.

[96]Walter Houghton, The Victorian Frame of Mind (New Haven, 1957), p. 110.

in the future, and for that very practical reason, he
urged preachers to take care that they did not fall behind
their congregations: "When they have all been to Board
Schools, if they come and listen to you, it will be a
pity if their minds are taken off the solemn things which
you wish them to think upon because of deficiencies of
education. God may bless you; but wisdom tells us that
we should not let our want of education hinder the gospel
from blessing men."[97]

For those who think of the Victorians as linguistic
vigilantes, ever alert to bowdlerize the language, Spurgeon's
plain, vigorous utterances are a pleasant antidote.
Throughout his career he was as honest in his speech as
the Puritan divines he so admired. "I have said _damn_ where
God said 'damn'--I have not sweetened it into 'condemn,'"
he said. "Don't be squeamish in the pulpit," he admonished
his students, "like one who read'Jonah was three days and
three nights in--ahem--the society of the fish.'"[98] The

---

[97]The Soul-Winner, pp. 104-105.

[98]Williams, op. cit., p. 171.

crowds were delighted with his straightforwardness and his racy humor. While in later years his pulpit manner became more restrained, his language remained plain and to the point. As late as 1885, the Dean of Windsor--Randall Davidson, later Archbishop of Canterbury--wrote of going to hear Spurgeon preach on a recent expose of the white slave trade which had earned the editor of the Pall Mall Gazette, W. T. Stead, a jail sentence. Dr. Davidson decided not to take a female friend, "thinking that Spurgeon would be sure, after all the horrors which have been revealed this week, to preach a coarse and trying sermon." To his surprise, the preacher "did not say one word which was indiscreet or coarse or harmful."[99] That this particular Anglican divine should have expressed concern over Spurgeon's language is indicative of the suspicion his blunt speech aroused among his more "polite" contemporaries. Spurgeon had an answer for his critics: "Soft speaking for soft heads, and good, plain speech for

---

[99]G. K A. Bell, Randall Davidson, Archbishop of Canterbury (Oxford, 1952), 113-114.

the hard-handed many. Mincing words and pretty sentences are for those who wear kid gloves and eye-glasses."[100] Whatever his faults, Spurgeon was never dull. "Dull preachers make good martyrs," he said. "They are so dry they burn well."[101]

Mrs. Booth once said that reverence was a thing of the heart, a sentiment with which Spurgeon was in agreement. He believed that religion was intended to have joy in it, and that it was irreligious to go "moping miserably through God's creation." "I am not John the Baptist, nor a monk, nor a hermit, nor an ascetic, either in theory or in practice," he said. "To me, to smile is no sin, and a laugh no crime."[102] His sense of humor was spontaneous and irrepressible, enlivening everything he said or wrote. Nothing, of course, horrified his detractors more than his habit of introducing humor into his sermons. The Saturday Review cited his taste for "pulpit burlesque" as "a sure sign of intellectual decay,"[103]

[100]Sword and Trowel, VI (1870), 433-434.
[101]Pike, Speeches, p. 73.
[102]Autobiography, III, 56.
[103]Saturday Review, XXXIII (January 6, 1872), 17-18.

and argued that "if there is such rollicking fun at Newington, we must say that there is an infringement of the Act 22, George II. The Tabernacle ought to be licensed as a cheap theater at once."[104] To those who chided his irreverence, Spurgeon replied that if they knew how many jokes he had suppressed, "they would commend me for the restraint I had exercised."[105] As he remarked to his students, "I would rather see people laugh than I would see them asleep in the house of God."[106] The humor in his sermons was spontaneous, but the purpose was well-planned. His purpose was to win souls, and he realized that some people responded more readily to honey than to vinegar. "I sometimes tickle my oyster until he opens his shell, and then I slip the knife in."[107] He naturally saw humor in most human situations, and he had no scruples about using humor to sustain attention. He could make the transition from laughter to prayer naturally and easily. "He looked upon 'soul-saving' with the same sense of

[104]Ibid., XII (October 5, 1861), 352.
[105]Lectures, I, 346.
[106]Autobiography, III, 339.
[107]The Soul-Winner, p. 94.

reality that a brick-layer looks upon brick-laying, and he joked about it as a brick-layer jokes when something funny is suggested to him by an incident in his work," wrote a perceptive critic.[108]

Spurgeon's wit was best when spontaneous, though in later years most of the off-the-cuff witticisms were pared from the printed text of his sermons. He was ill-served by his devoted friends and students who carefully garnered every stray Spurgeon anecdote and witticism for preservation and publication. Perhaps of all his traits, his sense of humor has the most dated quality. Many of his remarks, amusing in a given context, wrenched from that context and transferred to the pages of a collection of "humorous sayings" will strike a present-day reader as more embarrassing than witty. Spurgeon's great forte was the pun, perhaps the least likely form of humor to age gracefully. A Victorian audience might have been convulsed to hear the preacher tell them, "Though you are

---

[108]E. T. Raymond, Portraits of the Nineties (London, 1921), pp. 260-261.

teetotalers, you must all come to your bier at last," or
"What are the wild waves saying? 'Let us s(pray)'"; but
a modern audience would be more likely to groan.[109] It
is certainly still possible to admire Spurgeon for his
unconventional attitudes toward preaching and for his
willingness to challenge pious stereotypes about reverence;
one may even chuckle at an occasional "Spurgeonism," but
he was not Sydney Smith, and attempts by his admirers to
elevate his puns to the stature of great wit have been
misguided.

Spurgeon knew very well that the only way to
sustain attention was to say something worth hearing, and
that unless people were interested in what was being said,
they would forget what had been said. He was a shrewd
judge of his own abilities, and he was also aware of his
limitations--"I owe more to variety than to profundity in
my preaching," he admitted.[110] His sermons are still

_____

[109]In _Sword and Trowel_, VII (1871), 46, Spurgeon
denied emphatically that he had ever made the pun which is
most frequently attributed to him, "I won't ask 'how are
your poor feet?' What I want to know is 'how are your
poor souls?'"

[110]Williams, _op. cit._, p. 172.

read because they are still capable of sustaining interest, and they are still interesting because Spurgeon filled them with stories, examples, and anecdotes to illustrate his points. He had a fact-gathering mind, and the ability to remember the facts he had gathered. "I have a shelf in my head for everything, and whatever I read or hear, I know where to store it away for use at the proper time."[111] He read rapidly, skimming as many as five books at at single sitting.[112] He read for practical reasons--works of history or literature were valuable to the extent that they were useful to him.[113] History was a series of capsule lessons, and literature a treasure-trove of moral precepts. He carried with him everywhere a small notebook in which

---

[111]L. O. Brastow, Representative Modern Preachers (New York, 1904), p. 391.

[112]Sketch, op. cit., p. 129.

[113]Among the books in his library (now at William Jewell College, Liberty, Mo.) were: Henry Grey, Classics for the Millions, Being an Epitome in English of the Works of the Principal Greek and Latin Authors; Francis Knight, Half-Hours in English History from the Roman Period to Elizabeth; Edward Shelton, The Historical Fingerpost, A Handy Book of Terms, Phrases, Epithets, Cognomens, Allusions, and etc. in Connection with Universal History. A number of similar volumes suggest that here was the stuff of which anecdotes were made.

he jotted down random thoughts, quotations from his reading,
or stray pieces of interesting information. His reading,
his listening, his observations were all grist for the
mill, producing a fund of informative matter for his sermons.
He once wrote a book entitled, The Bible and the Newspaper,
which demonstrated the manner in which seemingly insignificant items from newspapers could be employed as sermon
topics.[114] He remembered the bulk of what he read or heard,
and in consequence frequently impressed people with his
wide range of information. A doctor meeting him on a train
was amazed at his knowledge of medical lore, and a farmer
declared, "He knew more about sheep than I do; yet I've
been a farmer all my life." "Dear Father was a living
'Inquire Within Upon Everything,'" recalled his son.[115]

The great range of his knowledge was not matched
by any real depth. He knew only two subjects thoroughly--
the text of the English Bible and the writings of the
Puritan divines. Both were products of the same age, and
as an antiquarian, Spurgeon was more knowledgeable than

---

[114]The Bible and the Newspaper (London, 1878).

[115]Autobiography, III, 301.

many scholars concerning the literature of the seventeenth century. His one personal luxury was a large library, and his quest for original Puritan editions made him well-known among booksellers. He eventually assembled one of the largest private collections of Puritan editions in the country.[116] He read and reviewed many of the Biblical commentaries of his own day, but without any sympathy or much comprehension. He measured everything he read against the yardstick of a verbally inspired Bible and the pronouncements of the Puritans, and in consequence, found little to approve of in the scriptural commentaries of his own time. His theology was practical rather than theoretical, and it is as a preacher and an administrator that he must be judged, and not as a scholar or theologian. The Bishop of Ripon observed, "I once heard it said of Mr. Spurgeon that he possessed no first-rate gifts, but a good supply of second-rate gifts in first-rate order,"[117] an assessment that was not wide of the mark.

---

[116]Spurgeon's library contained over 12,000 volumes, of which approximately 1,000 were printed before 1700. The oldest volume is dated 1525. The bulk of the collection was purchased by the trustees of William Jewell College in 1905 for $3,500.

[117]Living Age, LXXX (1892), 313-314.

Apart from his lectures and sermons, the bulk of Spurgeon's printed works consist of collections of short anecdotes and proverbs, intended to teach preachers how to illustrate their sermons with lively, pungent material. Typical is The Salt Cellars, Being a Collection of Proverbs, Together with Homely Notes Thereon. "I would go far to see a proverb book which I do not know," he said,[118] and he was rarely without a common-sense maxim or bit of proverbial wisdom tailored to meet the needs of any situation. Intellectually, he wallowed in wise-sayings. The quintessence of his prose style was the racy, common-sense proverb. A few examples from his popular work, John Ploughman's Talk, illustrate Spurgeon's gift for coining proverbs:

Of two evils, choose neither.
Mind your till and till your mind.
Promises don't fill the belly.
An old fox is shy of the trap.
When the goose drinks as deep as the gander,
pots are soon empty, and the cupboard is bare.

Better late than never, but better never late.

---

[118]Autobiography, IV, 105.

No flies will go down your mouth if you keep your mouth shut.

By perseverance the snail reached the ark.

While many of the proverbs attributed to Spurgeon are not strictly original, the total number credited to him is substantial. In the standard, short scholarly reference for quotations, Burton Stevenson's Book of Quotations, Spurgeon is credited with seventy-one citations, as compared to twenty-four for Luther, thirty-two for Donne, and fifty-nine for Kingsley. Calvin, Dale, Manning, and Liddon are not cited at all, Farrar is cited twice, Parker only once. Only Sydney Smith and George Herbert among English preachers rank above Spurgeon in total number of citations.[119] Obviously such a statistical survey of quotations cannot be pushed too far. The fact that Spurgeon is cited in Stevenson seventy-one times and Calvin not at all does not mean that Spurgeon has more stature than Calvin, or that George Herbert, with over one hundred citations, is more important than Spurgeon. The evidence

---

[119]Burton Stevenson's Book of Quotations, eighth edition.

merely substantiates the point that Spurgeon's fondness for coining proverbs made him very quotable.

Spurgeon's most popular work was John Ploughman's Talk, Being Plain Talk for Plain People in Pure Saxon. The book sold 400,000 copies before 1900, and is the source for most of the proverbs associated with Spurgeon's name. The fictional character, John Ploughman, was modelled on Will Richardson, a farmer whom Spurgeon had known in Stambourne, but it was also Spurgeon's nom de plume and represented something of an alter ego. John Ploughman emerged as a simple farmer, honest, thrifty, straightforward, and opinionated. He had no use for strong-minded women, college degrees, fancy dress, politicians, or lawyers. People with similar prejudices enjoyed John's ramblings, bought the book for a shilling a copy, and produced a demand for further instruction that led to several more editions of Talk, as well as John Ploughman's Pictures, and John Ploughman almanacs--a wise word for every day of the year. There was a great deal of Spurgeon in this sturdy, fictional ploughman. John, like

his creator, was "a square-toed, flat-footed believer,"
with "no trimming in him."[120]

John Ploughman, with all his prejudices, was
thoroughly English, and so was Spurgeon. He was, as Dr.
John Watson observed, "as characteristic an Englishman
as our generation has produced, and possibly, after Mr.
Gladstone, the ablest."[121] Spurgeon, like John Bright,
had the build of John Bull, and a face so plain and
homely that it was impossible to feel intimidated in his
presence. It was said of Canon Liddon that his face
was that of "a monk by Fra Angelico," but Spurgeon was
compared in his youth to a hair dresser's assistant, and
described in his maturity as a "gentleman farmer out on
a holiday." He never succeeded in looking much like the
conventional image of a man of the cloth. The Archbishop
of Canterbury, meeting him for the first time, was startled
to find that "Mr. Spurgeon is certainly uglier than I had
believed."[122] Even in an age when sheer physical bulk was

[120]Wilkinson, op. cit., p. 194.
[121]Fullerton, op. cit., p. 275.
[122]Benson, op. cit., p. 275.

not unusual, Spurgeon was bulky enough to inspire editorial
comments concerning his diet. He was not a handsome man,
but perhaps his physical appearance had a certain appeal
to his predominantly middle-class congregation. In his
very physical solidarity Spurgeon projected an image of
substantial, reassuring, well-fed prosperity. One would
be far more likely to look for Spurgeon in a canvas by
Breughel than Fra Angelico.

By birth, education, and temperament Spurgeon
belonged to the class of middle-class Nonconformists
Matthew Arnold labeled, "Philistine." A modern critic,
picking up the label, describes Spurgeon as "a cultural
and theological Philistine," and "a boor beside Newman,
Robertson, and Dale."[123] Yet it is perhaps precisely
because he was a cultural Philistine that Spurgeon enjoyed
the great influence that he did with ordinary people.
W. T. Stead wrote of Spurgeon that he was "a journalist
of the pulpit," who understood that "if you want to
influence the minds of your fellow men you must not be

---

[123]Horton Davies, op. cit., p. 172.

too far in advance, you must not be out of sympathy even with their prejudices and stupidities."[124] If he was a Philistine, so were the people he was trying to reach; if his tastes were mediocre, so were the tastes of his audiences. "It is because he is so ordinary," wrote a reporter in 1884, "so closely in sympathy with the ordinary, that his success is so gratifying, revealing as it does, the willingness of the most commonplace of English classes to accept even a commonplace Christianity, if it is placed before them in a way that comes directly home."[125] He was not the theological illiterate that some of his critics claimed, but he was largely self-educated, and his approach to learning remained thoroughly pragmatic: "I value books for the good they may do men's souls," he said.[126] As a result of this attitude, his literary preferences were frequently mediocre, and his aesthetic sense warped. He thought Sir Walter Scott "the greatest mind God ever created,"[127] and he considered "In the Children's Hospital"

---

[124]Review of Reviews, V (March 1892), 172.

[125]Spectator, LVII (June 1884), 8112.

[126]Autobiography, II, 153.

[127]Williams, op. cit., p. 53.

Tennyson's finest poem.[128] He was reduced to tears by
Mrs. Prentice's The Little Preacher, and he had words of
praise for such maudlin productions as How Little Bessie
Kept the Wolf From the Door and Jessica's First Prayer.
He declared that Watts' hymns were greater poetry than
Paradise Lost, and The Sinner's Friend was of greater
worth than all the works of Homer.[129] Art galleries and
museums bored him, because the exhibits were "either the
same thing over and over again, or else productions which
convey no thought, suggest no lessons, and embody no
great idea." In his opinion, most museums contained far
too many paintings of "groups of beer-boozers, or knights
doing nothing, and nobodies in fine clothes."[130] He
confessed in public, "my taste is very bad," but such a
candid admission would be more likely to win than to repel
Spurgeon's typical audience. In his tastes, as in his

[128]C. H. Spurgeon, The Old Gospel and the New
Theology (London, 1887), pp. 5-6.

[129]Autobiography, II, 153.

[130]C. H. Spurgeon, My Run to Naples and Pompeii
(London, 1873), p. 6.

appearance, he was thoroughly unpretentious, and all the
more persuasive to an unpretentious audience.

Spurgeon not only shared the tastes of the masses,
he shared certain of their vices as well. His fondness
for smoking big cigars in public made him one of the most
prominent smokers in Christendom. He made no attempt to
conceal his habit, and once defended smoking in terms which
scandalized less broad-minded souls. In 1874, an American
evangelist, Dr. Pentecost, was visiting the Tabernacle and
invited to preach. Unaware of his famous host's indul-
gence, Dr. Pentecost digressed from the text of his sermon
to vigorously condemn the vice of smoking. Spurgeon's
congregation, fully aware of their pastor's habit, was
horrified, but Spurgeon remained calm throughout the sermon.
When Dr. Pentecost had finished, however, Spurgeon added
his own footnote to his guest's remarks. He disagreed
with the visitor's remarks concerning smoking, he informed
the congregation; moreover, as a smoker, until he found
an eleventh commandment, "Thou shalt not smoke," he would
continue smoking "to the glory of God."[131] The remark was

_____

[131]Williams, op. cit., pp. 76-77.

widely publicized, and led non-smokers to deluge Spurgeon
with angry protests. To one irate critic, Spurgeon
replied:

> Dear Sir: I cultivate my flowers and burn my weeds.
> Yours Truly,
> C. H. Spurgeon.[132]

It is worth noting that one grateful tobacco company,
fully aware of the value of such an endorsement, began to
feature Spurgeon's round face on tobacco packages.

The Pastor of the Tabernacle, to the horror of
teetotalers, also enjoyed an occasional drink. Spurgeon
had reached maturity in a society and at a time when
moderate drink was not frowned upon. He knew that the
Puritans had not been teetotalers, and annoyed abstainers
by referring to beer as "the Puritan drink" He drank
beer, wine, and brandy in moderation through most of his
life. As the total abstinence movement gained strength
in the second half of the century, great pressures were
exerted upon Spurgeon to take the pledge. For some time
he refused. In March 1865, he pinned the Band of Hope blue

---

[132]Ibid., p. 78.

ribbon upon his twin sons, but added, "I am not a
teetotaler myself, and it is not likely I ever shall
be,"[133] and in 1868 he announced, "we will never put our
conscience under any man's heel, be he a teetotaler or
vegetarian."[134] In 1871 he poked gentle fun at a Band
of Hope calendar for children, describing it as "ghastly,"
and observing, "the snakes are on every page, and seem
to be fond of coiling around bottles with the corks in;
we think they are more likely to be there when the corks
are out."[135] In 1877 he specifically denied that the
Bible commanded abstinence: "The wines of the Bible were
intoxicating. . . . Our Lord did not ordain jelly or
syrup, or cherry juice to be the emblem of his sacrifice."[136]
He was irritated by the pronouncement of The Temperance
Manual that "those who use alcoholic beverages are aiding
in increasing the wickedness, augmenting the guilt, and

---

[133]Pike, Life, II, 168.

[134]Sword and Trowel, IV (1868), 565.

[135]Ibid., VII (1871), 476.

[136]Ibid., XIII (1877), 437.

perpetuating the wretchedness of their fellow men,"
pointing out that "such a censure would have included in
one sweep one whom we call 'Master and Lord.'"[137]

Spurgeon's stubborn determination to follow
Timothy for his stomach's sake provoked bitter personal
attacks. Neal Dow, an American temperance leader, published a diatribe accusing "a famous London preacher,"
who suffered from gout, of drinking a quart of beer and
a stiff portion of brandy every day, with the result
that "his face is big and flabby, with as much expression
as if it were a mass of putty. . . . He eats like
Dr. Johnson."[138] Though Dow later denied that he had
Spurgeon in mind, his remarks were justifiably resented
by Spurgeon. In the end, Spurgeon gave up alcohol,
probably less because of the pressures of the total
abstainers than for reasons of health. The temperance
movement welcomed the tardy sheep with open arms. On
October 14, 1882, the Blue Ribbon Chronicle printed on

[137]Ibid., VII (1871), 380.

[138]Letter to the New York Witness, December 11,
1878. Scrapbook clipping.

its cover a full-color portrait of "the popular preacher
and Blue Ribbonite," C. H. Spurgeon. And so Spurgeon
became a total abstainer, but without noticeable enthusi-
a s m. Unfermented wine replaced the previously fermented
variety at the Tabernacle communion table--though stories
circulated that a suspicious deacon had taken the "unfermented" wine to a chemist for analysis and it had proven
to be 19 percent alcohol. A Tabernacle Total Abstinence
Society was formed, with Spurgeon as honorary chairman,
but his warmth toward the group can be gathered by his
opening admonition that they were not to "wear a lot of
peacock's feathers and putty medals, nor to be always
trying to convert the moderate drinkers." Spurgeon did
not enjoy being dictated to, especially on such a personal
matter as drink, and his support of the movement was at
best grudging. He was primarily concerned with saving
souls, and he suspected that the abstinence movement
emphasized a particular problem to the detriment of the
central issue of man's sinful nature. "Nothing less than
to see men new creatures in Christ must satisfy us," he
declared. "Many will utterly slay drunkenness, and hang
a bit of blue ribbon over its grave, and yet all the while

remain utterly bad at heart."[139] Spurgeon never confused

abstinence with Godliness nor did he assume that all

teetotalers were superior to drinkers. Asked in 1882 to

endorse a man for the school board who was a fellow member

of the Band of Hope, he replied, "Do you think I am

going to support a donkey just because he has a piece

of blue ribbon on him?"[140]

While by modern standards Spurgeon's attitudes

toward smoking and drinking appear both cosmopolitan and

tolerant, his attitude toward other, seemingly far less

harmful worldly pleasures are in marked opposition to his

easygoing tolerance of liquor and tobacco. While he found

no difficulty in approving of moderate drinking, he

vigorously condemned social dancing and the theater. He

once said that the only form of social dancing which he

could approve was that in which the two sexes danced

separately--a remark which prompted Punch to feature "a

delightful ball, according to the Reverend Spurgeon,"

in which grim, haloed deacons danced a stately form to

---

[139]Williams, op. cit., p. 167.

[140]Christian World, October 19, 1882.

the "Spurgeon Quadrille."[141] Following the Puritans,
Spurgeon held that mixed dancing led to carnal thoughts;
moreover, as a Baptist he could not forget that "the
first Baptist had his head danced off," forgetting, so
it seems, that whatever Salome's sins, she had danced
alone. He was equally opposed to the theater, though he
loved to read Shakespeare aloud. Strange as his opinions
may seem by modern standards, they reflected his early
training and background. Raised in the Puritan tradition,
he saw nothing evil in enjoying moderate drink, but
social dancing or the theater, for him as for the "saints,"
were symptoms of moral depravity. Toward the end of the
century, the traditional evangelical opposition to the
theater began to fade, just as the total abstinence movement gained strength. Spurgeon, true to his training,
refused to change his attitude toward the theater, and
yielded to the teetotalers only with reluctance.

Narrow and opinionated in many ways, Spurgeon was
remarkably tolerant on racial questions, and seemed to be

---

[141]Punch, XXXIV (January 16, 1858), 23, 26.

without any racial prejudices.   In common with many
English evangelicals, he bitterly castigated the institution of slavery in the United States.   Early in his London
ministry, he invited a fugitive slave, John Andrew Jackson, to address the congregation at the New Park Street
Chapel, and then followed the slave's account of his
trials with a forthright denunciation of America's
"peculiar institution."

> Slavery is the foulest blot which ever stained a
> national escutcheon, and may have to be washed out
> with blood. America is in many respects a glorious
> country, but it may be necessary to teach her some
> wholesome lessons at the point of a bayonet--to carve
> freedom into her with a bowie knife or send it home
> to her heart with a revolver. Better far should it
> come to this issue, that North and South should be
> rent asunder, and the States of the Union shivered
> into a thousand fragments, than that slavery should
> be suffered to continue. Some American divines seem
> to regard it, indeed, with wonderful complacency.
> They have so accustomed themselves to wrap it up in
> soft phrases that they lose sight of its real char-
> acter. They call it a "peculiar institution," until
> they forget in what its peculiarity consists. It is
> indeed a peculiar institution, just as the Devil is
> a peculiar angel, and hell is a peculiarly hot place.
> For my part, I hold such miserable tamperings with
> sin in abhorrence, and can hold no communion of any
> sort with those who are guilty of it.[142]

---

[142]Carlile, op. cit., pp. 159-160.

Spurgeon's outspoken anti-slavery remarks were pared from

the text of the American edition of his sermons by his

American publishers in order that they might not offend

a portion of his American audience. When Henry Ward Beecher

wrote to Spurgeon, protesting these expurgations, Spurgeon

replied: "I believe slavery to be a crime of crimes, a

soul destroying sin, and an iniquity which cries aloud

for vengeance."[143] He then published a letter in the

Watchman and Reflector--which was widely reprinted in

American journals--declaring: "I do from my inmost soul

detest slavery anywhere and everywhere, and though I

commune at the Lord's Table with men of all creeds, yet

with a slave-holder I hold no fellowship of any kind or

sort."[144] His pronouncements drew a quick response. The

Times reported in July 1860, that a large crowd had

gathered in front of "a Virginia courthouse" for a cere-

monial burning of Spurgeon's sermons.[145] From 1860 until

the postwar years, the sale of Spurgeon's sermons in the

---

[143]Ibid., p. 166.   [144]Ibid., p. 161.

[145]The Times, July 23, 1860.

United States was negligible. It was a price he paid
cheerfully for the right to speak his mind freely. There
were a few Blacks in his college--including one ex-slave
from the United States. When the Fisk College Jubilee
singers visited the Tabernacle after the war, he told the
audience that he thought the ladies "very handsome," and
he could not imagine anyone owning them, "except a gentleman owning one of the ladies as his wife."[146] Certainly
Spurgeon had little opportunity to meet or know many
Blacks and his hostility to slavery was a part of his
evangelical inheritance; nevertheless, he was more outspoken than most on the evils of slavery, and he paid a
price for his opinions that many did not. There was a
fundamental decency behind his racial attitudes which went
beyond conventional toleration.

An even more significant indication of Spurgeon's
attitude toward racial questions can be gathered from his
pronouncements in the celebrated Governor Eyre Controversy,
a case which brought the issue of racial prejudice home to
mid-Victorian Englishmen with a directness which the

---

[146]Maurice Davies, op. cit., p. 345.

remoter issue of slavery in the United States could not.
The controversy had its origin in October 1865, when a
Black uprising in the crown colony of Jamaica was suppressed
with awesome force by troops acting on the orders of the
colonial governor, Edward Eyre.[147] Nearly five hundred
Blacks were killed outright or following summary court
martials. Hundreds more were tortured and imprisoned, and
a thousand homes were burned. One of those executed after
a trial marked by irregularities was George William Gordon,
a mulatto member of the Jamaica House of Assembly and a
political opponent of Governor Eyre. Gordon, a Baptist
lay-preacher, was accused of being the leader of the
uprising. When the news of the Jamaica rebellion reached
Britain, public opinion was sharply divided over the wisdom
of Eyre's conduct. Was he a hero who had "saved Jamaica
for the crown," or was he the wanton murderer of hundreds
of innocent Blacks? Even more important, was there one
standard of British justice for whites, and another for
Blacks? A Jamaica Committee headed by John Stuart Mill

---

[147]My summary is based upon Bernard Semmel,
Democracy Versus Empire (New York, 1969).

and Thomas Hughes was formed and began a three-year long battle to bring Eyre to justice for his crimes. The Jamaica Committee was countered by a Pro-Eyre group led by Carlyle, Ruskin, and Kingsley. The major issues raised during the controversy were legal ones, yet underlying the legal questions was the specter of racial prejudice and fear. The Eyre Case became, in Leonard Huxley's phrase, "the touchstone of ultimate political convictions."[148]

Spurgeon was not a member of the Jamaica Committee, but he was closely associated with two of its most prominent members, Thomas Hughes and Samuel Morton Peto. Peto, a member of parliament for Bristol and a Baptist layman, had laid the foundation stone for the Tabernacle. In addition, Spurgeon was a supporter of Edward Underhill, Joint Secretary of the Baptist Missionary Society, and one of Eyre's most persistent critics. In December 1866, Underhill came to the Tabernacle at Spurgeon's request to speak on the "Present State of Jamaica." In supporting the actions

[148]Ibid., p. 12.

of the Jamaica Committee, Spurgeon was certainly influenced by the fact that the martyred Gordon had been a Baptist lay-preacher, but he also had a genuine sympathy for the oppressed Blacks of Jamaica. Though Eyre was eventually exonerated, Spurgeon was confident that history would reverse the verdict. Writing in March 1868, he declared:

> That Mr. Gordon was innocent of the crimes alleged against him is as clear as noonday, and that he was a Christian hero, a soldier of liberty, and a defender of the right, is evident to most of us. His name and story will be forever intertwisted with the substance of Jamaica's history, and the day will come when statues will be erected in his memory, and their unveiling sanctioned by the presence of the highest authorities of the island.[149]

It is difficult to attach facile labels such as "evangelical," or "puritanical," or "anti-intellectual" to all of Spurgeon's attitudes because he drew his opinions from many traditions rather than a single one. In many of his opinions he was typically evangelical, but on some questions he stood virtually alone. His defense of drinking offended many evangelicals, but perhaps Spurgeon's loyalty

---

[149] In a review of D. Fletcher, "The Life of the Honorable George W. Gordon, the Martyr of Jamaica," in Sword and Trowel, IV (1868), 138.

was to an older tradition. Much of teetotalism resulted
from the replacement of inner conviction with outer show,
a development Spurgeon scorned. Although he frequently
lapsed into the familiar anti-intellectual arguments
against a learned ministry, he was an author, teacher, and
bibliophile, a man who spent his rare free hours surrounded
by books. Though many of his personal tastes seem maudlin
and sentimental, his abilities won the praise of men of
discrimination and culture. Though he ran the Tabernacle
with a firm and autocratic hand, he was a notoriously soft-
hearted and charitable man. The truth is that Spurgeon
was both autocrat and fierce democrat, authoritarian and
humane. Possibly because he was such an interesting combination of attitudes and emotions, he was one of the
most influential men of his day, and able to move as easily
in the society of archbishops and prime ministers as in
the company of farmers, chambermaids, and costermongers.
A tolerant, intolerant, democratic autocrat; an anti-
intellectual bibliophile; a Calvinist who offered salvation
to the whole world--the Pastor of the Tabernacle defies
easy stereotypes.

CHAPTER IV

EVANGELIST TO THE WORLD

It is a sight in Colorado on Sunday to see the
miners come out of the bowels of the hills and
gather in schoolhouses or under the trees while
some old English miner stands up and reads one
of Charles Spurgeon's sermons. They have
conversions right along.

. . . D. L. Moody

In 1855, in the second year of his London ministry,

Spurgeon began to publish weekly sermons. The sermons

were issued continuously until 1917, carrying Spurgeon's

message and name to remote points of the world. Spurgeon's

reputation was not limited to London. Though he preached

there to the largest Protestant congregation in the world,

his congregation was dwarfed by the multitudes who never

saw his face or heard his voice yet who knew Spurgeon

through his printed sermons. "I shall never see

Mr. Spurgeon on earth," said an Englishman dying in

Brazil, "but I shall tell the Lord Jesus about him when

I get to heaven."[1] It was such people who formed his largest congregation, his widest audience, and it was a congregation that encompassed the literate world.

When the first issue of The New Park Street Pulpit appeared in 1855, it was considered a trial venture, another supplement to the "penny pulpits" to which Spurgeon had already contributed an occasional sermon. He did not expect to publish a regular series, but the initial demand for his sermons was so great that the weekly issues were continued through the year, and then became a regular series. The young Spurgeon rejoiced at the success of his printed sermons, and with an innocent naïvete, told his New Park Street Congregation, "words that I spoke three weeks ago, eyes are now perusing, while tears are gushing from them as they read! Glory be to God most high!"[2]

The first five volumes of the series, The New Park Street Pulpit, were composed of single sermons of eight

---

[1]Autobiography, II, 162.

[2]The New Park Street Pulpit, I (1855), 344.

pages of small type each, which sold individually for a
penny. At the end of the year, the single sermons were
gathered together, and the approximately fifty-two issues
published as a single volume. At the time when the series
became <u>The Metropolitan Tabernacle Pulpit</u>, the duty on
paper was abolished, which allowed Spurgeon's publishers
to expand the eight pages of small type to twelve pages
of larger, more readable type. Until the firm of Passmore
and Alabaster became Spurgeon's publishers, the distribu-
tion of his sermons was rather haphazard, and some booksellers refused to carry the weekly sermons. In Cambridge,
where Spurgeon had a local following from his Waterbeach
days, the bookshops refused to stock his sermons, and they
had to be purchased from a local green-grocer.[3] Even
when the shops were willing to carry his sermons, critics
found his use of advertising to promote their sale another
instance of his deplorable "sensationalism." As his
reputation grew, the criticism was muted and the hostility
of the booksellers faded. When his publishers took offices

---

[3]Charles Ray, <u>A Marvelous Ministry</u> (London,
1905), p. 22.

on Paternoster Row, it seemed to symbolize the
respectability of their enterprise.

Spurgeon's weekly sermons had a normal circulation of 25,000, although that figure was frequently higher,
especially upon the occasion of certain topical sermons
such as the Mutiny or the death of the Prince Consort.
His best-selling single sermon, on "Baptismal Regeneration,"
sold 350,000 copes when printed as a pamphlet. By 1863,
when the five-hundredth weekly issue appeared, his sermons
had already sold more than eight million copies. At the
time of his death in 1892, fifty million copies had been
sold, a figure which has since doubled.[4] Issued continuously in a series of thirty-seven volumes, the series
continued even after Spurgeon's death. There was such a
backlog of sermons remaining that the series continued
until May 10, 1917, when the last sermon, number 3,653
was issued. Even at that late date, there were still
unpublished sermons, but a paper shortage brought on by
the war caused the publishers to abandon the series.

---

[4]A. C. Underwood, A History of the English
Baptists (London, 1947), p. 219.

Spurgeon's sermons were published in forty languages, including Arabic, Bengali, Chinese, Hindi, Maori, Telegu, and Urdu, as well as the major European languages. They were also published in Braille. Spurgeon never traveled further from London than Southern Italy, but his sermons traveled all over the world. When Dr. Livingston went to Africa on one of his missions, he carried with him a copy of one of Spurgeon's sermons. Years later, his daughter discovered the sermon in one of his trunks. It was well-thumbed, but intact, and bore the penciled comment, "very good, D.L."[5] Similar stories could be told about other, less celebrated travelers who carried with them into their own particular wilderness copies of Spurgeon's sermons as a last, tangible link with the civilization they left behind.

Over the years, Spurgeon collected amazing evidence concerning the far-reaching influence of his printed sermons. The sermons were printed, with Spurgeon's permission, in newspapers in Australia and the United States, and many

---

[5]Fullerton, op. cit., p. 221.

who would not purchase a religious tract read Spurgeon's sermons as they appeared in newspapers. One woman living in an English village wrote to say that she had been converted through reading one of his sermons which had been printed in an Australian newspaper and wrapped around a package sent to her in England. "Rough dwellers in the wild," living "far away in the bush," or "far away in the backwoods,"[6] wrote letters to Spurgeon telling him how much his sermons had benefited them. A correspondent in Minnesota wrote assuring him that in a community of less than six hundred people, several families subscribed to his sermons,[7] and from Corpus Christi, Texas, a semi-literate eighty-two year old man wrote a note to "Rev. Spurgeon, Tabernacle, London," recounting the good his sermons had done the local Christians in faraway Texas,

---

[6]The phrases are Spurgeon's. He had a romantic idea of the frontier. To judge by his comments, he believed most Americans of the late nineteenth century still lived in "the backwoods," and carried bowie knives.

[7]G. Holden Pike, Charles Haddon Spurgeon, Preacher, Author, Philanthropist (New York, 1892), p. 234.

as "the no lawe hear."[8]   A commander of a British garrison

in India recalled to Spurgeon that his troops had gathered

under the trees each Sunday to hear one of Spurgeon's

sermons read aloud.[9]   Spurgeon treasured each piece of

evidence regarding the power of his printed sermons,

declaring that one message "from some poor woman in the

backwoods of America" was "more precious to me than a big

bank-note."[10]   He observed that a single sermon, "Compel

Them to Come In," had led almost three hundred people to

testify that it had been the instrument of their conversion.

Of a sermon preached in 1856, Spurgeon wrote, "more than

thirty years afterwards, I received the joyful news that

a murderer in South America had been brought to the Savior

through reading it."[11]   It is certainly true, as W. T. Stead

observed, that Spurgeon "collected trophies of souls."

---

[8]The Ms. letter is in the Spurgeon papers, Spurgeon's
College, London. Spurgeon wrote on the margin of the
letter: "It is a speciman of hieroglyphics worthy of
preservation."

[9]Autobiography, IV, 193.

[10]Williams, op. cit., p. 52.

[11]Autobiography, II, 161.

The wilder and more improbable the testimony, the more
Spurgeon rejoiced in it, seeing factual evidence of the
wonderful power of the Word. When a cowboy wrote that
after reading one of Spurgeon's sermons he had "given up
bowie knives and revolvers," to "become like a child in
spirit," or a preacher in Tennessee testified, "nine years
ago I was a wild young man; but I was converted through
reading one of Mr. Spurgeon's sermons, and I am now pastor
of a large and influential church,"[12] Spurgeon accepted
the testimonials uncritically. He basked in such testimony
and was not inclined to be sceptical concerning its
validity. He continued to be amazed at the success of
his sermons in producing conversions, and professed to be
"more astonished at the fact than any other man can be,
and I feel no other reason for it but this--the sermons
contain the gospel, preached in plain language, and this
is precisely what multitudes need beyond anything else."[13]

Some of Spurgeon's subscribers put his sermons to
a very practical use. Many of his readers wrote to him

[12] Sword and Trowel, XX (1884), 200.

[13] Autobiography, II, 154.

reporting that his sermons were being delivered by other preachers. As early as October 1855, Spurgeon mentioned co his New Park Street congregation that he had heard "a canon of the Cathedral" was preaching from his sermons.[14] In Spurgeon's day, plagiarism in the pulpit was common. Some writers actually made a living supplying ready-made discourses of all shades of orthodoxy to preachers too-overworked or too lazy to prepare their own. The regular appearance of Spurgeon's sermons relieved not a few preachers and parsons from the burden of sermon-preparation. "Failing originality," concluded a reporter, "the next best method is to closely copy a man who is original; and in this respect, no one, save perhaps Whitefield himself, ever had so large a crowd of followers as Mr. Spurgeon."[15] Spurgeon's example spawned a multitude of imitators, who not only copied his style, but who appropriated his sermons as well. Spurgeon once had the unique experience of wandering into a rural Methodist chapel and hearing the local preacher deliver one of _his_ sermons. As he wryly

---

[14]_The New Park Street Pulpit_, I (1855), 344.

[15]Maurice Davies, _op. cit._, p. 117.

observed in 1879, "since so many have copied my style,
and so considerable a number have borrowed my discourses,
I submit that I am the orthodox example rather than the
glaring exception . . . an old-fashioned kind of body,
who is treated as an established part of the ecclesiastical
life of this great city."[16]

Spurgeon's sermons were a standard item on the
bookshelves of many homes in England and Scotland. One
zealous admirer, anxious to spread the good word, purchased
250,000 copies, had them specially bound "in the best
style," and then sent copies to every crowned head in
Europe, every member of parliament, every student in British
universities, and the principal householders in Ireland.
In the railroad stations in Scotland, Spurgeon's sermons
were sold side-by-side with the newspapers, and it was
said that his sermons could be found in two-thirds of the
homes of Ulster. How does one explain the phenomenal
sale of Spurgeon's sermons? One explanation is that the
individual sermons were cheap, and published in a

---

[16]Spurgeon, _Eccentric Preachers_ (London, 1879),
p. 9.

conveniently-sized tract format. The language of the
sermons was plain and direct, and the parables and stories
held the attention of the reader. These stories, anecdotes,
and parables also explain why the sermons were a popular
choice for reading aloud. Reading one of Spurgeon's sermons could serve as a source of inspiration and self-
improvement. W. T. Stead was perhaps typical of many
when he wrote that for years he read one of Spurgeon's
sermons every morning before going to work.[17] Spurgeon's
sermons appealed to that wide section of the reading
public who knew their Bible and relished their sermons.
The bond of a common Bible gave to nineteenth-century
society a cultural cohesiveness which is often forgotten.
It was an age in which speakers cited scriptures in House
debates without the need to explain their references.
As E. E. Kellett later recalled, it was not unusual to
encounter laymen who could recite the genealogy from Adam
to Christ, or name all the kings of Israel and Judah with
the years of their reign.[18]

---

[17]Review of Reviews, V (February 1892), 117.

[18]Kellett, op. cit., pp. 106-107.

People in the nineteenth century, lacking the
forms of instant communication available to modern man,
attached a significance to the printed word that we do not
today. For those isolated from society, books, newspapers,
sermons, and the ubiquitous tract could function as self-
contained links with civilization. Spurgeon's published
sermons provided a form of instant, convenient worship
for those isolated from a church. They could be read privately as devotional tracts; but significantly, they were
often read in a social context, as people gathered
together to hear them read aloud. Ian Maclaren (Dr. John
Watson) has described the way in which issues of Spurgeon's
sermons were avidly awaited by the people in the rural
Scots village of his youth. He recalled that when his
employer went into town each week to buy supplies, his
wife's parting admonition was always the same--"and John,
dinna forget Spurgeon!" "Spurgeon" was a weekly ritual
for the whole household. Gathered together around the
fire, the group would listen as one of the family read
aloud from the weekly sermons:

> Perhaps the glamour of the past is upon me, perhaps a
> lad was but a poor judge, but it seemed to me good

reading--slow, well-pronounced, reverent, charged with tenderness and pathos. No one slept or moved, and the firelight falling on the serious faces of the stalwart men, and the shining of the lamps on the good grey heads, as the gospel came, sentence by sentence, to every heart, is a sacred memory, and I count that Mr. Spurgeon would have been mightily pleased to have been in such meetings of homely folk. . . . Who of all preachers you can mention would have held such companies but Spurgeon? What is to take their place, when the last of these well-known sermons disappears from village shops and cottage shelves? Is there any other gospel which will ever be so understanded of the people, or move human hearts as that which Spurgeon preached in the best words of our tongue? The good man and his wife have entered into their rest long ago, and of all that company, I know not one now; but I see them as I write, against the setting of gold, and I hear the angel's voice, "Manasseh is saved," and for that evening and others very sacred to my heart I cannot forget Spurgeon.[19]

There were remote areas of the British Isles where these sermons represented virtually the only link the residents had to the outside world. There were places, it is said, where people failed to recognize the names of Gladstone or Disraeli, but responded at once to "Spurgeon."[20] The old

---

[19]Ian Maclaren (Dr. John Watson), "Dinna Forget Spurgeon," in His Majesty Baby and Some Common People (London, 1902), pp. 161-163. The sermon referred to, "Manasseh," was preached November 30, 1856 at the Surrey Gardens Music Hall. It is Number 105 in the New Park Street series.

[20]Sword and Trowel, XVIII (1882), 502.

Scot who expressed the wish that someday before he died
he could journey to London "to see Madame Tussaud's and
hear Mr. Spurgeon," suggests the place Spurgeon occupied
in the popular imagination of rural Britain.[21]

When Spurgeon left his London congregation for
brief trips into the countryside, his congregations were
crowded with the people who had been reading his sermons
for years. The Baptist paper, The Freeman, commented:

> The coming of Mr. Spurgeon to any city, town, or
> village, either in England, Wales, or Scotland, is
> an event which moves the entire population, Church
> and Nonconforming, rich and poor, church-going and
> non-church-going. In a city such as Manchester, the
> "upper ten" talk of it on the "Change, while down to
> the cabmen and bootblacks it is the theme of conver-
> sation. . . . No other preacher in this age wields
> such power, and it may be questioned whether anyone
> else has ever done it in these Islands save John Knox
> in Scotland and Christmas Evans in Wales."[22]

W. Y. Fullerton told the story of an old man who lived in
a country district which was to be visited by Spurgeon who
inquired of his employer if he might attend Spurgeon's
afternoon service, and was told that he could go only if
he had finished the entire day's work. The old man was up

---

[21]Contemporary Review, LXI (March 1892), 302.
[22]Cited in Pike, Life, III, 164.

before dawn working in the fields, and with every sweep

of his scythe he was heard to chant, "Spurgeon! Spurgeon!

Spurgeon!" until, working with inspired energy, he finished

his task early and was able to attend the service.[23] As

Joseph Parker wrote, "The visits of such men . . . formed

epochs in the history of agricultural Britain. How the

visits of great men were anticipated! What recollections

of their services were passed from mouth to mouth! How

young men felt encouraged in their best reading and in

their best religious service."[24]

Spurgeon's first volume of sermons sold 20,000

volumes in the United States, and from the beginning of

his ministry he had a large American audience for his

printed sermons. A common language and a common evangeli-

cal tradition have acted as strong links between the

United States and Britain, and at no time more than in the

nineteenth century. From the eighteen-forties on--with

the brief exception of the civil war years--there was a

constant exchange of evangelists between the two countries,

----

[23]Fullerton, op. cit., pp. 125-126.

[24]Parker, Autobiography, p. 365.

adding "a cosmopolitan flavor to what had previously been a provincial institution."[25] In 1849-1851, and again in 1858-1860, Charles Finney toured the British Isles, conducting revivals in London, Birmingham, Manchester, Edinburgh, and Aberdeen. The "Second Evangelical Awakening" of 1859 led two members of the Plymouth Brethren, Henry Moorehouse and George C. Heedham, to carry their message to the United States. Directing their appeal to the urban poor, the two specialized in Bible readings "in the old folk tradition."[26] Among the churches they visited was D. L. Moody's church in Chicago. Moody made his reputation in Britain in the famous Moody-and-Sankey campaigns which began in 1873. As Moody was packing the great halls of Britain, an itinerant English revivalist, Henry Varley, was filling Barnum's Hippodrome in New York preaching a gospel "calculated to impress people whose minds are not over-sensitive."[27]

----

[25]William G. McLaughlin, _Modern Revivalism_ (New York, 1959), p. 153.

[26]_Ibid._, p. 159.

[27]Cited from "a Unitarian paper," in _ibid._, p. 160.

It was natural that Spurgeon found an audience for his sermons in America. Their racy, common-sense approach to the gospel was perfectly suited to the American temperament. Dr. Joseph Cook of Boston remembered how these sermons had influenced him when he was a boy:

> I recollect vividly myself going into the empty upper rooms of those classic Latin commons at Phillips Exeter Academy, Andover, and reading aloud for an hour, nearly every Sunday morning from the sermons of this young and until recently unknown preacher of London. His light was beginning to fall upon this land as early as 1854, and it has been growing . . . ever since.[28]

The boy listening to Spurgeon's sermons in a Scots cottage and the boy declaiming the sermons to an empty classroom in America are evidence of the cultural link these sermons represented to the English-speaking world. Except for the years 1861-1865, there was a steady market for Spurgeon's sermons in the United States and a steady stream of American tourists coming to the Tabernacle. By 1879, 500,000 copies of his sermons had been sold in the United States, and the Christian Herald declared, "It is safe to say that no other preacher has had so extensive a hearing in the

---

[28]Review of Reviews, V (April 1892), 385.

United States as Charles H. Spurgeon."[29] In that same
year, a reporter for the Richmond Herald, reporting on a
European tour, wrote, "Of course I went to see Spurgeon.
I would as soon think of leaving London without seeing
Westminster Abbey or the Tower."[30] The Watchman (Boston)
reported that "during the tourist season, more of the
states of America are seated in his congregation than in
any congregation in the United States."[31] "Our first
question to returning friends," wrote a reporter for the
North American Review, "is, 'did you see the Queen? Then,
did you hear Spurgeon?'"[32] The New Englander, determined
to Americanize Spurgeon, described his features as
"unmistakably Indian!" In the magazine's opinion,
Spurgeon resembled "a good humored man of business, crossed
with Indian blood."[33] For the convenience of American

---

[29]The Christian Herald, January 1879, cited in
Autobiography, IV, 274-275.

[30]Richmond Herald, October 1879. Scrapbook
clipping.

[31]The Watchman, November 24, 1881. Scrapbook
clipping.

[32]North American Review, 86 (1858), 275.

[33]New Englander, XVI (1858), 281.

tourists determined to "hear Spurgeon," London bus drivers would begin to warn them about the impending appearance of the Tabernacle three miles in advance of the destination, and as the buses would roll over the bridge to the south side of the Thames, conductors would shout out, "Over the water to Charlie!"

Frederick Douglass was one of those Americans who came to know Spurgeon through his printed sermons, and felt compelled to visit the Tabernacle to see the man whose writing had so impressed him. As he confided to Spurgeon, the visit to the Tabernacle had been "the realization of an ardent desire born of reading some of your sermons in America."[34] "Everything that I could get hold of in print that he ever said, I read," testified D. L. Moody, who crossed the Atlantic in 1867 to see his idol. "My eyes just feasted upon him, and my heart's desire for years was accomplished."[35] Lucretia Garfield, performing the sad duty of gathering her husband's possessions and vacating the White House, discovered a folded program of

_____

[34]Autobiography, IV, 176.

[35]Ibid., 247.

a Tabernacle service, and wrote to Spurgeon that her grief was lessened by the memory of the inspiration she and her husband had felt attending one of his services.[36]

Because of his great reputation, Spurgeon received over the years a number of invitations to visit the United States. The Boston Redpath Lyceum Bureau tried for years to get him on the American lecture circuit, guaranteeing all of his expenses plus one thousand dollars in gold for every lecture that he delivered, but even such a lucrative offer failed to tempt him to cross the ocean. It was not uncommon for preachers to supplement their incomes by taking to the lecture circuit; Beecher, for instance, was a lecturer for the Redpath Lyceum Bureau, but Spurgeon apparently felt his pastoral responsibilities more heavily than Beecher did: Beecher, Spurgeon dryly observed, "is far from being as spiritual as he is spirited, and is more a model for an orator than a divine."[37] Money could not tempt Spurgeon to the United States, nor could the

---

[36]Ms. letter from Lucretia Garfield, August 29, 1882, in Spurgeon Papers, Spurgeon's College, London.

[37]Sword and Trowel, VII (1871), 131.

lure of the academy. Yale invited him to deliver one of the Lyman Beecher series of lectures on preaching, and R. W. Dale added his pleas to those of the university, but in vain.[38] He could not spare the time. American revivalists campaigned through Britain, and English evangelicals carried the good word to America, but Spurgeon sent his sermons and stayed in the Tabernacle. As he very characteristically explained to Dale, "I sit on my own gate, and whistle my own tunes, and am quite content."[39]

---

[38]Ms. letter from R. W. Dale, October 28, 1878; and Ms letter from Leonard Bacon, October 4, 1878, offering Spurgeon $600 plus expenses to come to Yale, are in Spurgeon Papers, Spurgeon's College.

[39]Dale, Life, op. cit., p. 339.

C H A P T E R   V

RITUALISM AND REGENERATION

The 1860's were for Spurgeon years of controversy
and commitment. The decade began with the opening of the
Metropolitan Tabernacle and ended with Spurgeon's emergence as a prominent spokesman for a newly aroused political
Dissent. With increasing militance, Spurgeon voiced Nonconformist grievances against the doctrine and practice of the
Established Church. In sermons, speeches, and tracts he bitterly castigated the "bastard popery" and hypocrisy of the
Anglican establishment. In June 1864, he touched off a
heated controversy with the publication of a sermon on
"Baptismal Regeneration." The sermon provoked a rancorous
debate in evangelical circles, sparked a pamphlet war, and
ended in Spurgeon's withdrawal from the Evangelical
Alliance. Spurgeon's conduct during the controversy
closely paralleled his behavior twenty years later during
the Downgrade Controversy which ended his association
with the Baptist Union. An analysis of this particular
sermon and the controversy it engendered is, therefore,

254

important for understanding Spurgeon, but such an analysis
can also illuminate the religious concerns of mid-
Victorian society.

The subject of Baptismal Regeneration was a complicated and touchy one for the Victorians, likely to
excite passions and exacerbate prejudices in a way that
seems almost incredible today. Spurgeon focused attention
upon the topic fifteen years after the controversial
Gorham Judgment, yet the nature of the debate which followed the publication of his sermon proved that the issues
raised in the Gorham case had not been forgotten. In
November 1847, the Reverend Mr. George Gorham was presented a living in the Diocese of Exeter. Since he was
rumored to hold extreme Evangelical views, his superior,
Bishop Henry Phillpotts, subjected him to fifty-two hours
of written and oral examinations on the Prayerbook. It
was Dr. Phillpott's conclusion that Gorham's views on
the subject of Baptismal Regeneration were heretical.
Gorham rejected the doctrine that the sacrament of Baptism
conveyed regeneration, arguing that it represented, but did
not confer, grace, unless preceded by genuine faith and
repentance. Bishop Phillpotts denied this symbolic

interpretation of Baptism and refused to institute Gorham.
He was upheld in his refusal by the Archepiscopal Court
of Canterbury (the Court of Arches), but Gorham appealed
from the Court of Arches to the highest ecclesiastical
appeals court in the country, the Judicial Committee of
the Privy Council. The Council, with a majority of laymen,
decided for Gorham on March 8, 1850, declaring that Gorham's views were not "contrary or repugnant to the declared
doctrine of the Church of England as by law established,"
since "Baptism is a sacrament generally necessary to salvation, but that the grace of regeneration does not necessarily accompany the act of Baptism."[1] Gorham was insti-
tuted over Phillpott's protests by fiat of the Archbishop
of Canterbury, who had concurred in the Privy Council's
decision. The decision was an important victory for the
Evangelical party, for many Evangelicals would have found
it impossible to remain within the Church had the Privy
Council upheld the High Church view of Baptism. For High
Churchmen the doctrinal shock was compounded by the
decision of a group of laymen to uphold Gorham and to

---

[1]J. C. S. Nias, Gorham and the Bishop of Exeter
(London, 1951), p. 96.

reverse ecclesiastical authority, revealing the frightening specter of state supremacy. Gladstone, who regarded the doctrine of Baptismal Regeneration as "the root" of the Prayerbook, had written Archdeacon Manning in December 1849, that "if Mr. Gorham is carried through . . . there [is] no doctrine of Baptismal Regeneration in the Church of England . . . there is no doctrine at all, and Arians or anybody else may abide in it with equal propriety."[2] Outraged that the state had intervened in a heresy case, Gladstone was sure that the Church's claim to Catholicity had been seriously undermined. He finally came to understand that the price the clergy would have to pay for full liberty of conscience was disestablishment.[3] Gladstone learned to live with state supremacy, but Manning would not, and a month after the Gorham Judgment was handed down, he made his submission to Rome. Manning was followed by a wave of converts, including Robert Wilberforce, James Hope-Scott, William Maskell, and T. W. Allies.[4]

---

[2]D. C. Lathbury, Gladstone Correspondence (London, 1910), I, 97.

[3]Philip Magnus, Gladstone, A Biography (London, 1954), pp. 95-96.

[4]Desmond Bowen, The Idea of the Victorian Church (Montreal, 1968), p. 99.

As a result of the Gorham Judgment an unwritten
compromise emerged by which both the Evangelical and High
Church clergy felt free to interpret the Prayerbook's
teachings on Baptism according to their own conscience.
Neither group accepted the views of the other, but the
decision of the Privy Council and the ambiguity of the
Prayerbook allowed the two groups to remain within the
same Church and to teach different doctrine from the same
text.   It was this tenuous compromise which Spurgeon set
out to expose in the summer of 1864, and the immediate
controversy resulting from his sermon is an indication of
a general awareness of the high stakes involved.   He chose
deliberately to reopen a dormant controversy, focusing
attention upon a subject which men of good will within
the Church had avoided discussing.   By taunting both sides
into an open defense of their views, he brought the wide
disparities in the teachings of the clergy on the subject
of Baptismal Regeneration to public attention.

Spurgeon was not the first prominent Nonconformist
to point to the doctrinal cleavage in the Established
Church.   Grattan Guinness had attacked the practice of
infant baptism in a pamphlet on "Believer's Baptism"

in 1860, and R. W. Dale had made a few headlines in 1862 when he delivered a lecture pointing to the contradictions in the teachings of the Prayerbook and the doctrine of the Evangelicals on the subject of Baptism. The year 1862 was the bicentenary of the Great Ejection of 1662, and the manner in which Nonconformists pointedly celebrated the occasion led to "some cooling in Evangelical-Nonconformist friendships,"[5] and, perhaps, started Spurgeon to pondering the nature of the Nonconformist alliance with the Low Church Evangelicals.

To understand Spurgeon's willingness to provoke controversy, it is necessary to realize that he equated silence in the presence of evil with complicity in evil. To know the truth and to remain silent was to participate in sin. "Trimming and temporizing, amiable silence, and unfaithful compromises are treason to God," he declared.[6] His belief that silence constituted "treason to God" is the key to understanding his behavior in a number of

---

[5]Ernest Payne, The Baptist Union, A Short History (London, 1955), p. 99.

[6]Sword and Trowel, II (1866), 4.

similar situations. Time and time again, Spurgeon refused
to keep his peace and remain silent, though the cost of
speaking his conscience was often a heavy one. Throughout
his ministry he was embroiled in controversies large and
small which led him to sacrifice friendship, monetary gain,
party unity, and denominational solidarity upon the altar
of "the truth." "When we observe an evil we shall point
it out; when we see a failure we shall speak of it as
such, and if perchance this injures the cause, let it be
injured. If truth hurts an interest or party, let it be
hurt."[7] "Pleas for charity to error are arguments for
the murder of souls," he wrote. "Life and death hang
upon the question of truth or falsehood; if lies be
propagated, or truth be clouded, the watchmen of the Lord
will have to give in their account for permitting it."[8]
"I will never modify a doctrine I believe to please any
man that walks upon earth."[9] His personal motto was
Cedo Nulli--"I Yield to None"--an aggressively revealing

---

[7]Ibid., IV (1873), 50.

[8]Ibid., XV (1879), 177.

[9]Sermons, seventh series (New York, 1861), p. 37.

choice. Early in his life he yearned to be "Valiant-for Truth," and if he did not always live up to the model he had chosen, he was never accused of resembling "Mr. Pliable."

As a boy, Spurgeon had become convinced that the practice of baptizing infants was unscriptural, and neither the fact of his own baptism nor the practice of his father and grandfather could deter him from condemning what he was convinced was unscriptural. "Truth is truth," he wrote of his grandfather, "even if he cannot receive it."[10] Believing that the sacrament of Baptism was meaningless unless accompanied by genuine faith and repentance, he had chosen to be re-baptized as a believer and to leave the Independent sect of his birth to join the Baptist communion. The practice of infant baptism and the doctrine of Baptismal Regeneration were frequent targets in his early sermons. In one of his earliest printed sermons he quoted the remark of William Jay that "Popery is a lie, Puseyism is a lie, baptismal regeneration is a lie," and elaborated:

---

[10]Letter to "Uncle," September 27, 1853, in Letters, p. 55.

So it is. It is a lie so palpable that I can scarcely
imagine the preachers of it have any brains in their
heads at all. It is so absurd upon the very face of
it, that a man who believes it puts himself below the
range of a common-sense man. Believe that every child
by a drop of water is born again! Then that man that
you see in the ring as a prize-fighter is born again,
because those sanctified drops once fell on his infant
forehead. Another man swears--behold him drunk and
reeling about the streets. He is born again! A pretty
born again that is! I think he wants to be born again
another time. Such a regeneration as that only fits
him for the devil; and by its deluding effect, may
even make him sevenfold more the child of hell. But
the men who curse, and swear, and rob and steal, and
those poor wretches who are hanged, have all been born
again, according to the fiction of this beautiful
Puseyite church. Out upon it! Out upon it![11]

"This aqueous regeneration" surpassed belief, he informed

his students. "Why there are those who pretend to save

souls by curious tricks, intricate maneuvers, and dexterous

posture-making! A basin of water, half-a-dozen drops,

certain syllables--heigh presto!--the infant is made a child

of God, a member of Christ, and an inheritor of the kingdom

of heaven!" "Such juggling," he declared, "can only be

carried out by certain favored persons who have received

apostolic succession direct from Judas Iscariot!"[12]

----

[11]Sermon delivered March 18, 1855, in New Park
Street Pulpit, I, 105.

[12]The Soul-Winner, pp. 233-234.

Spurgeon's hyperbole was unlikely to offend Evangelical Churchmen since they also rejected the High Church interpretation of the doctrine of Baptismal Regeneration. The issue was whether or not the Prayerbook contained the doctrine. Spurgeon believed that the Church of England Prayerbook plainly taught the doctrine of Baptismal Regeneration (and probably a majority of the Anglican clergy would have agreed that it did), and that the Evangelicals were closing their eyes to the fact. Worse, by remaining within the Church, although disputing a cardinal doctrine taught by the Prayerbook, the Evangelicals were guilty of hypocrisy and spiritual prostitution.

As early as June 1861, Spurgeon, speaking on the Nonconformist Burial Bill, had hinted that "the day is near when our affection for the good shall prove itself, not by a womanly sparing of the evil, but by a manly declaration of war against error, its adherents, and all who give it fellowship."[13] Describing the union of Church and state as a "spiritual fornication," Spurgeon delivered a violent diatribe against the Church couched in the

---

[13]Sword and Trowel, I (1865), 111.

metaphor of prostitution and the loss of chastity. He
ended the speech promising to "teach the peasant at the
plough to loathe the inconsistencies of your prayerbook,
and the pauper on the road shall know the history of your
ferocious persecutions in days of yore."[14]

On June 5, 1864, Spurgeon made his "manly declaration of war against error." "The burden of the Lord is
upon me," he told his congregation, "and I must deliver my
soul." "I have been loath enough to undertake the work,
but I am forced to by an awful and overwhelming sense of
solemn duty. . . . It is as much as my soul is worth to
hold my peace any longer, and whether you approve or not,
I must speak out."[15] Quoting the Prayerbook and the
Catechism as proof, Spurgeon attempted to demonstrate
that the Church of England taught the doctrine of Baprismal
Regeneration. "Here is a professedly Protestant Church,

---

[14]Ibid., 112.

[15]Baptismal Regeneration, A Sermon Delivered
June 5, 1864 (London, 1864). The sermon, Number 573 in
the Metropolitan Tabernacle Pulpit Series, was published
separately as a pamphlet. All quotations from the sermon
are from the pamphlet edition.

which every time its minister goes to the font, declares
that person there receiving Baptism is there and then
'regenerated and grafted onto the body of Christ's Church.'"

Although denouncing the doctrine of Baptismal
Regeneration as unscriptural, Spurgeon claimed to have no
quarrel with those who preached it. "God forbid that we
should censure those who believe that Baptism saves the
soul, because they adhere to a Church which teaches the
same doctrine. . . . I hate their doctrine, but I love
their honesty." His attack centered on the supposed
hypocrisy of the Evangelicals, who accepted pay from a
Church holding doctrinal positions which they could not
honestly espouse. By their example, he asserted, they
taught others to "lie to get a living." Moreover, this
hypocrisy was directly responsible for the growing number
of converts to Roman Catholicism. No longer was Roman
Catholicism in England a matter of "just a few titled.
perverts, and imported monks and nuns." Instead, "this
great city is now covered by a network of monks, and
priests, and sisters of mercy." The major responsibility
for this sinister development Spurgeon placed at the door
of the Evangelicals. The "false professions of men who

subscribe to doctrines they don't believe," disgusted the rank-and-file churchgoer, making them easy prey for the dogmatic security offered by Rome. Thus, the hypocrisy of the Evangelicals not only threatened their individual souls, but was a threat to the Protestant community at large.

Although Spurgeon had commenced his sermons professing to have no quarrel with those in the Church of England who believed that the Prayerbook taught the doctrine of Baptismal Regeneration, he was incapable of maintaining this resolution, and he soon digressed into an attack upon the ritual and practice of the High Church party. He equated the doctrine of Baptismal Regeneration with Puseyism, and cited the spread of the Puseyite teachings as a second factor contributing to the growing number of Roman Catholic converts. Puseyism, with its "toy-rags, wax candles, and millinery" was a halfway house down the path which led to "the gorgeous pomp of Popery." Spurgeon frequently lumped Tractarians, Puseyites, and ritualists together as examples of the pseudo-Popery of the Established Church. "Modern Tractarianism is a bastard

Popery, too mean, too shifty, too double-dealing to delude men of honest minds," he told his students.[16] "No longer can we say that Puseyism is Romanism disguised; it has removed the mask, and is now openly and avowedly what it has always been--ritualism, sacramentarianism, priestcraft, anti-Christ. Puseyism has cloathed itself with the beggarly rags worn by the Romish harlot in the dark ages, and thrown upon the dunghill because they were too full of leprosy to be endured by intelligent beings."[17]

Spurgeon's sermon on Baptismal Regeneration catered to all of the fears and prejudices of popular Protestantism. The language of the sermon, moreover, was both sensational and suggestive. "Do not talk to me of mild and gentle men, of soft manners and squeamish words," he told the congregation, "we want fiery Knox . . . we want Luther to tell the truth unmistakably in homely phrases." Spurgeon had done more than merely stir up the embers of an old controversy. Cloaking himself in the mantle of Knox and Luther, he had introduced personal elements into a doctrinal

---

[16]The Soul-Winner, p. 235.

[17]Sword and Trowel, II (1866), 340.

controversy which angered High Churchmen and Evangelicals alike. In the plainest language, Spurgeon had called the Evangelicals liars and the High Churchmen fools. Both, according to him, were guilty of leading the nation to Rome, the one by their treacherous example, the other by their adoption of Romish ritual. The sermon, appealing as it did to the strong anti-papal feeling of the English middle classes, was an immediate best-seller. The resulting controversy divided Nonconformists and threatened to destroy the rapport that had been established between the Evangelicals and their allies outside the Church. Conservative Churchmen had always considered Spurgeon a vulgar ranter; his sermon merely confirmed their impression. The Evangelicals, however, had been among his earliest defenders; they had prayed with him and for him, and many had contributed to his Tabernacle and his philanthropies. Naturally they felt that they had been betrayed. Spurgeon had not only reopened a doctrinal controversy, he had violated the accepted norms of good taste and gentlemanly conduct toward opponents. He had flung wild charges and personal innuendos out with zestful abandon, and then compounded his sins--in the eyes of his

critics--by launching a promotional campaign to sell the
infamous sermon. Instead of repenting his intemperate
attack, he seemed delighted by the furor it had caused.
When a friend warned him that he had gotten himself into
"hot water," he replied, "No, I do not feel the water to
be too hot. The truth is far otherwise. I am cool
enough; I am only the stoker, and other folks are in the
hot water, which I am doing my best to make so hot that
they will be glad to get out of it."[18] To another friend
he wrote:

> The good work grows in my hands; the battle thickens;
> the victory is all the nearer. My sermon on Bap-
> tismal Regeneration has stirred up the rattlesnakes'
> den; but as their venomous fangs cannot reach me they
> may rattle as they please. Of course I lose the
> friendship of the evangelicals, but I can bear that
> sooner than an ill-conscience.[19]

Instead of retreating, he grew jauntier and more defiant.
He preached additional sermons substantiating his position, he fired off letters to newspapers, and in a
flippant moment referred to a baptismal font as "a
spittoon." He installed a font in his own garden to serve
as a birdbath. "Spoils of war," he remarked.

---

[18]An All-Round Ministry, p. 403.

[19]Pike, Life, II, 108.

Spurgeon had been warned by his publishers that his sermon on Baptismal Regeneration would destroy the sales of his sermons "with a single blow." Perhaps he believed this; if so, he seriously underestimated his reading public as well as the market for sensational religious controversy. The sermon sold 350,000 copies the first year, and over 500,000 copies by the end of the century. Apparently parsons all over England felt compelled to preach sermons rebutting Spurgeon's charges, and far too many of these replies were published. Spurgeon collected one-hundred and thirty-five pamphlets replying to his sermon.[20] A contemporary cartoon pictured Spurgeon as Gulliver, pinned down by hundreds of Lilliputians in clerical garb. Spurgeon's sermons drew rebukes from clergymen embracing creeds ranging from Roman Catholicism to Calvinism, and anyone who reads even a fraction of the replies will concur with one of Spurgeon's earlier biographers: "If any industrious reader should succeed in wading through a complete set of the publications of

---

[20]Spurgeon's collection fills several bound volumes at Spurgeon's College, London.

this controversy, he will never be tempted to repeat the experience should he survive the first entertainment."[21]

The most vitriolic summary of Spurgeon's sermon came from a predictable source--the Saturday Review. It was the "height of the silly season," announced the Saturday Review, "the dull afternoon of the year, in the dark and backward abysm of time, when bees and wasps and apocalyptic frogs and the sorrows of curates occupy leading journals, and Mr. Spurgeon is not unnaturally the town's talk." Spurgeon's sermon was "a choice specimen of theological Billingsgate," and its author "a very ignorant person, utterly ignorant of theological history, of theological terms, and of the grammar of scientific truth." The journal was critical of the whole tone of Spurgeon's charges against the Anglican clergy, but conceded, "As it is impossible to make a silk purse out of a sow's ear, so it is absurd to expect a person like Mr. Spurgeon to possess either the information of a scholar or the manners of a gentleman, the language of refinement in controversy or humanities of Christianity in personal intercourse."[22]

[21]Pike, op. cit., 106.
[22]Saturday Review, XIV (September 17, 1864), 356.

The published replies of Anglican clergymen to Spurgeon's charges demonstrated how far apart the Evangelicals and High Churchmen were on the meaning of the Prayerbook's teachings on Baptism. The Evangelicals responded to Spurgeon's imputation of hypocrisy by denying emphatically that the Church of England taught Baptismal Regeneration,[23] while ritualists responded to Spurgeon's attack upon the doctrine by asserting it was proven in scripture.[24] In short, Spurgeon's assertion that the Prayerbook taught the doctrine of Baptismal Regeneration was denied by one segment of the Anglican clergy and affirmed by another. It was an awkward situation.

Even some of those most sympathetic to Spurgeon's position in the controversy were offended by the language of his sermon. Dr. John Campbell, the editor of the

---

[23]See, for instance, "London Vicar," The Spurgeon Antidote on Baptismal Regeneration (London, 1864), and the Rev. B. G. Johns, The Doctrine of Holy Scripture and the Church of England on Baptismal Regeneration: A Reply to the Rev. C. H. Spurgeon (London, 1864).

[24]See, for instance, Charles Perry, Baptismal Regeneration the True Doctrine of the Church of England and Shown to Be a Cardinal Doctrine of the Gospel (Melbourne, 1869).

Nonconformist paper, the British Banner, felt that
Spurgeon's arguments were "unanswerable," yet he criticized
the sermon as being "marked by an acritude of spirit,
fitted to startle, scandalize, and exasperate."[25] Those
who disagreed with Spurgeon's arguments were much harsher:
"discordant, jarring, and vulgar,"[26] "hideous buffoonery,"[27]
"awful and presumptuous . . . a forerunner of Anti-Christ."[28]
Given Spurgeon's own blunt language and implications, the
abusive character of some of the replies is understandable.

The most damaging reply to Spurgeon's sermon came
from a fellow Baptist, Wriothesley Baptist Noel. In an
"Open Letter," Noel defended the Evangelicals from Spurgeon's
charges of hypocrisy and questioned the judgment of the
pastor of the Tabernacle in choosing the Evangelicals for
his target. "I greatly regret your harsh judgment of men

[25]Sword and Trowel, I (1865), 347.

[26]John Pulman, An Exposure of the Fallacies and
Misrepresentations in Mr. Spurgeon's Sermon on Baptismal
Regeneration (London, 1865).

[27]Johns, op. cit., p. 10.

[28]"Convert," Awful Progress of Infidelity in
Southwark: Scriptural Prophecies Fulfilled (London, n.d.),
pp. 1-2.

who are shown by their fruits to be, as much as yourself,

the children of God."[29] Noel suggested here the common

bond of a conversion experience which united Nonconformists

with their Evangelical brethren in what has been described

as "the Invisible Church."[30] Noel was a former Anglican

clergyman who had given up his living to become a Baptist

preacher. Rather than give lip-service to the doctrine

of the Prayerbook, he had chosen to live by his principles

and to become a Nonconformist. In fact, he had done pre-

cisely what Spurgeon had castigated the Evangelicals for

not doing. His action placed him in a unique position to

refute Spurgeon's charges. He was, moreover, highly

---

[29]Wriothesley Baptist Noel, Letter to the Reverend
C. H. Spurgeon Respecting His Attack Upon the Evangelical
Ministers of the Church of England (London, 1864).

[30]G. F. A. Best, "The Evangelicals and the Established Church in the Early Nineteenth Century," Journal of
Theological Studies, X (April 1969), pp. 69-70. Professor
Best argues that the Evangelicals remained members of the
Visible Church, where they had to put up with the company
of untrue Christians, while they joined their friends and
pious Dissenters in the Invisible Church of true believers.
"They would have liked to enjoy the advantages of both
worlds and churches at once." Spurgeon was determined to
force them to choose.

respected within his adopted denomination. As one of Spurgeon's friends wrote, "Mr. Noel was more than respected, he was something of a hero in our eyes."[31] He had served as president of the Baptist Union in 1855, and was reelected to that post in 1867. Far from being an apologist for the Anglican establishment, Noel was as rabidly anti-Catholic as Spurgeon, having been active in popular anti-Catholic agitation since the 1840's.[32] His authority within the Nonconformist community made his criticisms of Spurgeon's conduct extremely damaging. Spurgeon replied to Noel's criticisms of the tone of his sermon by suggesting that Noel's "aristocratic associations" had "refined his modes of expression, and it will be allowed that _for him_ his remarks are as severe as mine are _for me_."[33]

One immediate consequence of Spurgeon's quarrel with the Evangelicals was his decision to withdraw from

[31]Pike, _op. cit._, II, 98.

[32]Norman, _op. cit._, pp. 33, 36.

[33]_Two Letters from C. H. Spurgeon: One to the Evangelical Alliance Signifying his Withdrawal from that Association; and the other to the Christian Public, Proving that his Accusations against the Evangelical Clergy were Neither Novel nor Singular_ (London, 1864).

the Evangelical Alliance, an association of Churchmen and
Nonconformists holding common evangelical views. When
Spurgeon's sermon was published, the secretary of the
Evangelical Alliance had protested sharply, charging that
the sermon violated the spirit of the organization as well
as the specific bylaws of the Alliance. The General
Resolution of the Evangelical Alliance stated:

> That when required by conscience to assert or defend
> any views or principles wherein they differ from the
> Christian brethren who agree with them in vital
> truths, the members of the alliance will aim earnestly,
> by the help of the Holy Spirit, to avoid all rash and
> groundless insinuations, personal imputations, or
> irritating allusions; and to maintain the meekness and
> gentleness of Christ, by speaking the truth only with
> love.

Clearly Spurgeon's sermon had violated the spirit of this
agreement; whatever else his sermon might have been, it was
hardly "meek," "gentle," or "loving," though Spurgeon,
characteristically, tried to prove it had been all of
these things. In an "Open Letter to the Christian Public"
defending his decision to leave the Evangelical Alliance,
he denied that he had spoken rashly or hastily. "Of the
charge making personal imputations, I also plead not
guilty. I have imputed nothing; I have merely asserted

truisms of the most obvious character. . . . I have not

imputed such conduct to the brethren in question, I have

proved it."[34]   To the charge that he had failed to treat

the subject with the meekness and gentleness of Christ,

Spurgeon declared that he had been "as gentle and meek as

so crying an evil permitted me to be."   "In the solemn

protest which I have felt bound to utter against the

double-dealing of certain ministers, it has been sufficient

for me to feel that I have discharged by duty in the sight

of God; and had I stood alone I would not have been

dejected, for it is not dishonorable to be right even in

the minority of one."   Spurgeon's willingness to be "a

minority of one" in controversy was one of his most promi-

nent traits.   His behavior throughout the Baptismal

Regeneration controversy was irritating and arrogant,

and indicative of a stubborn side of his personality which

invariably surfaced in controversy.   In controversy,

Spurgeon epitomized "the dissidence of Dissent."   In a

revealing comment in 1876 he remarked that even if the

---

[34]Ibid.

Church were disestablished, he would still consider himself a Dissenter, a "Nonconformist to doctrinal errors" wherever they appeared.[35]

On September 10, 1864, Spurgeon formally withdrew from the Evangelical Alliance, "until such time as the brethren whom I have charged with duplicity shall clear themselves of sin, or you shall ease yourself of their patronage and association."[36] It was some time before Spurgeon was to be reconciled with the Evangelicals. In 1870 he was still critical of "Ministers under False Colors," writing "Treachery is never more treacherous than when it leads a man to stab at a doctrine which he has solemnly engaged to hold, and for the maintenance of which he receives a livlihood."[37] In a speech at Exeter Hall in that year he called for the "break up of the inclined plane down which weakly Nonconformists descend, by the halfway house of Evangelicalism, into the abyss of

---

[35]_Sword and Trowel_, XII (1876), 307.

[36]_The Times_, September 10, 1864.

[37]_Sword and Trowel_, VI (1870), 70.

Tractarianism."[38] Spurgeon's sermon on Baptismal
Regeneration signaled his emergence as a prominent spokesman for disestablishment and coincided with the beginning
of his career as a political Dissenter.

In long-range terms, the significance of the
Baptismal Regeneration Controversy became apparent twenty
years later during the Downgrade Controversy which ended
Spurgeon's association with the Baptist Union. As the
historian of the Baptist Union has observed, "the Baptismal
Regeneration Controversy . . . set Spurgeon on a course
which ended in his disruption of the Union twenty years
later."[39] In both cases, the controversy began with
Spurgeon's discovery of "a glaring evil" and ended with
his accusing all who did not agree with him of being hypo-
crites. In both cases, rather than remain within an
organization which "condoned evil," he withdrew to become
a lonely champion for "the truth." "Truth is not to be
judged by votes; numbers can neither create nor destroy
it," he wrote in 1864, a sentiment he would echo in 1887.

---

[38]Ibid., 467.

[39]Payne, op. cit., p. 99.

Shortly after his withdrawal from the Evangelical Alliance, Spurgeon joined with two other Baptist ministers, William Landels and William Brock, to found the London Baptist Association. Landels, "brave as a lion and true as steel,"[40] had written a pamphlet during the controversy taking Spurgeon's side against Noel.[41] London was Spurgeon's orbit, and his ties were closer to the London Baptist Association than to the larger Baptist Union of Great Britain. The Evangelical Alliance tolerated a theological diversity that was too broad for Spurgeon, so he withdrew to join with other like-minded Baptists in a smaller, doctrinally more cohesive association. Tragically for Spurgeon, even this small group was not small enough; and finally convinced that the London Baptist Association was theologically unsound, he withdrew from its ranks at the time of the Downgrade Controversy, charging that Landels, his former champion, was blind to the "downgrading of the gospel" in Baptist pulpits. Each time that Spurgeon

[40]Sword and Trowel, XII (1876), 529.

[41]William Landels, Baptismal Regeneration: Remarks on the Controversy (London, 1864).

withdrew from an association, his circle of friends grew
smaller and tighter, and the influences surrounding him
grew narrower and more restricted.

C H A P T E R   V I

A POLITICAL DISSENTER

Drawing a line between the affairs of Caesar and

the affairs of God has never been easy; in the history of

Christianity the task has presented what H. Richard Niebuhr

termed "the enduring problem."[1] Christian responses to

the problem of reconciling "Christ and culture" have varied

from a withdrawal from the world and rejection of "culture"

to an active attempt to proclaim Christ in culture through

a social gospel.[2] The problem of reconciliation, which

confronts all Christians, is an especially vexing one for

the clergy. Should a minister avoid controversy and preach

the traditional gospel, avoiding its social implications,

---

[1]H. Richard Niebuhr, Christ and Culture (New York, 1951).

[2]Niebuhr describes five "typical answers" to the problem of reconciling Christ and culture. Spurgeon's position seems to be closest to what Niebuhr calls the conversionist response, wherein Christ is seen as the converter of man in his culture and his society.

or does he have a special responsibility to suggest the moral issues involved in social and political questions? "Do you say that it is not my business to regulate public affairs," said Henry Ward Beecher, "I tell you, it is the business of every man to whom God gives the opportunity, the understanding, the courage, and the impulse; and it is my business."[3] Spurgeon's response to the question of a minister's social responsibility was equally forthright: "We have long ago ceased to draw a boundary for our religion; we believe it should enter into everything and affect all our relationships. If we could not pray over politics we should doubt their rightness."[4] Spurgeon, like Beecher, was "a political preacher," and, inevitably, a subject of controversy as a result of his political activism. From 1868 to 1884, Spurgeon was a prominent spokesman for political Dissent and an ardent champion of Gladstonian Liberalism. As a public figure and a man of substantial influence he played a significant part in helping to shape the politics of Nonconformity.

----

[3]"Sphere of the Christian Minister, 1869," in Robert Cross (ed.), The Church and the City (New York, 1967), p. 172.

[4]Sword and Trowel, XV (1879), 245.

Walter James has written that "the origins of the English two-party system may be traced back to a difference of opinion between two sets of men over whether bishops were necessary."[5] It is not necessary to espouse the Whig view of history in order to see in the opposition of Churchman and Dissenter one of the major themes of English politics. In the United States, where Church and state are separated by law, it has rarely been possible to keep religion out of politics; in Britain it has been impossible. Through most of the nineteenth century Dissenters endured a variety of social and political disabilities, and it was natural that they would turn to parliament for relief. Inevitably, every major issue of the period--from education to Ireland--became a subject of sectarian controversy and an opportunity for reviving old slogans--"No Popery!" or "Church in danger!"

When Spurgeon left the country to come to London, a Dissenter could not take a degree at Oxford or Cambridge, a fact which tended to bar professional and political

---

[5]Walter James, The Christian in Politics (London, 1962), p. 106.

285

advancement. Although the repeal of the Test and Corporation Acts in 1828 had removed the religious test for holding office, it was forty years before Dissenters were brought into the Cabinet. In law, Dissenters were still liable for Church rates, even though the Census of 1851 had revealed how precarious the Anglican numerical superiority was. In country districts Dissenters frequently had little alternative to marriage by Church rites although burial in the churchyard was denied to them. As Dr. Kitson Clark has pointed out, although the disabilities of Dissenters were enforced for ostensibly religious reasons, they were more truly symbolic of a social division in English society:

> The disabilities imposed upon Dissenters were probably at least in part maintained because of the low esteem in which classes lower than their own were held by those who governed the country, and the privileges of the Church of England were certainly attacked as being the most notorious part of the whole iniquitous mass of privilege by which the aristocracy maintained itself.[6]

The disabilities were more strigently enforced in the country than in the towns; Spurgeon, as a countryman,

---

[6]G. Kitson Clark, The Making of Victorian England (London, 1962), p. 39.

brought all of his rural suspicions concerning the
Establishment with him when he came to London in 1854.

Spurgeon's views on English history were simple
and Whiggish. In political terms, he identified the Tory
party with royal tyranny and Anglican oppression. The
Whigs had been the Champions of the Protestant Constitution,
authors of the Glorious Revolution, and the defenders of
the Reform Bill. For Spurgeon, history was shaped by the
action of heroes and villains, and his villains were
blackest when they called themselves "priests." His
attachment to the principles of Whiggery was romantic and
rhetorical; his commitment to Gladstonian Liberalism was
personal and emotional. As a nineteenth-century Dissenter,
it was highly unlikely that Spurgeon would have been a
Tory. Nevertheless, there were varying shades of political
Dissent. H. J. Hanham has divided the Nonconformist
Liberals into three categories: the party loyalists, the
social reformers, and the militants.[7] Spurgeon's consistent
support of Gladstone's policies indicates that he belonged

---

[7]H. J. Hanham, Elections and Party Management (London, 1959), p. 117.

to the camp of party loyalists. In the last analysis,
only one issue could shake Spurgeon's loyalty to his
party. Tragically for the Liberal-Nonconformist coalition,
that one issue was the specter of Roman Catholicism.

Spurgeon's most active political partisanship
spanned the period from the campaign to disestablish the
Church of Ireland to the battle over Home Rule, roughly
the twenty years between the late 'sixties and the late
'eighties. In the period before, Spurgeon was largely
preoccupied with denominational concerns. After he broke
with Gladstone on the Home Rule question, his interest in
politics declined, and his last years were dominated by
theological controversy. The middle period (1868-1884) in
Spurgeon's career was the period of his greatest political
activity and influence, the years in which he labored not
only for eternity but also for a kingdom of heaven on
earth. He was a preacher first, and his congregation
remained his primary responsibility, but success in his
profession enhanced his authority in the secular world.
He was a political Dissenter because he was concerned with
issues, but he was an influential political Dissenter
because he was a famous and successful preacher, and the

measure of his success is the weight given to his
opinions on subjects having little to do with the business
of saving souls. As a star of the pulpit, he was a public
figure--his face was the blazing highlight of a fireworks spectacular at the Crystal Palace, he appeared on
the cover of Vanity Fair, Madame Tussaud's cast his
portly image in wax--and his opinions carried the authority
of his reputation. He was not a politician, but he spoke
out on political questions, and his opinions were frequently decisive with people who suspected the advice of
politicians. His opinion was solicited on virtually every
controversial subject of the day, and he was rarely
reluctant to speak his mind. Was Spurgeon opposed to
pigeon-shooting, hoop-skirts, or women in the pulpit? He
was, and the world was soon informed. If he expressed
an opinion on capital punishment (he supported it), or
vivisection (he opposed it), that opinion was quickly
passed along to the readers of those newspapers and periodicals which considered an article on "Mr. Spurgeon on
vivisection," a newsworthy subject--the readers, perhaps,
of Wit and Wisdom, who in response to a poll in October
1887, voted Spurgeon "the greatest ecclesiastical figure
of the nineteenth century."

In the early years of Spurgeon's ministry when he was pilloried in the popular press and cruelly lampooned as half-mountebank and half-clown, his endorsement would have been regarded by many politicians as a very mixed blessing indeed. Just at the time when his ministerial efforts were winning him broad support and serious consideration, he provoked the old charges of sensationalism anew with his sermon on "Baptismal Regeneration." The controversy resulting from the sermon did not die quickly, and it was some time before many of the Evangelicals trusted Spurgeon again. In the meantime, he kept his name before the public by joining the active campaign to disestablish the Church of England, the cause which first brought him into the political arena.

Spurgeon's emergence as a political Dissenter naturally provoked opposition. Even many fellow-Dissenters felt that ministers should avoid politics. The attacks upon him took many forms, ranging from sharply worded suggestions that he confine his energies to preaching, to the mischievous act of a group of vandals who painted his fences in Conservative colors during a general election.

He replied to his critics in a variety of ways, sometimes blandly denying that he was an active political partisan, at other times asserting his right to be as politically active as he pleased. He usually tried to disarm his Dissenting critics with a humorous answer, as when he assured a member of the Plymouth Brethren who had warned him to "leave politics to the devil and mortify the old man," that he was actually doing just that, since "my old man is a Tory, and so I make him vote Liberal." During the General Election of 1880, he received a letter rebuking him for leaving "his high and lofty position as a servant of God," to enter "the defiled arena of party politics." He replied:

March 22, 1880

Dear Sir,
    Your letter amuses me, because you are evidently a rank Tory, and so hearty in your political convictions that, in spite of your religious scruples, you must needs interfere in politics and write to me. If there is anything defiling in it, you are certainly over head and ears.

    However, dear sir, I thank you for your kindness in wishing to put me right, and I can assure you that I vote as devoutly as I pray, and feel it to be part of my love to God and my neighbor to try to turn out the Government whom your letter would lead me to leave alone.

You are as wrong as you can be in your notion;
but as it keeps you from voting, I shall not try to
convert you, for I am morally certain you would
vote for the Tory candidate. In things divine we
are probably at one; and you shall abstain from
voting <u>as unto the Lord</u>, and I will vote <u>as unto
the Lord</u>, and we will both give Him thanks.

Yours Truly,

C. H. Spurgeon[8]

Spurgeon drew a line between his role as pastor

of the Tabernacle and his role as a political Dissenter,

but he drew the line less precisely than many of his

critics would have preferred. He refused to loan the

Tabernacle to groups inspired by what he termed "purely

political purposes," but he approved of John Bright

addressing the Liberation Society at the Tabernacle,

because he believed disestablishment was "a divine and

not mere party cause." When Dr. Parker, another active

political Dissenter, toyed with the idea of announcing his

candidacy for the London School Board, Spurgeon proclaimed

his opposition to clergymen seeking public office,

pointedly condemning "certain preachers" who sought "to

be active partisans of Whigs or Tories, busy at canvassing,

---

[8]<u>Autobiography</u>, IV, 125-126.

and eloquent at public meetings for rival factions."[9]
However in several general elections Spurgeon engaged in
these very activities. How could he, on the one hand,
condemn preachers who became "active partisans," and on
the other hand, write speeches, edit platforms, form
associations, and issue handbills endorsing candidates for
office? The answer is that Spurgeon's definition of
"political activist" was at least as ambiguous as his
definition of Calvinism. He defined "political activist"
in a manner designed to satisfy himself but few others.
Spurgeon denied that he ever used his pulpit to lobby for
any political cause; that as a private citizen he spoke
out on political questions only under certain limited conditions. And what were the conditions? In July 1884,
he declined an invitation to address a Reform Rally in
Hyde Park, but declared, "Whenever topics which touch upon
the rights of men, righteousness, peace, and so on, come
in my way, I endeavor to speak as emphatically as I can
on the right side. It is a part of my religion to desire

---

[9]Sword and Trowel, IX (1873), 108.

justice and freedom for all."[10] Thus, in his own mind,
Spurgeon distinguished between "mere" politics and issues
touching upon rights, peace, righteousness, and so on.
Needless to say, these topics were sufficient to keep him
reasonably busy.

Preachers who become involved in politics know
that they will be criticized, and Spurgeon anticipated
opposition. What was puzzling, however, was the apparent
double standard of much of the secular press which vigorously condemned political Dissent as sectarian meddling,
yet found nothing reprehensible in bishops voting in
parliament to protect their own vested interests. Spurgeon
pointed to this hypocrisy in a sharply-worded editorial
in the Sword and Trowel in February 1873:

> Cease to be a man, and you will be a pious dissenter;
> but speak out and show the slightest independence of
> mind, and you will be an odious political dissenter.
> Be thankful for the toleration which you enjoy, and
> eat your humble pie in the corner, and the rector
> will condescend to meet you at the Bible Society's
> meetings; but dare to call your soul your own, and
> you shall be put into the black books . . .[11]

---

[10]Autobiography, IV, 132.

[11]Sword and Trowel, IX (1873), 107.

Spurgeon was not one to be thankful for small blessings or content with condescendence.

Spurgeon's grandfather had lived on comfortable and pleasant terms with the local rector at Stambourne. The two had been friends as well as neighbors, and the kindly and more affluent rector had been generous in tangible ways. James Spurgeon belonged to an older generation of English Dissent, grateful for toleration and reluctant to shatter the status quo by an attack upon the Anglican Establishment. The emergence of militant Dissent in the middle of the nineteenth century destroyed the old complacency. Certainly until the eighteen-forties there was little organized support for disestablishment. A combination of factors helped to create the climate in which a militant disestablishment campaign was nurtured--the growing popularity among Dissenting groups of the theory of voluntaryism; the Oxford Movement, with the corresponding revival of ritualism within the Established Church; the disappearance of unadulterated Independency, and a new emphasis upon denominationalism which in turn led to the creation of strong unions within the individual sects capable of rallying denominational opinion; and the

staggering implications of the religious census of 1851.[12]
The example of the Scottish disruption of 1843 certainly
prompted English Dissenters to think along similar lines--
in 1844 the British Anti-State Church Association was
founded. Ten years later the group changed its name to
The Society for the Liberation of Religion from State
Patronage and Control; commonly known as the Liberation
Society. The Liberation Society, under the energetic
leadership of Edward Miall, a member of parliament and
the editor of The Nonconformist, signaled a new phase in
the politics of English Dissent.

The disestablishment campaign naturally centered
on parliament, where a series of legislative victories
beginning with the movement to abolish university tests
in 1850 pointed to the growing political awareness of the
Nonconformists. A committee was formed to elect Nonconformists to parliament; by 1868, the committee chairman,
Samuel Morley, claimed sixty-three members in the House
of Commons and tallied ninety-five votes sympathetic to

---

[12]W. G. Addison, Religious Equality in Modern
England (London, 1944), pp. 80-93). See also, John Vincent,
The Formation of the Liberal Party (London, 1966), pp. 67-75.

disestablishment.[13] The campaign received great impetus

from the Reform Act of 1867 which brought household

suffrage to the boroughs, generating what H. J. Hanham

described as "something of a revolution in the political

status of urban Nonconformists." As their political power

increased, the Nonconformists became "the largest, most

active, and most highly principled section of the Liberal

party."[14] Spurgeon's role in forming and rallying this

section of the liberal coalition provides an interesting

example of the strengths and weaknesses of political

Dissent.

Spurgeon came to London in the year that the Libera-

tion Society took its new name and commenced its active

campaign for disestablishment. His career spanned the

period of the most active drive to disestablish the Church

of England, and for most of that period he was a prominent

participant in the movement. Certainly everything in

Spurgeon's background was tailored to make him hostile to

an established church. Steeped in those classics in the

_____

[13]Ibid., p. 93.

[14]Hanham, op. cit., p. 117.

folklore of martyrdom, Foxe's <u>Book of Martyrs</u> and Bunyan's <u>Pilgrim's Progress</u>, he had a healthy suspicion of the tyranny of established religion. His childhood was spent in a house built by a man forced to leave his chapel as a result of the Great Ejection. His grandfather supplemented his income with gifts from the local rector, and his father was forced to clerk on weekdays in order to afford the luxury of preaching on Sundays. Spurgeon's first preaching experience had been in Cambridge, a city which must have served as a constant reminder to the impressionable boy of the inequities of a society which opened its doors only to the privileged members of the establishment. Though he lived in Cambridge, he could not obtain a degree at the University. He came to London to preach, and found himself mocked and patronized by state-subsidized preachers who lacked his ability and his audience. His ministry weathered their hostility and eventually won their respect. But <u>mutual</u> respect was a long time in coming. The "Bishop of Newington Butts" lived long enough to become friendly with his neighbor, the Archbishop of Canterbury, but in the long interval which preceded their friendship, Spurgeon felt great bitterness against the Anglican establishment.

As the idea of religious voluntaryism gained
support among Dissenters, Spurgeon's personal success was
frequently cited as a potent argument against the need
for state support of religion. At thirty-five, he was
the most popular preacher in the country, pastor of the
largest independent congregation in the world, and director
of a diversified philanthropic organization. Everything
he had accomplished he owed to his talents and the contributions of his followers. The state gave him no rates, no
living, no cathedral. None of his institutions were sub-
sidized by the state, yet all flourished. In short, his
ministry was an effective rebuttal to the argument that
unless the state supported religion it would perish. His
example was prominent in the writings of those who sought
to prove the advantages of voluntaryism to a reluctant and
unbelieving Anglican community. Churchmen grew weary of
refuting his example. Dr. Benson tactfully sidestepped
the issue, declaring that it would be impossible to
imagine Spurgeon in any established church, since he was
"absolutely the 'raison d'etre' of Nonconformist

association,"[15] while Bishop Wilberforce, more to the point, asked if he did not envy the Nonconformists their Spurgeon, replied, "it is written, 'Thou shalt not covet thy neighbor's ass.'"[16]

In 1856, when Edward Miall first moved the disestablishment of the Church of Ireland, the motion failed, 143-93. Despite this setback, several events in the next decade reversed the government's attitude toward the Irish Church and ended in a notable victory for the Nonconformist foes of the establishment. In July 1865, Gladstone, rejected by Oxford, went "unmuzzled" to Lancashire, an event of great significance for subsequent Liberal policies; in 1867 the Reform Bill created a new electorate more responsive to the Radical demands for the disestablishment of the Irish Church; finally, the revival of the Irish question by the Fenians focused attention upon the

---

[15]Benson, op. cit., III, 275.

[16]Fullerton, op. cit., p. 116. Wilberforce was also the source for another famous Spurgeon joke: "What is the difference between Westminster Abbey and the Metropolitan Tabernacle?" Answer: "At the Abbey the pulpit is in the nave and at the Tabernacle the knave is in the pulpit."

whole issue of Anglo-Irish relations. As Gladstone was to tell the Queen in 1868, he believed that his mission was "to pacify Ireland."

Led by Miall, Bright, and Joseph Chamberlain of Birmingham, Radicals began after 1867 to campaign in earnest for the disestablishment of the Church of England. The first target was Ireland, where the gross inequities of an Anglican minority established over a Roman Catholic majority offered a tempting opportunity to exploit the whole question of disestablishment. Many, like Gladstone, opposed to the disestablishment of the Church of England, became convinced that justice demanded the disestablishment of the Church of Ireland.

Prior to 1867, Spurgeon's political activity had been negligible. He now became convinced that the time was opportune for a frontal assault upon the Established Church, and he brought to the campaign all of the energy he could muster. Coincidentally, he was reaching the largest live audiences of his career. In 1867, the Tabernacle was closed for repairs, and Spurgeon moved his congregation to the Agricultural Hall, an auditorium frequently used for reform meetings. His crowds at

Agricultural Hall averaged 15,000 through the spring and summer of 1867. On April 14, at the peak of the debate over the Reform Bill, Spurgeon addressed nearly 25,000 at a single service.

In March 1868, Gladstone introduced his resolutions calling for the disestablishment of the Church of Ireland. In his March editorial for Sword and Trowel, Spurgeon took up the cause, urging Dissenters in "all our towns and counties" to be "looking out for Dissenting representatives to send up to the next parliament. . . . We must disendow the Irish Church, and abolish church rates at once, and to do this there ought to be a strong Nonconformist element in the house. Truth and righteousness demand of Christian electors that they should bestir themselves."[17] The following month, speaking before the YMCA, he issued a call-to-arms: "I do not think peace is always the most desirable, delightful, and healthy thing; but a good fight brings out the muscles and puts them into play."[18] A few days later, John Bright came to the Tabernacle and

---

[17]Pike, Life, II, 201.

[18]Ibid., 249.

addressed a meeting of the Liberation Society. Spurgeon
began to distribute petition forms urging the disestablishment of the Irish Church--all of the graduates of the
Pastors' College endorsed Gladstone's Irish Church Bill.
On May 5, Spurgeon spoke to the Liberation Society, proclaiming the forthcoming fight over disestablishment "our
Battle of Waterloo," and, even more significantly, maintained that it was the duty of Christian ministers to
indoctrinate their congregations with "right principles"
so that they would vote the "right way."[19] At approximately the same time he advocated the formation of a Nonconformist Alliance to represent all the sects in a
unified demand for the rights of Dissenters.

Spurgeon's sudden emergence as a political Dissenter
did not pass unnoticed. His attack upon the establishment
and his championship of voluntaryism brought forth two
interesting rebuttals, one appearing in Matthew Arnold's
Culture and Anarchy, the other in a speech by Samuel Wilberforce, the Bishop of Oxford, in the House of Lords.

---

[19]Ibid.

Matthew Arnold was the son of a famous clergyman, and was firmly committed to the ideal of an established national church. Although Arnold was frequently critical of Dissenters, he conceded that Spurgeon was a man of great ability. On November 9, 1866, he was taken by William Forster to a lecture by Spurgeon, and wrote later to his mother that it had been "well worth hearing." The lecture, he wrote, "was a study in the way of speaking and management of the voice . . . a most striking performance, and reminded one very much of Bright's. Occasionally there were bits in which he showed unction and real feeling; sometimes he was the mere dissenting Philistine; but he kept up one's attention for more than an hour and a half, and that is the great thing. I am very glad I have heard him."[20] Arnold, while admiring Spurgeon's style, did not subscribe to his principles, and he had already begun planning the work which he hoped would "deliver the middle class out of the hands of their

---

[20]George W E. Russell (ed.), Letters of Matthew Arnold (London, 1895), I, 342-343. Spurgeon recalled that on the occasion he was heard by Arnold he was feeling "very unwell."

dissenting ministers."[21]   On July 17, 1868, he wrote to

his mother concerning the Irish question:

> The Protestant dissenters will triumph, as I was sure
> they would. But I am equally sure that, out of the
> House and the fight of politics, I am doing what will
> sap them intellectually, and what will also sap the
> House of Commons intellectually, so far as it is ruled
> by Protestant dissenters; and more and more I am
> convinced that this is my true business at present.[22]

The result was Culture and Anarchy, published in 1869.

Spurgeon's name appears at several points in the text, and

it seems clear from the references that Spurgeon epito-

mized the intellectual weaknesses of Dissent which Arnold

sought to expose and render powerless.

Arnold first noted the role that Spurgeon had

played in the disestablishment campaign, and criticized

him for a speech in which he had argued that he preferred

to leave an established Anglican church in Ireland if the

alternative was an established Roman Catholic Church.

There had been some proposals that a dual establishment

be set up in Ireland, and Spurgeon had responded quickly

to the proposal that parliament endow the Roman Catholic

hierarchy:

---

[21]Ibid., 227.   [22]Ibid., II, 17.

> That they would be willing sooner to endow Popery,
> than to lose their own self, stamps the whole party
> consenting to such a scheme with the black brand of
> hypocrisy and covetousness. These, forsooth, are
> your Protestors, par excellence! Why they would
> sooner endow the powers of the pit than to lose the
> golden fleece![23]

Spurgeon objected to _all_ religious establishments, but forced to choose between two evils, he preferred an established Protestant church to a dual establishment. The establishment of Roman Catholicism was not a price he was willing to pay for the partial disestablishment of Anglicanism. Arnold's opinion was that Spurgeon's argument was all too typical of the narrow-minded Dissenter's opposition to giving Irish Catholics "their fair and reasonable share of church property."[24]

The second reference to Spurgeon concerned the Metropolitan Tabernacle, which Arnold described as not nearly "so impressive and affecting as the public and national Westminster Abbey, or Notre Dame."[25] This was

---

[23]_Sword and Trowel_, V (1869), 381.

[24]Matthew Arnold, _Culture and Anarchy_, edited by J. Dover Wilson (Cambridge, 1960), p. 68.

[25]_Ibid._, pp. 171-172.

an aesthetic judgment, and it seems reasonable to suppose
that most qualified critics would concede that the stolid
architectural charms of the Tabernacle do not compare to
the gothic beauty of the Abbey or Notre Dame. The issue
involved more than aesthetics, however; for the Tabernacle
had become a proud symbol of the virtues of voluntaryism,
and it is certainly significant that Arnold singled it
out for attention.

Arnold described Spurgeon as "a born Hebraiser,"[26]
that is one who took an uncritical interpretation of the
Bible as the rule for all conduct; one who sacrificed all
sides of life to the religious side. From Arnold's view-
point, Spurgeon embodied all of the parochial and narrow
qualities of Dissent which kept it separate from the
national mainstream. Arnold sought to bring Dissent within
the national pale, into "the main current of national life,"
and he saw the Established Church as one guarantee that
there would always be a national "public arena of life and
discussion." For Arnold, therefore, Spurgeon was a
Philistine, preaching the virtues of a narrow and bigoted

---

[26]Ibid., p. 173.

creed. Certainly judged by Arnold's standard, Spurgeon
was a Philistine, and his message tailored to appeal to
the worst instincts of other Philstines. Yet, although
Spurgeon's tradition was outside the National Church, that
tradition has surely done as much as the Church of England
to mold and discipline English society. Arnold's opinion
of Spurgeon is now a mere literary footnote, but it is
worth recalling that the political fact which inspired
the opinion was Spurgeon's prominence in the disestablishment
campaign.

Arnold had attacked Spurgeon as a symbol of voluntaryism by arguing that what Nonconformist voluntaryism
had accomplished was insignificant when compared to the
advantages of a national, established religion. Bishop
Wilberforce argued against voluntaryism by maintaining
that Spurgeon's success was atypical rather than the rule
as an example of voluntaryism. During a debate on the
Irish Church question in the House of Lords, Bishop Wilberforce presented the case against voluntaryism, and cited
Spurgeon in proof of his argument. In a speech on June 29,
1868, Wilberforce observed that Spurgeon--"one to whom a
great many look up"--had been guilty of great inconsistency

in arguing that the Church of Ireland should be put upon
the voluntary system. He read a letter from Spurgeon to
the Liberation Society in which Spurgeon had declared
that since the Irish Church represented "the best of the
clergy," they should be the "first to be favored with
the great blessing of disestablishment. They would only
be called to do what some of us have for years found
pleasure in doing--namely to trust the noble spirit of
generosity which true religion is sure to invoke."[27] Then
the Bishop read another letter from Spurgeon, written to
the Baptist Union in January 1867, lamenting the fact
that "hundreds of poor but faithful ministers of Jesus
Christ who labor in our midst in word and doctrine . . .
are daily oppressed by the niggardliness of the churls
among us."[28] How could Spurgeon reconcile his belief in
the advantages of voluntaryism with the facts of Baptist
experience? According to the Bishop, Spurgeon's faith
in voluntaryism was condemned by his own testimony.
Wilberforce's argument was a strong one, although his

---

[27]Great Britain, Hansard's Parliamentary Debates,
third series, CXCIII (1868), 199-200.

[28]Ibid., 200.

manner of presenting it was offensive. He made a passing
reference to Spurgeon's gout, which drew laughs from the
peers, and he read the quotations from Spurgeon's letters
in a whining nasal tone, which he perhaps fancied to be
the style of the Anabaptist Caliban.

The joking reference to Spurgeon's gout seemed
singularly inappropriate coming from a Bishop, and both the
Daily News and the Morning Star questioned Wilberforce's
taste.[29] Spurgeon answered Wilberforce in a sermon preached
on July 5, and in a letter to The Times on July 4. He was
unconcerned with the charge of inconsistency: "Every man
who speaks freely what he believes and follows truth with
a confident unreserve will be open to the charge of inconsistency. . . . If I advocate the voluntary system, must
I close my eyes to its failures, or be impeached for folly?
Must I defend its working as absolute perfection, or else
be grossly unreasonable in preferring it?"[30] The controversy continued in the press for some time, stoked by
pamphlets and tracts issued by Spurgeon and his supporters.

---

[29]Wilberforce protested that he meant no slight,
as he suffered from gout himself.

[30]The Times, July 4, 1868.

At the art of invective, the Bishop of Oxford was
no match for the Bishop of Newington Butts. Although
Wilberforce's speech in the House of Lords was his first
public recognition of Spurgeon's existence, Spurgeon had
singled out the Bishop of Oxford for chastisement on
several occasions before July 1868, and the Bishop of
Oxford must have been aware of Spurgeon's criticisms if he
did not deign to dignify them with a rebuttal. In 1867,
Wilberforce, perhaps anxious to quell suspicions that he
had extreme High Church views, had made a speech in which
he suggested that the Methodists might rejoin the Anglican
community, since "the great religious differences which
now divide us, exist more upon the memory of past evils
than upon the existence of a present necessity." The suggestion drew a violent rejoinder from Spurgeon. In a
November editorial in Sword and Trowel entitled "Best
Oxford Soap," Spurgeon observed that "The Bishop of Oxford,
of saponaceous renown, has lately distinguished himself
upon two or three occasions in a manner eminently calculated to increase his repute among persons devoid of
understanding." Wilberforce's suggestion that the religious
differences between Methodist and Churchman were based

upon memory rather than fact prompted Spurgeon to charge

that the statement was "either a willful falsehood or a

miraculous hallucination."[31] Spurgeon warned Wilberforce,

"no revision of the Prayerbook, nor reformation of spirit

would remove our conscientious objection to the very

existence of a state church! The thing itself is evil

and must be removed."[32] In an impassioned declaration,

he demanded,

> Would he have us become Puseyites and array ourselves
> in motley and adore a god of bread, and trust in cere-
> monies? Would he have us return into a bondage which
> our fathers could not endure? Are we to crouch at the
> feet of priests, and give up our wives and daughters
> to the sway of father confessors? Does he really
> believe that there is no necessity for Dissent from a
> church which has now become so like to the anti-Christ
> of Rome that if a hue and cry were raised for Babylon's
> twin sister, she would certainly be arrested?[33]

The same theme was sounded in a series of tracts

which Spurgeon's publishers, Passmore and Alabaster, began

to issue in the summer of 1868. "Tractarianism owed its

origin to tracts," Spurgeon reasoned, "why not accomplish

---

[31]Sword and Trowel, III (1867), 514.

[32]Ibid., 516.

[33]Ibid.

its downfall by tracts?"[34] The illustrated Tracts for the Times, with short texts by Spurgeon, touched upon a variety of contemporary issues and sold for 6d. a hundred. In May--one month before Wilberforce's speech--one of the tracts featured three Anglican priests in full regalia (embroidered robes, long skirts, girlish simpers), with an accompanying warning that "the distinction between the Popery of Rome and the Popery of Oxford is only the difference between prussic acid and arsenic: they are both equally deadly, and are equally to be abhored."[35] A companion tract, "The Church of England the Bulwark of our Liberties?" asserted that the Church was no more the protector of Protestant liberties than "are the beefeaters of the Tower or the cream-colored horses in the royal stable." Far from being the "protector of our liberties," the Church of England had "hanged and imprisoned our forefathers," "clipped ears, slit noses, and branded cheeks." The Establishment should be aware that "the sons of Ironsides are not yet departed from among us, and we who could

---

[34]Autobiography, III, 162.

[35]Sword and Trowel, IV (1868), 203-2-4. The tracts were re-printed in Sword.

not use carnal weapons have yet our free press, our
unfettered pulpit, and our open Bibles, and feel safe
enough while these are our weapons of war." In political
matters, Spurgeon wrote, Dissenters "do not owe the
Church of England a brass farthing." Moreover, the disestablishment of the Church of Ireland was only to be the
preamble: "Therefore laying the axe at the root of the
system, we demand the abolition of every union between
church and state, and the disallowance on the part of
Caesar with things which belong to God."[36] In August
1868, the month following the controversy with Bishop
Wilberforce, Spurgeon issued another Tract for the Times,
certainly the single most offensive of the series, which
pictured an Anglican priest kneeling at a trough with a
corpulent pig wearing a papal tiara. The accompanying
text explained that the pig represented the Roman Catholic
Church and the trough stood for the overworked Irish
peasantry, perpetually forced to feed pig and priest.
"Let every true Protestant help to deliver the Irish Church
from her present condition, and may God defend the right."[37]

---

[36]Ibid., 227.   [37]Ibid., 413.

Several of Spurgeon's tracts appear in Gladstone's papers; perhaps Spurgeon sent them to him, though what Gladstone may have thought of these colorful pieces of propaganda is not recorded.

Parliament was dissolved on November 11, and the question of Irish disestablishment was left to the electorate. Spurgeon urged all Christians to pray for "that noble statesman, Mr. Gladstone," and issued an election tract proclaiming, "the cry of 'No Popery' ill becomes the mouth of a Church of England clergyman, when it is by men of his cloth that the ceremonies of Rome are being forced upon us: the fox with the hen in his mouth might as well cry out, 'no robbing of hen roosts!'"[38] The result of the election was gratifying to Spurgeon and the parliamentary Radicals, for the Liberals were returned with a majority of one hundred and twelve. There seemed no limit to the future of political Dissent: "In December 1868, Dissenters and Radicals dreamed dreams and saw visions."[39]

------

[38]Ibid., 509-510.

[39]Addison, op. cit., p. 124.

On March 1, 1869, the government bill to
disestablish the Church of Ireland was introduced into
the House of Commons. Gladstone was the man of the hour
for Dissenters, as a letter from Spurgeon to Gladstone,
written on April 16 suggests:

> The Tabernacle
> Newington
> April 16

To the Rt. Honorable
W. E. Gladstone, Esq.

Sir,

    As one among thousands I have watched your career
with an almost affectionate admiration; not only
because for the most part I have agreed with your
politics, but because I have seen in you a man actuated
by a sense of right, in contradistinction to the
pitiful shifts of policy.

    I have been made bold to write to you this one word
to say that in your present struggle to do justice to
Ireland by the disestablishment of the Church of the
few, you have not only the zealous cooperation of
Dissenters interested in politics, but the devout prayers
of those to whom it is a matter of solemn conscience
that our Lord's kingdom is not of this world. We see
in you an answer to many a fervent petition that the
day may come when the Church of Jesus may believe in
her Lord's power and not in human alliances. Whether
you would personally go with us in that view is not the
point, but going as far as you do, so purely, so con-
scientiously we invoke the aid of the God of Providence
to help you.

    I felt ready to weep when you were threatened with
so much contumely by your opponents in your former
struggle, and yet I rejoiced that you were educating
the nation to believe in conscience and truth. It is
nothing to you that I sympathize with you, and yet in

moments of vexation a child's word may cheer a strong man; and it is for this that I felt that I must say to you that I trust you will be sustained under the yet more virulent abuse which will certainly come upon you. The sense of right will be to you as a sword and buckler, and if again deserted by recreants as you may be, you will stay yourself upon the Eternal God in whose custody the jewels of right and justice are ever safe.

I do not expect even a line from your secretary to acknowledge this. It will content me for once in my life to have said 'Thank-you' and 'God-speed' to such a man.

Yours very respectfully,

C. H. Spurgeon[40]

The humble, gracious tone of Spurgeon's letter would have surprised those who had encountered only the sharp side of his tongue and pen. Gladstone had entered parliament in the year of Spurgeon's birth; the preacher, at thirty-five, was a boy no longer, yet the awe and admiration the younger man felt for the older are transparent. For Nonconformists, there was cause for rejoicing at last, for in Spurgeon's words, policy was now directed by a man "actuated by a sense of right."

The Government's disestablishment bill passed its third reading in the House of Commons on May 31, 1869, but

---

[40]Ms. letter, April 16, 1869. Gladstone Papers, British Musuem, CCCXXXV, f. 133.

opposition from the bishops and conservative peers made
it seem likely that the bill would encounter delay and
possibly rejection in the House of Lords.   On July 13,
Spurgeon wrote again to Gladstone, announcing that the
London Baptist Association, "of which I am this year the
President," had passed a resolution urging the peers to
accept the bill.   The Association represented 25,000
communicants, "and probably 100,000 hearers," he wrote,
offering to "send you this resolution in the way most
likely to strengthen your hands with the public."[41]   Suggesting a meeting with Gladstone for the following Thursday
morning, he enclosed a handwritten copy of the London
Baptist Association's resolution:

> Resolved:
> That this meeting believes that the Irish Church Bill
> as it left the House of Commons was formed in justice
> and was eminently calculated to promote the social
> order and religious prosperity of Ireland, it was
> therefore heard with deep regret that the House of
> Lords has adopted amendments which violate the funda-
> mental principle of the Bill and they earnestly and
> respectfully entreat her Majesty's government and the
> Liberal majority to use their utmost endeavors to

---

[41]Ms. letter, July 13, 1869.   Gladstone Papers,
British Musuem, CCCXXXVI, f. 145.

> maintain the Bill in its integrity, to yield to no
> compromises, but to urge on this great and just
> measure until it shall become the law of the land.

At the same time, Spurgeon wrote an editorial in <u>Sword and
Trowel</u> sharply critical of the "tyrannical action" of the
House of Lords in delaying the bill, and suggesting that
the bishops ought to be removed from the upper house
immediately, since "with one or two exceptions they are
always the friends of everything oppressive."[42] For Gladstone, a man with High Church sympathies, the circumstances
of the summer of 1869 must have been awkward. The Baptists
cheered him on and the bishops refused to budge. Finally
it was pressure from the Queen and Dr. Tait, the Archbishop
of Canterbury, which brought the recalcitrant bishops into
line, and on July 26, the bill passed into law.

Gladstone had warned his Lancashire constituents
in 1868 that the question of Irish disestablishment was
quite distinct from the question of English disestablishment, but in spite of this warning most Dissenters
obviously regarded the victory in Ireland as a prelude

---

[42]<u>Sword and Trowel</u>, V (1869), 381.

to a greater victory in England. When Miall moved to
disestablish the Church of England in 1869, the motion
received eighty-nine votes; by 1873, the same motion mus-
tered only sixty-one votes. In retrospect, 1869 appears
as a high-water mark in opposition to the Established
Church. Dissenters continued their efforts to keep the
issue prominent--Spurgeon warned that voters must continue
to keep the question paramount in their minds: "It is to
be hoped that no Nonconformist will vote for a man who
will not aid in the disestablishment of the Anglican Church.
Liberal and Tory alike are useless to us if they will not
do this much for us."[43] But attempts to make the disestablishment question the test of true Liberalism were
unavailing. The country was diverted by other issues, and
Gladstone was never persuaded that the time was appropriate
for raising the question.

Spurgeon continued to be a strong advocate of
religious voluntaryism, but in later years he grew philosophical about the issue of disestablishment. He came

---

[43]Ibid., IX (1873), 476.

to believe that disestablishment was almost a providential

carrot for Liberals to use in keeping the donkey of Dissent

in line, and he strongly suspected that without the carrot,

the donkey would seek other pastures. In a speech on

disestablishment in May 1877, he remarked: "I sometimes

think that some of you rich Dissenters would not always

be for Liberal measures if you got this carried--that you

would some of you become Conservatives. . . . You are kept

to do justice for others by suffering injustice your-

selves."[44] He repeated the idea in an interview in 1884:

> I sometimes think it is a providential arrangement
> that the State Church should be permitted to exist,
> in order to bind the Nonconformists hand and foot to
> the Liberal party. If that were once removed a con-
> siderable section of wealthy Nonconformists would go
> over to the Conservatives. Wealth is naturally con-
> servative. But in Nonconformists the political con-
> servative tendency of riches is kept in check by the
> constant sense of bitter injustice inflicted upon them
> for conscience sake, and as long as that is kept
> ranking in their minds they will remain with the
> Liberal party, even though in many things they may
> prefer the politics of the other side.[45]

---

[44]Pike (ed.), Speeches, p. 144.

[45]Pall Mall Gazette, XXXIX (1884), 11-12.

This was a very astute analysis of the Liberal-Nonconformist
alliance. Obviously a man who viewed disestablishment
as "a providential arrangement" which bound Nonconformists
"hand and foot to the Liberal party" was no zealot consumed by holy fires. These were the words of a party
loyalist who was prepared to be pragmatic about this
particular issue.

Nonconformist disenchantment with the Gladstone
administration was quick to develop following the initial
victory in Ireland. The refusal of the ministry to consider the disestablishment of the English Church coupled
with the Education Act of 1870 and the Licensing Bill of
1871--both anathema to many Dissenters--alienated all but
the staunchest loyalists from the government. The controversial Education Act especially antagonized Dissenters,
and Spurgeon's role in defending the Act and W. E. Forster
from the attacks of the militant Dissenters clearly places
him in the party loyalist category. Throughout the
lengthy controversy surrounding the attempt to frame a
national education policy, Spurgeon played the part of a
mediator, attempting to arrange some compromise which

would bring Dissenters together in support of a national system of public education.

Spurgeon's attitudes toward a national education system changed between 1866 and 1868. In common with many old-fashioned Dissenters, his first response to the idea of a state-supported educational system was negative. As a champion of voluntaryism, be believed that private, sectarian education was consistent with the voluntary principle. However, in practice a voluntary system worked to the disadvantage of Dissenters, and increasingly the old faith in complete voluntaryism began to fade. Spurgeon at one time considered establishing a "really first-class school," to teach "the principles advocated by Mr. Spurgeon," but as the response to his proposal was negligible, he abandoned the scheme. By 1868 he appeared to have forsaken the voluntary principle in education. "Education of a secular sort has been too long withheld by the bickering of the rival sects," he declared in April, "the nation is now in such a humor that it will have no more of such unenlightened bigotry, but will insist upon it, that every child shall be taught to read and write."[46] "The great question of the hour seems to be a national system of education. We should like to see a system of universal application which would give a sound education to children, and leave the religious training to the home and the agencies of the church of Christ."[47] Spurgeon's proposal--which closely paralleled Forster's Bill--was that the state continue aid to established Church and Dissenter schools, but that it provide for free secular schools where none existed, and compel all children to attend one or the other.[48]

The home of the militant National Education League which pressed for free, unsectarian, compulsory education was Birmingham; its leaders were R. W. Dale and Joseph Chamberlain. Spurgeon's sphere of influence was London; and within that sphere, and specifically in heavily-populated South London, he exercised important influence in moderating the demands of the Birmingham Radicals. Both Spurgeon and the Birmingham League demanded "secular

---

[46]Sword and Trowel, IV (1868), 147.

[47]Ibid., 139.   [48]Ibid., 140.

education," bus disagreed on what "secular education"
meant. When Spurgeon argued for secular education he
did not mean a _completely_ secular education, and his
advocacy of Bible-reading in the schools involved him in
a dispute with the leaders of the Birmingham League.
Spurgeon objected to teaching any specific _doctrine_ in
state schools, but he was horrified at the demands of
Radicals that public education should be made truly
secular.

Spurgeon objected to doctrinal teachings in the
schools for three reasons: first, he personally disagreed
with much of the doctrine which would be taught; second,
he believed that doctrinal instruction would be used to
buttress the religious status quo; and third, he doubted
that religious instruction in schools could ever be an
effective way to win souls. "The lads of the village
might generally carry in a hollow tooth all the religion
they receive at the charity school," he commented.[49] His
attitude toward doctrinal instruction in the parish schools
was a reflection of his own experience and his rural

---

[49]_Ibid_., 147.

325

background. He strongly suspected that the chief purpose of much of the religious instruction in the parish schools was to reinforce the established social system. In 1865 he had observed, "Episcopalian priests are much at home in teaching ignorant rustics to order themselves lowly and reverently to all their betters,"[50] and in 1868 he protested that too many children in parish schools were being taught lessons "about behaving one's-self lowly and reverently to one's betters in a manner suitable for an American Negro previous to the late war. . . . It will be highly beneficial to the morality of youth to dispense with this miserable farrago, in which the false of super-stition and the true of law are hopelessly jumbled."[51] "There will be a great outcry about the divorcing of religion from education," he wrote in April 1868, "but we shall not join in it, partly because it is useless to cry over spilt milk--the thing must be, and there is no preventing it; and yet more, because we think we see our way to a great real gain out of a small apparent loss."[52]

---

[50] Ibid., I (1865), 390.   [51] Ibid., IV (1868), 148.
[52] Ibid., 147.

At no time did Spurgeon advocate removing the
Bible from the state schools, and Radical demands to dispense with Bible-reading puzzled and infuriated him. As
G. F. A. Best has noted, the struggle over formulating a
national educational policy was marked by "two irreconcilable ideas of what really was 'religious' education--
the doctrinal idea and the undenominational idea."[53]
Spurgeon, in common with many Dissenters, objected to
doctrinal instruction in state schools, but accepted the
nondenominational use of the Bible as an educational tool
suited to buttress the rather nebulous ideal of a "national
faith." "Denouncing the establishment for cramming the
catechism down the infant rustics' throats was one thing,
but 'banishing the Bible from the schools' was another."[54]
When Forster's bill was being debated in the summer of
1870, Spurgeon announced that he would "counsel Christians
to refuse to send their children to the schools if the
Bible be excluded."[55] He went to Exeter Hall to participate

---

[53]G. F. A. Best, "The Religious Difficulties of
National Education in England, 1800-1870," Cambridge Historical Journal, XII (1956), 161.

[54]Ibid., 172.

[55]Sword and Trowel, VI (1870), 285.

in a debate over Bible-reading in the schools and was
delighted when the secularist position won only twenty
votes. "The workingmen of London are not prepared to with-
hold from their children the Book of God," he declared.[56]
When news filtered into London of the attempt by French
radicals to establish a Commune in Paris, Spurgeon saw
Paris radicalism as a reflection of too-little Bible-
reading. "Paris is full of anarchy," he asserted,
"because [Paris is] steeped in atheism."[57]

In August 1870, the Education Act passed into law.
The system which resulted was neither generally free nor
compulsory education, but rather an attempt to fill in the
gaps in the existing system. Dissenters had prevailed
in their insistence that there be no distinctive catechism
taught in the state schools, but they were dissatisfied
with other provisions of the act, especially with clause
twenty-five which permitted school boards to pay the fees
of poor children at either board or voluntary schools.
To many Dissenters, this appeared to be an attempt to

---

[56]Ibid., 332.

[57]Ibid., VIII (1872), 10.

subsidize parish schools out of rates, and by 1874, over
three hundred Liberal candidates were pledged to repeal of
clause twenty-five.[58] No single group was wholly
satisfied with the act, which was the result of a series
of compromises.

Spurgeon had reservations about the act, but in
spite of his doubts, he worked to get Nonconformist
acceptance of its basic goals. "The bill is a compromise,"
he wrote in an editorial in the Sword and Trowel, "give
it a fair trial. Education, if it be not utterly irreligious, need not be feared by the free churches of England,
nor need they quarrel over every petty detail of its
management while their power at the headquarters of government is what it is." Spurgeon urged Dissenters to move on
to the next task, that of electing good men to the new
school boards, and he was quick to offer advice on the
selection of appropriate candidates. In rural districts,
he warned, Dissenters should support only other Dissenters,
but in London, "we should vote not so much to secure

----

[58]Addison, op. cit., p. 134.

Dissenters as to elect men who will not use the government
educational machinery for party or sectarian purposes."[59]
On November 16, 1870, Spurgeon wrote letters to the major
dailies endorsing the candidacy of W. R. Selway to the
London School Board. He urged that no clergymen be
elected, and suggested the election of at least one workingman, as they were the class "more immediately concerned
in the present movement."[60]

He continued to work through the 'seventies to
bring the warring Dissenting factions together on the
school question. He became a particular champion of
W. E. Forster. Forster, a Quaker who shared the representation of Bradford with Miall, had been the responsible
minister in the house for the Education Act, and consequently became the target for Dissenters' frustrations.
Spurgeon was one of the few prominent Dissenters to defend
the beleagured minister, whom he described as "an honest,
warm man."[61] His interest in Forster continued through
the election of 1880--in Spurgeon's scrapbook for that

---

[59]Sword and Trowel, VI (1870), 528.
[60]Pike, Life, II, 366-367.
[61]Ibid., 156.

year there is a telegram to Spurgeon from Forster's

headquarters, confirming his victory at Bradford.

"Mr. Spurgeon," declared a reporter for the

Weekly Dispatch, "continues to be the greatest single

influence in South London in favor of Liberalism. At

elections, School Boards and Parliamentary, his followers

display an energy and discipline which leave nothing to

be desired. It would be hard to find a better Radical

than Mr. Spurgeon."[62] But even for a party loyalist,

---

[62]Weekly Dispatch, November 9, 1879. Scrapbook
clipping. Spurgeon's "Radicalism" owed more to seventeenth-
century Independency and memories of past wrongs than to
the secular Radicalism of the Benthamites. Spurgeon had
a radical view of what he believed were the oppressions of
an entrenched social class, insofar as that class was represented by the Anglican Establishment. He had a rather
romantic view of "the Christian workingman," but he had
little knowledge of or contact with workingclass politics.
His approach to social problems was individualistic,
emphasizing philanthropy rather than state action. He was
close to "great Radical capitalists" such as Samuel Morley
and Sir Morton Peto. He belonged to the group of Radicals
Professor Vincent has described as "political Calvinists,"
whose "really important attitudes had nothing to do with
the industrial revolution, much to do with the English Civil
War," in op. cit., p. xxix. Vincent's analysis of the parliamentary Radicals distinguishes between the secular Radicals and the Dissenting Radicals who lived "in the world of
Samuel Smiles, in its second generation," p. 35. Spurgeon
was an important part of the constituency which this group
represented.

there are limits to loyalty. Strong party man though he
was, there was one issue upon which Spurgeon refused to
compromise, and it finally caused him to break with his
party leadership. "No Popery" was a rallying cry that
would always threaten to turn Spurgeon into a one-man
Gordon Riot. Truly, as a journalist commented, "The Roman
Catholic Church was to him the scarlet woman of the
Apocalypse who sat upon the seven hills, who was drunk
from the blood of the Saints, and who was only prevented
from making a meal of Mr. Spurgeon and his flock by our
Protestant Constitution."[63] Churchmen and Dissenters alike
exploited the prejudice against Roman Catholics to suit
their own ends, but few Englishmen were more violent in
their hatred of Rome than the Pastor of the Tabernacle.
He was incapable of moderation on the subject, though
characteristically, he denied unusual bias: "I am not
an outrageous Protestant," he wrote. "I rejoice to confess
that there are some of God's people even in the Romish
Church."[64] In spite of his disclaimer, his anti-Catholicism

---

[63]Review of Reviews, V (1892), 250-251.

[64]Autobiography, II, 364.

was notorious. The <u>Saturday Review</u> was not far from the truth in maintaining that "denunciation of the Roman Catholics generally, or of the Pope or of his priests in particular, form a necessary condiment to every intellectual feast held in the Tabernacle."[65] When a fellow-Baptist once told Spurgeon that he had attended a Roman Catholic Mass in Paris and had "felt very near the presence of God," Spurgeon retorted that the experience proved the truth of the text: "If I make my bed in hell, behold thou art there!"[66]

When Gladstone made tentative offers to protect the Pope during the Italian crisis of 1871, Spurgeon was furious. "Mr. Gladstone misrepresents the nation when he makes the dignity of the Pope a <u>legitimate</u> object of the national notice of Great Britain," he declared. "We are Liberals, but we cannot take this even from the most Liberal of Cabinets. O, for an hour of Oliver Cromwell in the senate to denounce truckling of this sort."[67] He

---

[65]<u>Saturday Review</u>, XVII (1864), 226.

[66]E. T. Raymond, <u>Portraits of the Nineties</u> (London, 1921), p. 362.

[67]<u>Sword and Trowel</u>, VII (1871), 87.

was also quick to protest Gladstone's appointment of a Roman Catholic convert, the Marquis of Ripon, as Viceroy of India. How, asked Spurgeon, could one "sworn to allegiance to the Pope" represent Her Majesty's Government in India? For Gladstone "to put Papists to the front," Spurgeon declared, does not increase my esteem for him."[68] Spurgeon's politics were colored by the turbulent history of English Nonconformity. The man did not forget his boyhood lessons.

By 1874, even party loyalists had become alienated from the government. As G. M. Young wrote, "In its six years of office, this great but unfortunate administration contrived to offend, to disquiet, or to disappoint, almost every interest in the country."[69] In March 1873, the government was defeated in the House of Commons on a bill which would have allowed Protestants and Catholics to attend the universities in Ireland on the same basis. Disraeli refused to take office without an election, and

---

[68]Autobiography, IV, 126.

[69]G. M. Young, Victorian England, Portrait of an Age (New York, 1954), p. 161.

the government limped on for nearly a year until the
General Election of 1874 returned the Tories to power.
The Liberal coalition of 1868 had evaporated, and Spurgeon's
verdict on the election results suggests one reason why:
Liberals will remain out of power, he declared, "until
they learn that the helots who have followed at their
heels, who have really won their victories, mean to be
free themselves." Meanwhile, "may the Liberals keep out
until they know their friends."[70]

The Nonconformists were defiant, but their defiance
was short-lived. What alternative did they have to
Liberal leadership? They might bring the Liberal government down, but they had little influence in the government
of the Conservatives. Gladstone's great authority with
the Nonconformists was that they saw in him a man of moral
purpose--in Spurgeon's words, "a man actuated by a sense
of right." As Dr. Kitson Clark writes, they "recognized
in the ring of his voice, in his choice of words, in the
sanctions to which he appealed, the same spirit as that

[70]Pike (ed.), Speeches, p. 144.

which possessed them."[71] Whatever his failures of judgment
or administration, Gladstone had the ability to transform
political issues into moral issues and to capitalize upon
the strong "sense of right" of the Nonconformist electorate.

It was Disraeli's foreign policy which provided
the Liberal opposition an opportunity to raise the question
of conscience, and in so doing, provide Gladstone with
the moral issue his political psychology demanded. In 1876
a revolt in Bulgaria was brutally crushed by the Turkish
army. The atrocities made it clear that Turkey had no
intention of keeping the promises made following the
Crimean War to extend the rights of subject Christian
peoples within the Turkish Empire. Disraeli, anxious to
preserve Turkey as a buffer against Russian expansion into
the Balkans, failed to understand the moral revulsion
many Englishmen felt at the atrocities of the "Terrible
Turk." R. T. Shannon's researches on the Bulgarian agitation of 1876 have pointed to the episode as "the most
convincing demonstration of the susceptibility of the

[71]G. Kitson Clark, in "Introduction," to
R. T. Shannon, Gladstone and the Bulgarian Agitation, 1876
(London, 1963), xxii.

High Victorian conscience" to moral agitation.[72] Within

six weeks of the news of the "horrors," nearly five hundred

demonstrations against the government's policy of support

of the Turks had occurred throughout Great Britain. Glad-

stone, who had retired from the leadership of the Liberal

party in 1875 to devote his remaining years to writing upon

religious questions, was a late convert to a well-organized

Bulgarian agitation. Gladstone had at first little aware-

ness of the political potential of the agitation. "Far

from being a decisive agent, Gladstone was practically

carried into the agitation by others."[73] Perceiving at

last that the Bulgarian agitation was "a stirring of truly

popular moral passion," Gladstone tardily joined the

crusade, producing in September 1876, his celebrated

pamphlet on the "Bulgarian Horrors." For Gladstone the

issue was one of supporting a Christian people or supporting

a government of "abominable and bestial lusts," engaged in

activities "at which hell itself might almost blush."[74]

---

[72]Ibid., p. 15.   [73]Ibid., p. 90.

[74]Magnus, op. cit., p. 242.

Disraeli dismissed the anti-Turkish agitation as a smokescreen obscuring the real threat of Russian aggrandizement in the Balkans, and when the Russian government declared war on Turkey in 1877, his view seemed vindicated. It was preposterous to see Russia as the champion of Christendom. "The Emperor of Russia," he confided to Lady Chesterfield, "cares as much for the Christians as you do for Spurgeon."[75]

Whatever Lady Chesterfield may have thought of Spurgeon, Spurgeon's opinion of Disraeli was a matter of public record. When Disraeli had threatened war with Russia in November 1876, inspiring the famous music hall refrain which added "jingoism" to the language, he had seemed to capture the bellicose mood of much of the country. On November 30, the Pastor of the Tabernacle took note of his country's belligerent mood, and prayed that "the extraordinary folly of our leaders" would not "lead this country into war." Lest that happen, he prayed, "change

---

[75]Marquis of Zetland (ed.), The Letters of Disraeli to Lady Bradford and Lady Chesterfield (London, 1929), I, 21.

our rulers, O God, as soon as possible."[76] The following

month, writing in an editorial in Sword and Trowel, he

declared, "When we see war threatened on behalf of a

detestable tyranny, contrary to all the dictates of humanity

and religion, we cannot do otherwise than to implore the

Judge of all the earth to save us from such an astounding

wickedness, and to remove from office the man whose rash

bravados give rise to our fears."[77] Spurgeon's remarks

were given wide publicity in the European press.[78]

Spurgeon's opinions are indicative of the growing

Nonconformist hostility to the belligerent foreign policy

of the Tory government. In Spurgeon's case, the hostility

was grounded not only in the crisis of the moment, but on

---

[76]The Times, November 30, 1876.

[77]Sword and Trowel, VII (1871), 87.

[78]Dr. Shannon, in op. cit., 167-168, noting that
Spurgeon refused to join in the plans for a "Bulgarian
Sunday," concludes that "there is little evidence of deep
moral involvement" in the question for Spurgeon. I think
that Spurgeon refused to join in the organized agitation
for personal reasons. First, he was in ill health during
much of the year, and at the height of the agitation in the
summer of 1876, was touring Scotland. He was thus removed
from his London base. He was also not on especially good
terms with R. W. Dale, the leader of the clerical portion of
the agitation. Spurgeon was still nursing a grudge against
the Birmingham Congregationalist for his part in the school
controversy a few years earlier. Finally, Spurgeon was at
his best when he was at the center of the stage. He was fond
of neither committees nor organizations, especially when
directed by others.

an aversion to war and the politics of imperialism
generally. It is commonly argued that Protestantism, and
especially the Protestant mission movement, was an
important source of the nineteenth-century imperialist
thrust; if so, Spurgeon's views are certainly atypical.
His hatred of war was deep, and he strongly rejected the
idea that the gospel could be spread by conquest. As
early as 1854, speaking before the London YMCA, he had
protested the British bombardment of Canton:

> Whenever England goes to war, many shout, "It will
> open a way for the gospel." I cannot understand how
> the devil is to make a way for Christ; and what is
> war but an incarnate fiend, the impersonation of all
> that is hellish in fallen humanity. . . .For English
> cannon to make way in Canton for an English missionary,
> is a lie too glaring for me to believe for a moment.
> I cannot comprehend the Christianity which talks thus
> of murder and robbery. . . . I blush for my country
> when I see it committing such terrible crimes in China,
> for what is the opium traffic but an enormous crime?[79]

In August 1870, writing as "John Ploughman," Spurgeon
addressed an open letter to the Emperor of France, and
King of German suggesting that they settle their differences
by personal combat--"why don't you strip and go at it

---

[79]Autobiography, III, 44.

yourself as our Tom Rowdy and Big Ben did on the green;
it's cowardly of you to send a lot of other fellows to
be shot on your account." The letter was an eloquent
indictment of the folly of war:

> Did either of you ever think of what war means? Did
> you ever see a man's head smashed, or his bowels ripped
> open? Why, if you are made of flesh and blood, the
> sight of one poor wounded man, with the blood oozing
> out of him, will make you feel sick. I don't like to
> drown a kitten; I can't bear even to see a rat die, or
> any animal in pain. But a man! Where's your hearts
> if you can think of broken legs, splintered bones,
> heads smashed in, brains blown out, bowels torn, hearts
> gushing with gore, ditches full of blood, and heaps of
> limbs and carcasses of mangled men? Do you say my
> language is disgusting? How much more disgusting must
> the things themselves be? And you make them! . . . Do
> you fancy that your drums and fifes, and feathers and
> fineries, and pomp, make your wholesale murder one whit
> the less abominable in the sight of God? Do not
> deceive yourselves, you are no better than the cut-
> throats whom your own laws condemn; better, why you are
> worse, for your murders are so many. . . . Emperor and
> King, who are you? Though the great folk flatter you,
> you are only men. Have pity upon your fellow men. Do
> not cut them with swords, tear them with bayonets, blow
> them to pieces with cannon, and riddle them with shots.
> What good will it do you? What have the poor men done
> to deserve it of you? You fight for glory, do you?
> Don't be such fools. I am a plain talking Englishman
> and I tell you the English for glory is DAMNATION, and
> it will be your lot, O kings, if you go on cutting and
> hacking your fellow men.[80]

---

[80] Sword and Trowel, VI (1870), 352-353.

Spurgeon was equally critical of the "periodical war madness" of his own people. In April 1878, when Britain seemed on the verge of involvement in the Russo-Turkish war, and pro-war mobs demonstrated in London, he observed:

> England, at set seasons, runs wild with the war lunacy, foams at the mouth, bellows out "Rule Britannia," shows her teeth, and in general behaves herself like a mad creature: then her doctors bleed her, and put her through a course of depletion until she comes to her senses, settles down to her cotton-spinning and shop-keeping, and wonders what could have ailed her?[81]

"When war begins, hell opens," he wrote, and it was a conviction he held regardless of jingoistic appeals to crown, race, or country.

In the summer of 1878, Spurgeon renewed his correspondence with Gladstone. In May, he wrote to Gladstone requesting that he act as chairman of his annual orphanage society meeting. He knew that Gladstone's presence would assure good publicity for his orphanages, for as he complained, "as Dissenters it matters not what works of

---

[81] Ibid., XIV (1878), 145. Spurgeon's comments must be viewed as a reaction to the pro-war agitation in London which gave the impression that the country was closer to war than was the case. See, Hugh Cunningham, "Jingoism in 1877-78," in Victorian Studies, XIV (June 1971), 429-453.

philanthropy we may achieve, no notice is taken of us in highest quarters."[82] He assured Gladstone that the orphanages were non-sectarian, but Gladstone was unable to accept the invitation. He softened his refusal by extending an invitation to Spurgeon to join him for dinner. Spurgeon declined, explaining, "My work cannot be done except by keeping to it hour by hour. Social enjoyment has long since been out of the question with me. I do not dine out or breakfast out once in a year nor can I. I may add that I do not feel in spirits for going into company more than I am forced to do."[83] Spurgeon was obviously annoyed with Gladstone for refusing to publicize his orphanages. He was in poor health, and he was certainly not a social gadfly; nevertheless, his social life was not so austere as his churlish note suggests.

Whatever his annoyance with Gladstone, Spurgeon was aware that the alternative was more Disraeli; and that alternative was sufficient to keep him a Gladstonian; as

[82]Ms. letter, May 18, 1878. Gladstone Papers, British Museum, CCCLXXI, 44456, ff. 332.

[83]Ms. letter, May 21, 1878. Gladstone Papers, British Museum, CCCLXXXI, 44456, ff. 338.

he remarked to a friend, even when Gladstone's policies disturbed him, "yet I am a Gladstonite despite all this."[84] In May 1879, Spurgeon was again demanding from the pulpit that the Lord intervene to rid the country of its iniquitous ministers:

> We once hoped that peace was the favorite policy of England, but now Britannia thrusts her fists into everybody's face, and recklessly provokes hostility. The present ministry has sent the nation back half a century as to its moral tone; and it has laid up in the records of divine justice a sad amount of retribution, which is even now, in a measure, being meted out to the land. . . . It is our prayer that God may forgive the present belligerent ministers and either remove them from their offices or reverse their policy.[85]

In November 1879, when Gladstone commenced his great Midlothian campaign, sharply criticizing the moral bankruptcy of the Disraeli government, Spurgeon was very ill. A severe attack of gout made it impossible for him to approach his duties with his customary energy. "The wheels of life go round with a motion clogged and painful," he wrote in January 1880. He decided to go abroad to

---

[84]Letter to Mr. Watts, July 19, 1880, in Autobiography, IV, 126.

[85]Sword and Trowel, XV (1879), 245.

escape the cold, damp London winter. Before leaving for Mentone he wrote an editorial endorsing Gladstone's speeches and urging the formation of "Christian Consultation Committees" in each parliamentary district to advise the electorate. He denied that the proposal had a partisan purpose. "It is not for the Christian to descend into the dirt and treachery of politics, but . . . to draw politics up into the light and power of Christ. . . . The United States has shown us what horrible corruption is engendered by Christian men refusing to be the salt of the world; let it not be so among us."[86]

Spurgeon continued to issue advice to the voters from his retreat at Mentone. In February 1880, he wrote to the South London Express urging the election of the Liberal candidate, Andrew Dunn, at the forthcoming by-election at Southwark. Dunn was a personal friend, and had addressed the students at the Pastors' College on several occasions. When Spurgeon returned to London in the middle of February, his first sermon was a forthright attack upon the jingoistic policies of the government. A report of his

---

[86]Ibid., 41.

sermon in The Times declared that he had said, "England is following a dangerous policy. Her rulers were making bloody wars and oppressing nations, and they encouraged and consoled themselves with the reflection, 'we are a great people; and by Jingo, do what we like, and it will all come out right in the end."[87] The Western Mail characterized the sermon as "a violent attack upon her Majesty's government," and reported Spurgeon had accused the English people of worshipping a new god, Jingo.[88] The sermon was widely reported in the foreign press; the New York Herald-Tribune reported the speech as its first item in its column on foreign news.

Spurgeon had misjudged the temper of the London electorate, and his attack upon jingoism proved to be poorly timed. At the end of February, his friend, Andrew Dunn, was defeated by a Tory candidate. Southwark had always been a Liberal stronghold, and Spurgeon had gone out of his way to endorse Dunn. Unquestionably, the Tory victory at Southwark encouraged Disraeli to conclude that

---

[87]The Times, February 16, 1880.

[88]Western Mail, February 1880. Scrapbook clipping.

the times were propitious for the Tories, and in March
1880, parliament was dissolved in preparation for a general election in April. Spurgeon had come to regard
Southwark as something of a pocket-borough, and he took
Dunn's defeat in a very personal way. Determined to
reverse the judgment of February, he devoted the month
before the general election to feverish activity in behalf
of the Liberal candidates in South London.

It is possible to gauge the extent of Spurgeon's
activity in the election of 1880 by studying some of the
momentoes of the campaign which are preserved in his scrapbook for that year. A number of handbills, clippings, and
telegrams suggest that Spurgeon was very busy indeed. A
typical handbill, addressed to "the Liberal electors of
Lambeth," from "your friend and neighbor, C. H. Spurgeon,"
declared:

> Do you sorrow over the warlike policy which has thrust
> might into the place of right, and invaded weak nations
> with but scant excuse? Then return the two candidates
> who are opposed to the Beaconsfield ministry.
>
> Do you believe that constant bluster creates political
> uneasiness, and disturbs our peaceful relations with
> other nations, and thus hinders trade and commerce?
> Then send to parliament Liberal candidates to strengthen
> the hands of Mr. Gladstone.

Do you believe that great questions of progress at home should no longer be pushed into a corner? Then increase the number of men who are in the advance guard of liberty. Lovers of religious equality, your course is plain, and you will not leave your duty undone. With hands and heart support the men who would rid religion of state patronage and control. You who would ease the national burdens by economy and retrenchment, vote for Messrs. McArthur and Lawrence. You who would promote temperance cannot support the party whose most eager partizans belong to the opposite camp. Imagine another six years of Tory rule, devoid alike of peace and progress, and you will rouse yourself to do your duty, and all hazards of a repetition of the Southwark disaster will be far away.

To insure that there would be no repetition of "the Southwark disaster," Spurgeon addressed another leaflet to the voters of that borough:

How many wars must we reckon on between now and 1886? What quantity of killing will be done in that time, and how many of our weaker neighbors will have their houses burned and their fields ravaged by this Christian (?) nation? Let those who rejoice in war vote for the Tories. . . . Southwark once led the van in advance Liberalism, and now it has come to be represented by two Conservatives! . . . "Wipe out the stain" of defeat at the last election. Vote for Messrs. Cohen and Rogers.

Cohen and Rogers, the two Liberal candidates in Southwark, plastered the borough with posters bearing Spurgeon's attack upon one of the Conservative candidates, a Mr. Cattley, for paying his workers only two-pence halfpenny

for an hour of overtime. The Standard, reporting later
on the Liberal victory at Southwark, quoted an anonymous
workingman who pointed to one of these signs and said,
"That's whats done it."[89]

Spurgeon's well-known enthusiasm for Liberal candidates was the source for one of the most frequently repeated
stories concerning him. In 1880, the noted atheist,
Charles Bradlaugh, was a candidate for the United Liberal
Party in Northampton. His supporters passed our leaflets
quoting Spurgeon as saying, "I would vote for the devil if
he were a Liberal," and urging voters to "throw theological
prejudice to the winds," and vote for Bradlaugh. Spurgeon
vigorously denied that he had ever made this remark, but
the story circulated for years. He finally had cards
made up bearing this message:

> I certainly would not vote for the devil under any
> circumstances. Nor am I able to conceive of him as
> so reconstructed as to become a Liberal. I think he
> may have had a considerable hand in the invention of
> many a story which of late has been published concerning
> me.[90]

---

[89]The Standard, April 3, 1880. Scrapbook clipping.

[90]Ray, op. cit., p. 386.

Although Spurgeon denied endorsing the devil, he did

insist that the voters of Northampton had the right to

elect an atheist to parliament. As early as 1868,

defending the Liberal M. P. for Lambeth, Mr. Lawrence,

against Conservative charges of religious heterdoxy, he

had written:

> At an election, if a man is solid in other respects,
> we cannot discuss his soundness in theology. To do
> so would be persecution. It is one of our first
> principles that a man's civil rights are not affected
> by his religion. If the office sought had been that
> of teacher of religion we should have examined the
> candidate with the Westminster Confession; but as the
> duties were such as any honest Liberal can discharge,
> we did not note the color of Mr. Lawrence's hair, his
> views on the planet Jupiter, or his opinions upon the
> origin of the species. For a horde of graceless Tories
> to set up for defenders of orthodoxy is a transparent
> piece of hypocrisy.[91]

Ten years later he reiterated his belief that there was

no relationship between a man's orthodoxy and his right to

sit in parliament.[92] When many of the Nonconformist

Liberals turned their backs on Bradlaugh and attempted to

deny him his seat, Spurgeon declared that parliament could

---

[91]Sword and Trowel, III (1868), 567.

[92]Pike (ed.), Speeches, p. 141.

not deny a man his seat either because of his religion or his lack of it. Spurgeon was extremely narrow in many of his views; yet it is worth some balancing in the scales to recall that he supported Bradlaugh when it was not popular to do so. He preserved a clipping from the free-thinking paper, the National Reformer, which must have pleased him. Annie Besant, condemning the Liberals who had voted against seating Bradlaugh, praised Spurgeon for his defense of Bradlaugh's right to be seated. "Mr. Spurgeon's religion is of a manlier order. No one can question his intense abhorrence of Mr. Bradlaugh's atheism, but being a Liberal in fact instead of only in name, he calmly declared to the bigots who attacked him . . . that people of every faith and people of no faith had a right to parliamentary representation. . . . Mr. Spurgeon belongs to Verta brata, not to the mollusca."[93]

It was sometimes said of Spurgeon that he was the only Radical who could send two members to parliament. Perhaps this was an exaggeration. Though the candidates Spurgeon endorsed in 1880 were victorious, it was a year

---

[93]The National Reformer, April 25, 1880. Scrapbook clipping.

of Liberal victories, and the biggest coattails belonged
to Gladstone. Certainly, however, his energetic cam-
paigning for the Liberals in 1880 should put to an end
the fiction that Spurgeon believed that politics and the
pulpit should not be mixed.[94] As he announced to the
London Baptist Association, the results of the general
election "filled him with unspeakable delight."[95]

In his first post-election communication to Gladstone, Spurgeon addressed the Prime Minister as "honored
Chief."[96] A few months later he wrote, "How glad I am
that you have been spared to us after such a session. May
one gracious for long continue you to us, that those who
love righteousness and honesty may not lose a leader so

---

[94]See, for instance, the comment of Horton Davies:
"Spurgeon took the pietistical view that preachers should
keep politics out of the pulpit," in Worship and Theology
in England, p. 345.

[95]Cited in Pike, Life, III, 239.

[96]In the letter (March 1, 1881), Spurgeon enclosed
eighty pounds from "a contrite one," who felt that he had
cheated the government of that amount, and had sent the sum
to Spurgeon in the hopes that he could straighten the matter
out. Spurgeon forwarded the money to Gladstone, who ack-
nowledged with a receipt. An otherwise insignificant episode, it does suggest that there were some who saw Spurgeon
as a suitable mediator between citizen and state.

able. I rejoice that I live to see the day in which right is thought to be a possible policy."[87] In this letter he invited Gladstone to attend a Tabernacle service, promising to seat him where he would not be observed. When Gladstone wrote in January 1882, requesting two tickets for a Tabernacle service, Spurgeon confessed to the Prime Minister, "I feel like a boy who is to preach with his father to listen to him. I shall try not to know that you are there at all, but just preach to my poor people the simple word which has held them and their thousands these 20 years."[88] On January 10, Gladstone and one of his sons met Spurgeon in the vestry and then accompanied the preacher onto the platform for the service.

The visit of the Prime Minister to the Tabernacle was widely publicized, as both must have expected. Spurgeon felt compelled to write a note to Gladstone apologizing for all the publicity which had surrounded his visit, assuring the Prime Minister that he had told no one of their plans, for he hated the idea of "dodging a

_____

[87]Ms. letter, August 23, 1881. Gladstone Papers, British Museum, CCCLXXXIII, 4471, f. 98.

[88]Ms. letter, January 5, 1882. Gladstone Papers, British Museum, CCCLXXXIX, 44474, ff. 14.

man's footsteps and reporting everything he says."[99] The

visit sparked the inevitable rumors in the press about a

new political alliance, or as one account had it, "Mr. Glad-

stone Spurgeonized." The Saturday Review declared Glad-

stone's motives were surely political, noting that

"Mr. Spurgeon is worth in point of votes at least two

bishops." The editors found it appropriate that the two

enjoyed each other's company, as "they both share what may

be called the demagogic idiosyncrasy."[100] Someone com-

posed an acrostic upon the subject and sent a copy to

Spurgeon:

    G--reat in evasion and equivocation
    L--eader of all the ritualists in the nation
    A--and yet to the rationalists an inclination
    D--isregarding fear, his party to uphold
    S--o that be done, his country may be sold
    T--ruckles to Rome, the Romish vote to win
    O--r to the House, held atheist Bradlaugh in
    N--ot long since Enraght's ritual he approves
    E--ven as now, Spurgeon's Dissent he loves.[101]

---

[99]Ms. letter, January 11, 1882. Gladstone Papers,
British Museum, CCCLXXXIX, 4474, f. 30.

[100]Saturday Review, LIII (January 14, 188), 42.

[101]The Acrostic, V, 134. Scrapbook clipping.

On June 14, 1884, Spurgeon celebrated his fiftieth
birthday, and a Golden Jubilee service was held in the
Tabernacle. Tributes were delivered by colleagues,
students, businessmen, members of parliament, and prominent laymen. The celebration went on for two evenings
even though an anonymous message telling of a Fenian plot
to blow up the Tabernacle prompted the police to send a
special guard. During the ceremony, a message was read
from Gladstone in which he asked "to unite my voice with
the voices of thousands in acknowledging the singular
power with which you have so long testified before the
world, . . . and the splendid uprightness of public character and conduct, which have, I believe, contributed perhaps equally with your eloquence and mental gifts to win
for you so wide an admiration."[102] A manuscript draft of
the letter in the Gladstone papers (together with a copy
of the final manuscript) suggests the care with which the
tribute was composed. "Among all the kind words which have

[102]Ms. letter, June 14, 1884. The original is at
Spurgeon's College. A copy is in the Gladstone Papers,
CCCCI, 4486, ff. 279.

been addressed to me this week," Spurgeon replied, "none has given me greater pleasure than yours."[103]

Gladstone told Spurgeon that he believed they shared in common a strong sense of loyalty to their particular denominations, and that "both you and I belong to the number of those who think that all convictions, once formed, ought to be stoutly maintained."[104] Spurgeon replied that Gladstone had "expressed with precision my idea of duty amid the strife of opinions. A distinct, and conscientious holding of truth, and a decided and resolute obedience to it are perfectly consistent with hearty love of those whose convictions run in another direction."[105] It was well that the two had agreed to disagree in a gentlemanly fashion, for the were soon to find themselves on opposite sides of a controversy which split the Liberal party into rival factions.

Gladstone's ability to make political issues moral questions was his greatest political strength; it was also potentially his greatest political weakness. A conscience

---

[103]Ms. Letter, June 21, 1884. Gladstone Papers, British Museum, CCI, 4486, ff.290.

[104]Letter of June 18, ibid.

[105]Letter of June 21, ibid.

roused can be dangerous in politics. Gladstone was
prompted by his conscience to bring home rule to Ireland;
but many were forced for reason of conscience to oppose
him. Many of those Nonconformists most active in the
Bulgarian agitation—notably Dale and Forster—refused
to follow Gladstone in the cause of Ireland ten years
later.[106]

Spurgeon's name, conceded The Times, was "one of
power among the Nonconformists,"[107] and his decision to
oppose Gladstone on the home rule question was widely
interpreted as proof that the Liberal-Nonconformist
alliance had finally disintegrated. Spurgeon had been a
consistent champion of Liberal causes including some
measures—notably the Education Act—which Dissenters
generally had opposed. However Spurgeon's fundamental
loyalty was to his Protestant convictions, and he could
not support the cause of a Roman Catholic majority at
the expense of Protestant Ulster. As he explained to a
citizen of Cardiff:

---

[106]Shannon, op. cit., p. 281.

[107]The Times, June 3, 1886.

I feel especially the wrong proposed to be done to
our Ulster brethren. What have they done to be thus
cast off? The whole scheme of home rule is full of
dangers and absurdities as if it had come from a madman, and yet I am sure Mr. Gladstone believes he is
only doing justice and acting for the good of all. I
consider him to be making one of those mistakes which
can only be made by great and well-meaning men.[108]

The comment quickly found its way into all the dailies and

was soon featured on posters which appeared in London

announcing the opinions of "Mr. Bright and Mr. Spurgeon on

the Home Rule Bill."[109] Spurgeon's phrase, "as if it had

come from a madman," was especially unfortunate, for it

was quoted out of context to suggest that Spurgeon had

called Gladstone a madman. "It may help Mr. Spurgeon to

be more guarded in his utterances," observed the Daily

News, "to learn that his recent charge of madness against

Mr. Gladstone is placarded all over Bristol today."[110]

Spurgeon's name figured prominently in the agita-

tion of the Liberal Unionists, but his heart was not in

---

[108]Quoted in Ellis, Spurgeon Anecdotes, p. 126.

[109]The remarks are featured on one poster approximately 4' by 2½' in the poster collection of the British
Museum.

[110]Daily News, June 2, 1886.

the fight. He was torn by two loyalties--a personal
loyalty to Gladstone and the Liberal party, and a deep-
seated emotional loyalty to the Protestant tradition. He
could not remain silent; to have done so would have been
completely out of character; but his voice was muted, for
the decision to oppose the "honored chief" was painful.
Spurgeon and Gladstone remained friends even though they
could no longer remain allies. Throughout the months of
Spurgeon's last illness, Gladstone sent messages and
inquiries; scattered through Gladstone's papers for this
period are the handwritten reports of Spurgeon's physi-
cians on the progress of the patient. Replying to one of
Gladstone's messages, Spurgeon summoned the strength to
write a few words across the bottom of a page--"my
heart's love to you."[111] It was his last message to his
chief.

In the post-civil war United States, evangelical
Protestantism was frequently a force for political con-
servatism. Spurgeon's American friend, D. L. Moody,

---

[111]Ms. letter, Gladstone Papers, British Museum,
CCCCXXVIII, 44513, ff. 68, 69.

"never had any doubt that the best man was always the candidate of the Republican party." Moody surrounded himself with wealthy businessmen, and he felt the problems of labor could be resolved if the workers would only "get to know Jesus." "The nation is crying reform," said Moody in 1877, "but there will be no true reform until Christ gets in our politics."[112] In Victorian England, however, the circumstances of an established church and the political and social disabilities of Dissenters forced evangelical Nonconformists into an alliance with parliamentary Radicals in an attempt to end the privileges of an entrenched Establishment. "We are made to do justice for others," Spurgeon perceptively commented, "because we suffer injustice ourselves." Spurgeon became politically active because he saw in the Liberal-Nonconformist alliance the only opportunity to purge the system of injustice. Thus, although deeply conservative in his theological views, unlike Moody, he espoused the politics of reform. Spurgeon's commitment to Liberalism was based upon more than expediency, however. He was among the last of the

[112]McLaughlin, op. cit., p. 278.

Nonconformists to revolt against his party in the period after 1870, and among the first to rally the opposition against Disraeli. He was deeply loyal to Gladstone, and only the threat of Rome could force him to sever his traditional allegiance to his party.

Spurgeon never questioned the fundamental assumptions of nineteenth-century Liberalism or ever doubted that the Liberal creed was sufficient for the future. The teachings of the "social gospel" had no appeal for him; nations would not be redeemed "through gymnastics and sing-song . . . or sanitary regulations, social arrangements, scientific accommodations, and legislative enactments."[113] "Socialism," he assured W. T. Stead, was "too extreme" to ever have any appeal in England.[114] "The working classes of England are made of redeemable material afterall," he argued, "and those who believe in them can lead them."[115] He looked to "the Christian workman" as "the hope of the

---

[113]An All-Round Ministry, p. 331.

[114]Pall Mall Gazette, XXXIX (June 19, 1884), 11.

[115]Sword and Trowel, VII (1871), 222.

age,"[116] and he had no fear of advancing democracy. "I have no fears about the future, nor any terrors about the growing power of the democracy," he said in 1884. "I do not think that the great body of Englishmen will ever go very far wrong in matters of political justice when the case is fairly put before them."[117] Shaftesbury warned Spurgeon that he would live "to see the streets of London swim with blood." "I think not," Spurgeon replied, "I think not."[118] Spurgeon's political creed was that of a moderate man who rejected extremist solutions, denying both the utopias of revolutionaries and the fears of class war expressed by frightened conservatives. He remained confident that the future would have no terrors for those who trusted in the essential good sense of the mass of the people. A simple creed, perhaps a naíve creed, but not an unattractive one.

---

[116]Ibid., VIII (1872), 9.

[117]Pall Mall Gazette, XXXIX (June 19, 1884), 11.

[118]Benson, op. cit., 277.

C H A P T E R   V I I

DEFENDER OF THE FAITH

In November 1883, while Spurgeon was vacationing
at Mentone, he received a letter from Lord Shaftesbury
lamenting "the open, avowed, boasted modern infidelity"
apparent everywhere, and warning the preacher that he
would "come back and find that socialism, contemptuous
unbelief, and an utter disregard for anything but that
which makes the world the 'be-all' and the 'end-all' of
our existence, have attained vastly increased proportions
during your absence."[1] Shaftesbury's somber tidings of
increased materialism and scepticism could not be dismissed
as readily as his fears of an imminent political holocaust,
for Shaftesbury's tidings of the growth of worldliness
and the declining commitment to the old values undoubtedly
confirmed Spurgeon's own forebodings that "the spirit of
the age" had even begun to infiltrate Baptist pulpits.[2]

---

[1]Autobiography, IV, 179.

[2]See below, pp. 413-417.

"Religion," observed a writer for the Westminster Review
in 1882, "no longer commands the absorbing interests of
all classes, as it did but a century or two ago. Religion
has come to be regarded as a holiday suit, to be donned
on special occasions and on Sundays. Practically all that
is left to religion is a shadowy belief in a Deity and in
a future life."[3] The writer attributed the decline of
religious faith to four factors: Science, the rise of
historical evidence, the separation of morality and religion, and the decline of the priesthood.[4] The files of
nineteenth-century periodicals are filled with similar
obituaries of traditional religion; article after article
commenting upon "the decay of faith" or "the decline of
the pulpit" testify to the absorbing interest many had in
the struggle between the old faith and "the spirit of the
age." Indeed, far more energy was expended upon analysis
than upon invention; for many writers, the outcome of the
struggle between religion and materialism had already been

---

[3]"The Decay of Faith," Westminster Review, LXII
(July 1882), 75.

[4]Ibid., 59-84.

determined, their task was one of merely recording the inevitable triumph of modern thought. There seemed to be a general awareness of spiritual bankruptcy. The last twenty years of the century, wrote Alfred North Whitehead, "closed with one of the dullest stages of thought since the time of the First Crusade."[5] Conventional Christianity, many had concluded, was an anachronism; religion, if it survived at all, must adapt itself to the age. Those who dared to look ahead to the twentieth century predicted a very different "Church of the Future."[6]

Not all, of course, were willing to concede that traditional Christian dogma was a casualty of the nineteenth century. A few remained firmly committed to the faith of their fathers and determined to resist attempts to "tone down, or in any way to adapt the Gospel of Christ to suit the fancy of the nineteenth century."[7] And of those determined to bear witness to the validity of the old

[5]Alfred North Whitehead, Science and the Modern World (New York, 1959), p. 96.

[6]See, for instance, W. T. Stead, The Church of the Future (London, 1891), p. 8.

[7]William Booth, "What is the Salvation Army?" Contemporary Review, XLII (August 1882), p. 176.

truth, none was more determined than C. H. Spurgeon. He was ready with his heart, his voice, his pen, and, if necessary, with his life. In a sermon at the Tabernacle in 1887, he likened himself to the Roman sentinel at Pompeii, and "as [the sentinel] stood to his post even when the city was destroyed, so do I stand to the truth of the atonement though the Church is being buried beneath the boiling mudshowers of modern heresy."[8]

Spurgeon was undeniably attracted to the example of Christian martyrdom. He was fond of quoting Bishop Latimer's famous admonition to Bishop Ridley as the two-faced martyrdom at Oxford: "Be of good comfort, Mr. Ridley, and play the man. We shall this day light such a candle in England by God's grace as I trust shall never be put out." These words served to remind Spurgeon that he was a participant in a great English tradition of Protestant witness. He was also attracted by the nature of the challenge, to "play the man," to endure, and through manly endurance, to attain grace. He must have recalled Latimer's

---

[8]Autobiography, IV, 253.

challenge many times in the last years of his life, when, engaged in what he called "the greatest fight in the world," he endeavored to remain true to what he believed to be the tradition and faith of his fathers. A lonely Victorian Elijah, standing fast against the modern priests of Baal, he sought, as others before him, to be a witness to the truth, to keep the faith, "to play the man."

Even as a young man, Spurgeon had not been receptive to new ideas. Most of his theological opinions were well-formed by the time he was twenty, and even in mid-Victorian society his theology had struck many as quaint and old-fashioned. He had been an unusually opinionated young man, and although maturity softened the tone of his rhetoric it did not lessen the edge of his dogmatism.

By Victorian standards, Spurgeon was regarded as self-educated. What he knew of Biblical criticism and theology was the result of independent reading, and not the consequence of systematic study. It is possible to gather from the contents of his library some idea of the depth of his reading in contemporary scholarship and Biblical criticism. As one would expect, the majority of books in his library are works of religious history or

Biblical commentaries. All of the standard works of the
Puritan divines are there--many in the original editions--
as well as most of the important Biblical commentaries of
the eighteenth and early nineteenth centuries. Missing
from Spurgeon's library, however, are many of the seminal
works of higher criticism which so strongly challenged the
traditional interpretation of the Bible in the second half
of the century. There are few volumes dealing with
political theory or philosophy, and even fewer devoted to
natural science. He owned a first edition of The Voyage
of the Beagle, but not a copy of The Origin of the Species.
While the novels of Louisa May Alcott are present on
Spurgeon's bookshelves, Bentham, Eliot, and Mill are
missing. One cannot assume, of course, that because Spurgeon's library does not contain certain works that Spurgeon
had not read them. His wife declared, "his usual method
of dealing with a thoroughly bad book--either morally or
doctrinally,--was to tear it into little pieces too small
to do harm to anyone, or to commit it bodily to the flames."
While there is no way of tabulating how many volumes met
this fate, Susannah Spurgeon wrote that "this was the
sentence executed upon many volumes which cast doubt upon

368

the divinity of our Lord, the efficacy of His atoning
sacrifice, or the inspiration of the scriptures."[9] Even
if one concedes that Spurgeon read books which he did not
care to preserve in his library, it is still undeniable
that his pastoral responsibilities limited his time for
reading, which meant that increasingly in later years he
naturally preferred spending his leisure time with those
works which buttressed his views rather than those which
challenged his views. "I do not care to read books opposed
to the Bible," he said, "I never want to wade through mire
for the sake of washing myself afterwards."[10] In all
probability, Spurgeon's library is a fairly accurate
measure of the range of his reading, and a survey of its
contents suggests that his intellectual interests were
limited. He frankly admitted a certain lack of intellectual curiosity: "I do not know what may be the peculiarity
of my constitution, but I have always loved safe things,"

---

[9]Ibid., 272.

[10]Pike, Life, I, 151.

he wrote. "I have not, that I know of, one grain of speculation in my nature."[11]

Spurgeon died in 1892, before the term "funda-mentalist" was applied to those with his conservative theo-logical views. Had Spurgeon lived somewhat later, his insistence upon the literal interpretation of the scrip-tures coupled with his unstinting attack upon modernist scholarship would have placed him in the camp of the funda-mentalists. By the time of his death, he was generally recognized as one of the most prominent spokesmen in the English-speaking world for a traditional, conservative Christianity. Through his sermons he reached the largest audience of any minister of his day. His reputation and influence in the Protestant world were unrivaled, and an analysis of his arguments against modernism deserves con-siderable attention. He was an articulate champion of those who opposed the new scholarship and the new science, and it is not too much to suggest that his reputation and influence made Spurgeon's arguments against modernism virtually the definitive nineteenth-century rebuttal to

----

[11]Autobiography, I, 193.

the new theology. Whether he was right or wrong in his contentions, his position as a leading spokesman for a traditional Christianity commands attention to his arguments.

Spurgeon offered basically four arguments in defense of his conservative views. First, the validity of his faith was proven by his own experience. This highly personal argument was reinforced by Spurgeon's own success which so strongly appealed to the cult of the self-made man. Second, Spurgeon argued that his theology was the theology of the Puritans, and represented the best tradition of the English religious experience. He looked backwards to a Golden Age of Faith, when society had been ruled by Godly men, whose theological views were very close to his own. Third, in sharp contrast to the honest English manliness of his faith, the teachers of modern thought were offering an effeminate, watered-down gospel which was, moreover, foreign in its very origins. Finally, his views, while simple and dogmatic, were easily comprehended by those willing to make the leap across logic to faith. He offered dogmatic certainty while his opponents were

only able to offer the hypotheses of science; and science,
by its very nature, admits no final truth.

Spurgeon was intellectually stubborn, and he
deliberately limited the ground for any debate of his
views by insisting that there was in fact nothing to debate.
At bottom, all of his reasoning begins with the assumption
that theological argument is futile, because faith is
undebatable. "I do not believe that infidels are ever won
by argument," he maintained. Moreover, he perceived a real
danger in attempting to refute the arguments raised by
sceptics:

> Possibly our refutation of error may not have been
> perfect, and many a young mind may have been tinctured
> with unbelief through listening to our limited
> exposure of it. I believe that you will rout unbelief
> by your faith rather than by your reason; by your
> belief, and by your acting up to your conviction of
> the truth, you will do more good than by any argument,
> however strong it may be.[12]

Spurgeon's refusal to meet the critics upon their own
debating ground was naturally infuriating to them, but his
position had certain undeniable advantages. He

---

[12]The Soul Winner, pp. 115-116.

categorically denied that either "proof" or "reason" were admissible evidence to challenge or substantiate his views. Certainly his critics were right when they accused him of having a closed mind, but on the other hand, Spurgeon neatly avoided the difficulty of ever having to produce "evidence" or demonstrate "reason." It is impossible to imagine Spurgeon, like Bryan, trapped on a witness stand defending his beliefs. Spurgeon liked to tell about an acquaintance who attended his services regularly, but had never been willing to accept Christianity. The man tried time and time again to get Spurgeon to answer his arguments against Christianity, but Spurgeon refused to rise to the bait.

> One of these days I expect to see him converted; there is a continual battle between us, but I never answer one of his arguments. I said to him once, "If you believe that I am a liar, you are free to think so if you like; but I testify what I do know, and state what I have seen, and tasted, and handled, and felt, and you ought to believe my testimony, for I have no possible object to serve in deceiving you." That man would have defeated me long ago if I had fired at him with the paper pellets of reason.[13]

---

[13]Ibid., p. 116.

"A good many infidels have been converted," observed
D. L. Moody, "but not by argument."[14] Spurgeon simply
refused to become embroiled in any debate in which "the
paper pellets of reason" were admissible evidence. His
faith was "the strongest rock in the world," and it
required more than "mere" reason to budge him. "Believe
anything in science which is proved," he told his students,
"it will not come to much. . . . And then believe everything which is clearly in the word of God, whether it is
proved by outside evidence or not. No proof is needed
when God speaks. If he hath said it, this is evidence
enough."[15]

Spurgeon denied that his convictions represented
merely another point of view, for he claimed to be a spokesman for "revealed truth" and not simply opinion:

> We have received the certainties of revealed truth.
> These are things which are verily believed among us.
> We do not bow down to men's theories of truth, nor
> do we admit that theology consists in "views," and

---

[14]McLoughlin, op. cit., p. 261.

[15]Spurgeon, The Greatest Fight in the World
(London, 1896), p. 32.

"opinions." We declare that there are certain
verities--essential, abiding, eternal--from which it
is ruinous to swerve. . . . I have been charged with
being a mere echo of the Puritans, but I would rather
be the echo of truth than the voice of falsehood. . . .
Rest assured that there is nothing new in theology
except that which is false; and the facts of theology
are today what they were eighteen hundred years ago.[16]

To all new theories of Biblical criticism he had a ready

answer: "We care little for any theory of inspiration:

in fact we have none. To us the plenary verbal inspira-

tion of the Holy Scripture is a fact and not a hypothesis."[17]

Thus, Spurgeon defended his views by first denying that

any defense was necessary; he answered the new learning

with the assertion that anything new was necessarily false;

and he did so with an arrogant confidence which nonplussed

his critics as frequently as it irritated them. Dr. Parker,

who had experienced Spurgeon's scorn, summed up the atti-

tude voiced by many of Spurgeon's critics:

Mr. Spurgeon was absolutely destitute of intellectual
benevolence. If men saw as he did they were orthodox;
if they saw things in some other way they were heterodox,

---

[16]An-All Round Ministry, p. 17. Cf. Booth, "Let
me boldly say we have never imagined anything new to be
learnt, and have no expectation of learning anything new,"
in op. cit., p. 176.

[17]Greatest Fight, p. 27.

pestilent, and unfit to lead the minds of students or
inquirers. Mr. Spurgeon's was a superlative egotism;
not the shilly-shallying, timid, half-disguised egotism that cuts off its own head, but the full-grown,
over-powering, sublime egotism that takes the chief
seat as if by right. The only colors which Mr. Spurgeon
recognized were black and white.[18]

Although Spurgeon asserted that faith needed no

defense, he defended his faith at great length, and being

the "superlative egotist" that he was, he naturally grounded

his defense in his own experience. All faith must ulti-

mately rest upon personal experience, but in Spurgeon's

case, his belief in the power of faith was greatly strength-

ened by his remarkable personal accomplishments. In

intellectual terms, Spurgeon was held captive by his own

success. He never lost his fascination for the details of

his own life story, nor his sense of wonder that "the

Essex bumpkin" could have come so far. "If I possessed

the powers of a novelist, I might write a three-volume

novel concerning the events of any one day in my life, so

singularly striking has my experience been," he wrote.[19]

---

[18]The Times, February 3, 1892.

[19]Autobiography, I, 3.

Indeed, as he confided to a friend, "My life seems to me like a fairy dream."[20]   Surely the glory belonged to God, and his experience was more evidence of the all-conquering power of faith.   "I preach the doctrines of grace because I believe them to be true; because I see them in the scriptures; because my experience endears them to me."[21] "Because my experience endears them to me" is the key to an argument that was unanswerable because rooted in a unique personal experience.   "When you can quote yourself as a living instance of what grace has done, the plea is too powerful to be withheld through fear of being charged with egotism."[22]   "I do not want proof that the Bible is true.   Why?   Because it is confirmed in me.   There is a witness which swells in me which makes me bid defiance to all infidelity."[23]   "They tell us sometimes that such and such statements are not true; but when we are able to reply that we have tried them and proved them, what answer is

---

[20]Williams, op. cit., p. 26.

[21]Sword and Trowel, XXIII (1887), 4.

[22]Thielicke, op. cit., p. 56.

[23]Pike, Life, I, 151.

there to such reasoning?"[24] Spurgeon did not question

the efficacy of prayer because his prayers were answered;

he did not question the Bible because his experience con-

firmed its promises. As he told W. T. Stead, "it is not

a matter of faith with me, but of knowledge and everyday

experience. I am constantly witnessing the most unmis-

takable instances of answers to prayers. My whole life is

made up of them."[25] Spurgeon declared that he could no

more doubt the power of prayer than the law of gravita-

tion, and for the best of reasons, because his prayers

received a prompt answer. "We ask God for the cash, and

he sends it," is a comment with more than a little of the

cash-register ring to it, but for Spurgeon, it was "a good,

solid, material fact, not to be explained away."[26]

W. Y. Fullerton wrote that only twice in his life did

---

[24]Thielicke, p. 105.

[25]Pall Mall Gazette, XXXIX (July 19, 1884), 11.

[26]Ibid. The fact that both the language of religion
and the language of sexuality drew heavily upon metaphors
from the world of business and finance is a revealing com-
mentary on the Victorian sense of values. See Steven Marcus,
The Other Victorians (New York, 1967), p. 27.

Spurgeon spend a whole night in prayer. "He was not indeed accustomed to remaining long on his knees, for his idea of prayer was the passing of a cheque over a bank counter; there is no need to urge that it be honored, all that was necessary was to wait until the answer came."[27] That Fullerton was correct is confirmed by Spurgeon's own analogy in referring to what he termed "the Bank of Heaven." "I believe in business prayers,--I mean prayers in which you take to God one of the many precious promises which he has given us in His Word, and expect it to be fulfilled as certainly as we look for the money to be given to us when we go to the bank to cash a cheque or a note."[28] Supremely confident, Spurgeon grounded his faith in his own experience, creating a mystique of his personal success which had a wide appeal to an age fascinated by the saga of the self-made man.

Spurgeon firmly believed that he and his followers were part of a tradition of Protestant witness which was

[27]W. Y. Fullerton, Thomas Spurgeon, A Biography (London, 1919), p. 88.

[28]Only A Prayermeeting, p. 32.

deeply rooted in the English religious experience. History,

for Spurgeon, like theology, was colored in black and white

and peopled with obvious villains and heroes. He fre-

quently raided the annals of the English past for evidence

to support his view that the best men in the past had been

those whose theological views most nearly approximated his

own. In arguing from history, he was never reluctant to

draw parallels between the past and the present. Giants

had once walked upon the earth, but now their heritage

seemed threatened by a generation unfit to share the stage

of history with their forebears.   "There lived in the

past men who believed with all their heart, soul, and

strength; held truth against all comers, as the Spartans

held Thermopylae. . . . Would God we had 10,000 such among

us in this time-serving hour! Above all things, the Church

needs a regiment of Ironsides--men of mettle, men of

truth."[29] Instead of sturdy Ironsides, Spurgeon saw all

around him,

   . . . striplings fresh from reading the last new novels
   correcting the notions of their fathers, who were men

---

[29]Sword and Trowel, VIII (1872), 9.

of weight and character. Doctrines which produced
the godliest generation that ever lived on the face
of the earth are scouted as sheer folly. Every little
man's nose goes up celestially at the very sound of
the word "Puritan"; though if the Puritans were here
again, they would not dare to treat them thus cava-
lierly; for if the Puritans did fight, they were soon
known as Ironsides; and their leader could hardly be
called a tool, even by those who stigmatized his as
a "tyrant."[30]

Two centuries after the last Puritan had put away his
sword, Spurgeon was still separating the world into Round-
heads and Cavaliers, and urging that the sons of Ironsides
take up the weapons as of old. "In the history of heroes,
there are none who show so much moral muscle and spiritual
sinew as those who make the word of God their necessary
food."[31] "The Godliness of Puritanism will not long survive the sound doctrines of Puritanism," he warned. "The
coals of orthodoxy are necessary to the fire of piety."[32]
It should be noted that Spurgeon used the words "Puritan"
or "Puritanism" very loosely. At times he used the terms
to refer to an idea, at other times in reference to a

_____

[30]Greatest Fight, p. 27.

[31]Sword and Trowel, XIX (1883), 83.

[32]Ibid., XXIII (1887), 62.

specific set of historical characters, and still other times to describe a moral or doctrinal position. Moreover, he was never very precise about those people in the past he considered Puritans. He sometimes described Puritanism as a philosophy that could be traced back to Wycliffe and the Lollards, and on occasion he spoke of Wesley and Whitefield as being part of a great chain of Puritan divines. In general, however, he meant by "Puritans" the seventeenth-century followers of Cromwell and by Puritanism a moral and theological outlook closely related to his own. Spurgeon was no historian, but he found history useful. "I believe that there is no period of history which may not yield something profitable," he maintained.[33]

As far as Spurgeon was concerned, no other generation of Englishmen ever managed to measure up to the standard set by the seventeenth-century Puritans. The brief period when Cromwell ruled England seemed to him in retrospect a Golden Age of Faith. When Cromwell passed from the scene, the character of English society began to degenerate. Speaking of the eighteenth century, he

[33]Spurgeon, Illustrious Lord Mayors, A Lecture (London, 1861), p. 23.

lamented, "In those days, believers did not quit themselves like men so fully as the Puritans did; they were made of softer metal; the world had alloyed their gold and debased their steel. The Nonconformists of the times of Anne and the first George were but dwarfs compared with the giants of times gone by."[34] Dwarfs replaced giants, and steel yielded to a softer substance. "These stern old men with their stiff notions are gone, and what have we in their places? Indifference and frivolity. We have no Round-heads and Puritans; but then we have scientific dressmaking and lawn tennis."[35] In the place of the "solid, substan-tial, and real" theology of Charnock, Owen, and Manton, Englishmen were offered Robertson, Maurice, and Voysey--"whipped cream and souffles . . . very pretty, but very much like nothing at all. In a cubic inch of Charnock and Owen, there is enough matter to cover acres of the new school of writing."[36] "Oak has given way to willow; every-body has grown limp. . . . There is no end to this limpness.

---

[34] Ibid.

[35] Barbed Arrows from the Quiver of C. H. Spurgeon (London, 1896), p. 50.

[36] Sword and Trowel, XXI (1885), 269.

It slobbers Judas Iscariot with affectionate kisses; and adds to its prayers a petition for the restoration of the devil."[37] "The velvet mouth is succeeding the velvet cushion. . . . We want a man just now to speak out as God tells him, and care for nobody."[38] "Modern scepticism is playing and toying with truth; and it takes to 'modern thought' as an amusement, as ladies take to croquet or archery. This is nothing less than an age of millinery and dolls and comedy."[39] The times demanded "more men and fewer molluscs" to speak the truth. The truth was there as it had always been for those with grace to know it: "We are satisfied with the truth which is as old as the hills and as fixed as great mountains. Let 'cultured intellects' invent another God more gentle and effeminate than the God of Abraham."[40]

The expressions Spurgeon used in describing the theology of the modernists are suggestive of his contempt.

---

[37] Ibid., XIX (1883), 27.

[38] Sermon delivered January 11, 1857, in The New Park Street Pulpit.

[39] Lectures, III, 51-52.

[40] Saturday Review, LV (February 3, 1883), 159.

Their teachings are compared to souffles, whipped cream,
velvet, jelly, slobbering kisses, ladies' games, dolls,
dress-making, and lawn tennis. Those he identified with,
however, were described as men of character, stiff, hard,
substantial, manly. "A man of God," said John Ploughman,
"is a manly man," and there "never was a more splendid
specimen of manhood than the Savior," said John Ploughman's
creator. In order to "play the man" you must first be a
man—as Spurgeon reminded his students, "we must be men
ourselves if we ever wish to move men." "A Christian is
no milksop; nay, of all men the Christian is, or should
be the most manly." "Manliness in religion is a mark of
nobility of soul, such nobility of soul as grace alone can
give. He who wears it is more than a match for ten
thousand slaves of custom who cut their cloth according
to fashion."[41] Spurgeon was convinced that modern thought,
if unchecked, would emasculate the evangelical tradition;
he feared a virile, manly Christianity would be replaced
by a "namby-pamby sentimentalism, which adores a deity
destitute of every masculine virtue."[42]

---

[41] Sword and Trowel, VIII (1872), 9.
[42] Autobiography, II, 274.

It was wholly in character that Spurgeon made this
particular argument against modern thought, for he had a
habit of referring to his opponents in various controversies as effeminate. In his celebrated sermon on Baptismal Regeneration he had pointedly criticized the
Puseyite preoccupation with "toy-rags, wax candles, and
millinery."[43] "How much of the extravagance of female
dress," he wondered, "could be traced to the man-millinery
of Anglican priests? . . . when men, and even ministers,
take to resplendent trappings, who can wonder that the
weaker sex exercises a larger liberty? For shame ye so-
called priests, put away your baby garments and quit
yourselves like men."[44] The way to heaven, he announced
in 1866, is not to be found "through ceremonies,
millinery-wax-gilt-artificial flowers-music-a kind of
celestial squeaking through the throat, instead of speaking
plainly."[45]

[43]Baptismal Regeneration, a sermon delivered June 5,
1884, No. 573 in the Metropolitan Tabernacle Pulpit series.

[44]Spurgeon, The Bible and the Newspapers (London,
1878), p. 34.

[45]Oliver Creyton (ed.), Spurgeon Anecdotes and
Stories (London, 1866), p. 152.

Richard Hofstadter has pointed out in another connection
that the term "man-milliner" was a common nineteenth-
century term of abuse.[46] Hofstadter noted that when the
American political boss Roscoe Conkling used the expression in his famous attack upon George Curtis and the civil-
service reformers, contemporaries were so shocked that
some reports deliberately deleted the expression from the
printed text of the speech.[47] It was probably not coincidental that Spurgeon used this suggestive phrase in referring to both the ritualists and to modernists. "They
might almost boast with the Pharisee that they are not as
other men are," he observed, "although it would be blas-
phemy to thank God for it."[48]

---

[46]Richard Hofstadter, Anti-Intellectualism in
American Life (New York, 1963), p. 189.

[47]Ibid., Conkling's remarks were made in 1877.
Hofstadter suggested that the term "man-milliner" referred
to a series of articles on fashion being published by Har-
per's. Since Spurgeon used the term as early as 1864, it
must have been in fairly common usage on both sides of
the Atlantic by 1877.

[48]Thieliecke, op. cit., p. 137. See also Norman,
op. cit., p. 198.

Spurgeon had been a weak, puny boy, afraid of cattle and of darkness, too weak to participate in games. The puny boy became a portly man, but his health remained poor. From the beginning of his ministry until his death there was not a year in which he enjoyed consistent good health. His chronic illness was complicated by an extremely emotional nature. He was subject to periodic attacks of despondency and melancholy which often seemed to have no apparent cause. Apart from a stoic acceptance of pain, he was not courageous in any of the ordinary physical meanings of the word. His biographers have all stressed his curious timidity, his fear of crowds, of horses, of even crossing the street alone. Superficially, it seems ironic that this apparently cowardly, physically weak man should be so quick to label those who disagreed with him as "superfine young men with roses in their teeth" lacking in "honest manliness." Yet it is partially because Spurgeon was so "unmanly" in many of the ordinary situations of life that made it mandatory for him to take a stand in the one area where he could "play the man," and play the man better than anyone--in defense of his beliefs. And somehow he succeeded in projecting from the

pulpit the very qualities of robust masculinity which
eluded him in his private life.

Yet to suggest that Spurgeon's constant stress upon
the masculine virtues resulted from a need to compensate
for his physical weakness is not the whole truth. The
argument was more than a product of personal idiosyncrasy,
for it was rooted in a cultural as well as a personal context. Spurgeon's physical weakness and timidity make his
argument from sexual manliness psychologically more interesting, but these are personal traits which no more explain
the full context of the argument that, for instance, Theo-
dore Roosevelt's boyhood puniness "explains" the belligerent
foreign policy of the Roosevelt administration. No doubt
both Spurgeon and Roosevelt were compensating to a certain
extent for physical weakness as children when they both
later became champions of the masculine virtues; but the
response was deeply cultural. Muscular Christianity and
the vogue of the strenuous life were both products of the
same nineteenth-century stress upon manliness, an emphasis
which was born out of a deep-seated cultural uneasiness.
As David Newsome has noted, "manliness" and "manly" are
words which appear so frequently in the writings of the

Victorians, one might reasonably conclude that "manliness was one of the cardinal Victorian virtues."[49] As the century drew to a close, more and more traditional beliefs were challenged, questioned, and discredited, and it was natural that the defenders of these beliefs were driven by an almost hysterical need to reaffirm the validity of the old ways. One obvious way to do this was to defend your own views as manly and to suggest that your opponents were weak, effeminate, "namby-pamby sentimentalists" preaching doctrines which threatened to emasculate the heroic traditions of the past.

A corollary to Spurgeon's defense of his theology in nationalist terms was his argument that higher criticism was foreign in its origins and therefore hostile to the English religious experience. Modern thought, like Roman

---

[49]David Newsome, Godliness and Good Learning (London, 1961), p. 195. Newsome traces the changes in the meanings of the words "manly" and "manliness" from mid- to late-nineteenth century. Originally the word "manly" was used to describe someone who was open, transparently honest; later the word described living life to its greatest potential, living for the higher good; finally the word came to have robust, masculine connotations. For Kingsley, Hughes, and Spurgeon, the opposite of "manly" was effeminacy.

Catholicism, he viewed as a sinister foreign influence seeking to sap the faith of Englishment and to undermine the strength of the English evangelical experience. Spurgeon's faith was the faith of his fathers; higher criticism was the faith of the fatherland. As Willis Glover has pointed out: "The fact that higher criticism in the first half of the century was so largely a German product enabled it to be branded not only as foreign, but as emanating from a specific nation which was not held in very high esteem by the English."[50] Much attention has focused upon the developing Anglo-German rivalry in the second half of the nineteenth century, but relatively little of this attention has centered upon the intellectual rivalry between the two powers. At least part of the hostility Spurgeon and other evangelicals directed toward German scholarship can be viewed as still another manifestation of the increasing tensions between the two nations.

[50]Willis B. Glover, <u>Evangelical Nonconformists and Higher Criticsm in the Nineteenth Century</u> (London, 1954), p. 39.

Spurgeon's attack upon German Biblical scholarship antedated the political unification of Germany. As early as 1860, Peter Bayne, the editor of the Unitarian paper, The Dial, had criticized Spurgeon and Dr. John Campbell, the editor of The British Banner, for their anti-German pronouncements. Spurgeon was reprimanded for declaring that "the English language is a slave to the German," and reminded that "the land of the Reformation has a claim to at least a hearing in the matter of Christian truth."[51] Bayne wrote that Spurgeon's attitude toward German scholarship was that of "a boarding-school miss," and urged the pastor to find a "more noble" way to serve the Christian cause than by attacking German Biblical scholarship.[52] Certainly at this period in his life whatever knowledge Spurgeon had of German scholarship would have been gained at second hand. It is extremely unlikely

---

[51]Peter Bayne, Terrorism for Christ's Sake, Or Mr. Spurgeon and Dr. Campbell (London, 1860), p. 3.

[52]Ibid., p. 58. In 1884 Bayne wrote to Spurgeon apologizing for this "scrap of mine which had its place among those 'paper bullets of the brain' whose impact did you, it seems, no harm." Autobiography, IV, 241.

that Spurgeon ever read Wilhelm Vatke, Carl Lachmann,
F. G. Bauer, or many of the other German scholars who laid
foundations for modern Biblical scholarship. Indeed,
Spurgeon was quoted by The Times as remarking that "some
of the German religious books or sermons were so almighty
dry," that they "could interest no persons unless they
wanted to have sin taken out of them in the same way as
Eve was taken out of Adam--in deep sleep."[53]

Spurgeon's initial objection to German scholarship
was a very practical one--he was of the opinion that
preachers who quoted any foreign language or remote work
of scholarship in a sermon had a very poor opportunity to
establish rapport with a typical congregation. "The devil,"
he was fond of saying, "has no use for your Germanic
objectives and subjectives," but "pelt him with Anglo-
Saxon," and he will turn tail. Gradually, however,
Spurgeon came to see in foreign scholarship something more
menacing. He became increasingly convinced that higher
criticism was not only contaminating preachers, but through
them, their congregations. In November 1870, he warned

---

[53]The Times, July 7, 1879.

of "the painful degeneracy of Protestantism in Germany,"
and attributed it to the spread of pernicious doctrine.
"Scholars there speak of Christianity as an Asiatic
religion; the majority of the educated classes have not
only rejected all creeds, but have also renounced the Bible,
the dogmas of which, they urge, have been exploded by
'scientific criticism.'"[54] "Germany has been made unbelieving by her preachers," he wrote in 1887, "and England
is following in her tracks."[55] By the 'eighties, Spurgeon
was convinced that even his own conservative denomination
had been tainted by the heresy of higher criticism. He
remained "an ungermanized believer," but he feared many
Baptists had gone astray, and were attempting to outfit
themselves in "the old Teutonic small-clothes."[56]

Spurgeon's power as a preacher lay in his utter
confidence in his own beliefs and in his ability to communi-
cate those beliefs in eloquent but simple terms. As
William Wilkinson wrote: "Perfect mastery of his own

[54]Sword and Trowel, VI (1870), 520-521.

[55]Ibid., XXIII (1887), 399.

[56]Ibid., 18.

system of doctrine was another secret of Mr. Spurgeon's power. Perfect mastery of it and perfect conviction of its truth went hand in hand together with him. He never stood before his hearers like a reed shaken by the wind. He stood solid on the rock, with the whole balanced weight of his personality."[57] Spurgeon was confident of his faith because it was based upon his own experience rather than resting upon theory or hypothesis. On the other hand, what could modernists offer in support of their arguments? The "laws" of science? the "lessons" of philosophy? The "new discoveries" of scholarship? All such evidence Spurgeon dismissed as presumptuous reasoning. When chided by his critics for his ignorance of science or higher criticism he stubbornly denied the need to know anything which contradicted Scripture. For him, the "new discoveries" were the old heresies, and he boasted that he knew nothing of the "new ologies; we stand by the old ways. The improvements brought forth by 'modern thought' we regard with suspicion, and believe them at best to be dilutions of the truth, and most of them old, rusted heresies,

---

[57]Wilkinson, op. cit., p. 104.

tinkered up again, and sent abroad with a new face put
upon them, to repeat the mischief which they wrought in
ages past."[58]

    "What is man," wrote the psalmist, "that Thou art
mindful of him?" What is man's knowledge, asked Spurgeon,
when compared to the mind of his maker? "The high culture
of mortal man! Bah! How ludicrous it must seem to the
Eternal mind! Vain man would be wise, though he be born
like a wild ass's colt."[59] Is not all of man's knowledge
a pitifully small residue and all his learning mere hypothesis? What theory, what law, what truth has not been questioned, revised, altered, or abandoned altogether? To
Spurgeon, man's knowledge was finite and fallible, and he
put his trust in the truth which changeth not. "If it
ever becomes a matter of decision whether we shall believe
God's revelation or man's science we shall unhesitatingly
cry, 'Let God be true, and every man a liar.'"[60] "We are
accused of dogmatism; but we are bound to dogmatize when
we repeat that which the mouth of the Lord has spoken. We

---

[59]Sword and Trowel, IV (1868), 175.

[60]Spurgeon, The Clue of the Maze, pp. 74-75.

cannot use 'ifs' and 'buts' for we are dealing with God's
'shalls' and 'wills.' If he says it is so, it is so; and
there is an end of it. Controversy ceases when Jehovah
speaks."[61]

It is not necessary to sympathize with Spurgeon's
abrupt dismissal of the spirit of inquiry in order to see
the logic of his position or its usefulness as an argument.
Spurgeon did not attack scientific revelation directly,
attempting to prove that every statement in Genesis was
literally true; instead he denied the challenge of science
in a more basic and subtle fashion, by pointing out that
by the very nature of the scientific method, all scientific "discoveries" remained hypotheses. He placed his
trust in the unchanging, immutable truth as he knew it,
and abandoned his critics to the sinking ship of experiment.
"Is this thing called 'science' infallible?" he asked.
"The history of ignorance which calls itself 'philosophy'
is absolutely identical with the history of fools, except
where it diverges into madness."[62] For those troubled with

_____

[61]Sermon delivered Mary 11, 1888, in The Metropolitan
Tabernacle Pulpit series.

[62]Greatest Fight, p. 30.

the recent discoveries of science or scholarship, he offered a ready assurance: "There is little of theory in science today which will survive twenty years, and only a little more which will see the first day of the twentieth century. We travel at so rapid a rate that we rush by sets of scientific hypotheses as quickly as we pass tele-graph posts when riding in express trains."[63]

Spurgeon's knowledge of contemporary science was at best superficial. There is no evidence to support his boast that he had "read a good deal upon the subject" of evolution; indeed, his comments upon the topic suggest that he had only the haziest notions concerning evolutionary theory. The few books in his library which deal with scientific subjects are mainly works of "popular science" such as Through the Fields With Linnaeus or Consider the Heavens. Spurgeon was quick to ridicule Darwin, but betrayed little comprehension of the subtleties of Darwin's thought. In 1861, lecturing at the Tabernacle with a stuffed gorilla beside him, he told the audience that Darwin "is prepared to prove that our greatgrandfather's

---

[63]Ibid.

grandfather's father--keep on for about a millennium or two--was a guinea-pig, and that we ourselves originally descended from oysters, or seaweeds, or starfishes."[64] A few years later he expressed the hope that "Mr. Darwin could induce the earthworms which mar our lawns to develop into oysters, for now the blackbirds alone devour them, and then we should have a share of the spoils."[65] While he conceded that a person might believe in evolution and Revelation too, such a feat was possible only because "a man can believe that which is infinitely wise and also that which is only asinine. In this evil age, there is apparently nothing that a man cannot believe."[66] Personally, he assured his students, he was not prepared to throw away the scriptures because of "one or two curiously-shaped stones found in the company of the remains of ancient animals," and as far as he was concerned,

[64]"A quotation which everybody remembers in The Origin of the Species," observed the Saturday Review, XII (October 5, 1861), 352. The episode prompted Punch to wonder if the gorilla of the future would lecture on a stuffed preacher.

[65]Sword and Trowel, VII (1871), 531.

[66]Autobiography, IV, 134.

Darwin, Tyndall, and Huxley could "go to the aboriginal monkeys from whence they say they sprang."[67]

It is easy to demonstrate Spurgeon's ignorance of contemporary science, but his apparent ignorance is not really relevant to the substance of his argument against scientific discovery. In the first place, he was far less concerned with the menace of biology and geology than with the threat of higher criticism and "modern thought." Darwin, Huxley, and Tyndall did not disturb Spurgeon nearly as much as Strauss, Colenso, and the Essayists. In the second place, if he knew little of the actual discoveries of science, he knew enough to point to the fundamental weakness of scientific "truth." He was far too clever to join Huxley on a platform. Instead, he insisted, "All that we are certain of today is this, that what the learned were sure of a few years ago is now thrown into the limbo of discarded truth,"[68] and he was confident the future would consign what was currently regarded as true to the same limbo. He was probably correct in his expectation.

---

[67]Williams, op. cit., p. 150.

[68]Greatest Fight, p. 30.

Alfred North Whitehead was a student at Cambridge during
the last few years of Spurgeon's ministry. Commenting upon
those years, Whitehead observed:

> We supposed that nearly everything of importance about
> physics was known. Yes, there were certain obscure
> spots, strange anomalies having to do with the phenomena
> of radiation which physicists expected to be cleared up
> by 1900. They were. But in so being, the whole science
> blew up, and Newtonian physics, which had supposed to
> be as fixed as the Everlasting Seat, were gone. . . .
> Certitude was gone.[69]

The scientists of Spurgeon's day who believed that they
were in possession of certitude were fully as dogmatic in
their assertions concerning "scientific truth" as Spurgeon
was in his theology. But as Whitehead noted in discussing
"the fallacy of dogmatic finality," when it becomes a
question of clinging to certitude, "sceptics and believers
are all alike." Indeed, in their dogmatism, sceptics and
believers have a common bond. Spurgeon professed to have
less quarrel with honest atheists than with hypocritical
Christians, and cited with approval a sentence from
Huxley's Agnostic Annual in which Huxley maintained that

---

[69]Lucien Price, Dialogues of Alfred North Whitehead
(New American Library, 1956), p. 12.

"on the whole the 'bosh' of heterodoxy is more offensive
to me than that of orthodoxy; because heterodoxy professes
to be guided by reason and science, and orthodoxy does
not."[70] In defense of his opinions, Spurgeon wandered down
some strange logical paths, and none stranger than the
one which ended with this unsparing critic of modern
thought agreeing with the logic of Thomas Henry Huxley.

Spurgeon was neither a theologian nor a systematic
thinker. Shrewd, intelligent, and pragmatic, he had little
sympathy for those in search of more sophisticated answers
than he had to offer. In his defense of his theological
views he was neither logical nor rational, but he rejected
both logic and reason as criteria for determining theological truth. Although his arguments against modernism
were frequently lacking in logic, they had a great deal of
emotional appeal, and were convincing enough for those
willing to believe where they could not prove.

Spurgeon was unwilling to make the slightest con-
cession on any point which challenged his view of scriptural
authority. He believed in the plenary verbal inspiration

---

[70]Sword and Trowel, XX (1884), 90.

of scriptures, and regarded the attack upon <u>verbal</u>
inspiration as an attack upon inspiration itself.[71] Spurgeon, wrote W. T. Stead, kept his faith in its integrity,
"husk as well as kernel, and in his eyes the husk was
hardly less important than the kernel."[72] As far as
Spurgeon was concerned, if the scriptures were not infallible,
they were worthless--he conceded no degress of falliblity.
His view of the scriptures was one which has been characterized by H. G. Wood as based upon the "all-or-nothing"
fallacy, or the insistence that either <u>everything</u> in the
scriptures is inspired, or <u>nothing</u> is inspired.[73] "If the
book of Genesis be an allegory," Spurgeon declared, the
Bible is "an allegory all through."[74] If there were no
actual and material serpent tempting an actual and material
Eve, then there was no Christ, no incarnation, no

---

[71]<u>Greatest Fight</u>, p. 27.

[72]<u>Review of Reviews,</u> V (1892), 170.

[73]H. G. Wood, <u>Belief and Unbelief Since 1850</u>
(Cambridge, 1955), p. 70.

[74]Spurgeon, <u>The Teachings of Nature in the Kingdom
of Grace</u> (London, 1896), p. 23.

resurrection. "We will never attempt to save half the truth by casting any part of it away. . . . We will stand by all of it or none of it. We will have a whole Bible or no Bible."[75] "All or none!" was Spurgeon's creed, and the slightest deviation from that arbitrary standard he viewed as heresy--stark, crude, and menacing.

---

[75]Greatest Fight, p. 33.

C H A P T E R   V I I I

THE DOWNGRADE CONTROVERSY

Spurgeon devoted his whole life to preaching the gospel, and nothing less than the meaning of his life was at stake for him in the issue of scriptural infallibility. Could he question the message he had given to multitudes? How poignant his query--"If this book be not infallible, where shall we find infallibility?"[1] "Unless we have infallibility somewhere, faith is impossible."[2] Under- lining his question was his realization that his conserva- tive views were coming under increasing attack from a younger generation of preachers, including many within his own denomination. On his fiftieth birthday he told W. T. Stead, "In theology I stand where I did when I began preaching, and I stand almost alone."[3] He knew that he

---

[1]Greatest Fight, p. 33.

[2]Sword and Trowel, XXIV (1888), 260.

[3]Pall Mall Gazette, XXXIX (July 19, 1884), 11.

was regarded as the last of a line, and he recognized
that only his unrivaled position within his denomination
silenced a number of young preachers who regarded his
views as old-fashioned. Even within Baptist circles the
voices of modernism were being heard, and the drift in
the denomination was clearly away from the theologically
conservative emphasis of the Pastor's College. Spurgeon
became convinced that it was his mission to halt this drift
toward modernism, and in the last years of his life, he
cast himself in the role of a prophet, seeking to call an
erring people back to the faith which had sustained their
fathers. If they refused to turn, he could not force them
back, but the heavens would bear witness that he did not
remain silent. "It were better to die a lone Elijah than
to live delicately among the thousands of Baal's priests,"[4]
he wrote, and like Elijah, he felt compelled to testify to
the validity of the only truth he knew.

Had Biblical scholarship remained the concern
exclusively of scholars, the questions posed by modernist

[4] Sword and Trowel, XXI (1885), Preface.

critics would have remained merely academic for Spurgeon.
His concern was with preaching, and it was only when he
perceived the inroads which modernism had made into the
pulpit that he began to voice strong concern over the
issues raised by higher criticism. As Willis Glover has
shown, Spurgeon came to associate higher criticism with a
denial of evangelical teaching, and he linked the declining
influence of the pulpit to the spread of modernism.[5] "If
the pulpit is declining in power," he said, "it is due in
a great measure to the men who mistake error for freshness,
self-conceit for culture, and a determination to go astray
for nobility of mind."[6] Traditionalists like Spurgeon
feared that the result of the emphasis upon higher criticism
would be to place a barrier between the layman and the
Bible. "I am jealous lest the Bible should in any sense
be made a priest's book," said Joseph Parker. "Are we to
await a communication from Tübingen, or a telegram from
Oxford before we can read the Bible?"[7] Certainly there was

[5]Glover, op. cit., p. 166.

[6]Sword and Trowel, IV (1868), 227.

[7]Glover, op. cit., p. 230.

substance for these fears. Although other factors

undoubtedly contributed to the decline in lay Bible-reading,

the days when laymen could recite the Kings of Israel and

Judah in order were passing, and the interpretation of the

scriptures came increasingly to be regarded as the special

province of an educated clergy. This was the specter which

haunted Spurgeon's last years: a docile laity drifting

toward scepticism and a clergy too tainted with the heresy

of modernism to perceive the drift. Faith was being under-

mined by the very men whose task it was to sustain it.

"From the pulpit these traitors to God and to his Christ

have taught the people that there is no hell to be feared.

. . . The precious atoning sacrifice of Christ has been

derided and misrepresented by those who were pledged to

preach it. . . . From hundreds of pulpits the gospel is as

clean gone as the dodo from its old haunts; and still the

preachers take the position and name of Christ's minis-

ters."[8] "We have nowadays around us a class of men who

preach Christ, and even preach the gospel; but then they

preach a great deal else which is not true, and they destroy

---

[8]The Soul-Winner, p. 285.

the good of all they deliver, and lure men to error. They

would be styled 'evangelical,' and yet be of the school

which is really anti-evangelical."[9] "Avowed atheists are

not one-tenth as dangerous as those preachers who scatter

doubt and stab at faith."[10] "If the fundamental doctrines

of the gospel are kept back, and our congregations are

constantly plied with questions about inspiration, evolu-

tion, and progressive thought, our young people will

become Unitarians first, and infidels afterwards, as

surely as eggs are eggs."[11] "In proportion as modern

theology is preached," he declared, "the vice of this gen-

eration increases. I attribute the looseness of the age

to the laxity of the doctrine preached by its teachers."[12]

This was the drift Spurgeon set out to challenge,

resulting in the prolonged Downgrade Controversy, which

split the Baptist denomination into rival camps. For

Spurgeon, the pulpit had become "the Thermopylae of

[9]Greatest Fight, p. 31.

[10]Sword and Trowel, XXIII (1887), 399.

[11]Ibid., XXVI (1890), 5.

[12]Soul-Winner, p. 385.

Christendom," a metaphor which suggests that he had

forgotten the outcome of the battle and remembered only

the heroic stand of the defenders.

A number of years have passed since the Down-

grade Controversy split the Baptist Union, and all of the

principals in that struggle are now dead, but the subject

of the controversy remains a chapter in the history of

their denomination which the Baptists of Britain prefer

to forget.[13] The impact of Spurgeon's break with the

---

[13]The Secretary of the Baptist Union of Great
Britain, Dr. Ernest Payne, has written, "It cast a shadow
over the Baptist denomination for more than a generation
and there has been a general desire to say as little as
possible about it, lest the old wounds be opened." (The
Baptist Union, A Short History, p. 127.) The full story
of the controversy has never been told, and probably never
will be told. Spurgeon did not publish a full account of
his role in the controversy, and his wife, in compiling
his autobiography, chose "to conceal under a generous
silence, most of the documentary and other evidence which
could be produced to show the perfect uprightness, veracity,
and fidelity of my dear husband." (Autobiography, IV,
293.) At the time of the controversy, the religious and
secular press published conflicting accounts of the struggle
based upon the testimony of the chief participants, but
these accounts were superficial and highly partisan. All
accounts of the controversy which have been published since
have been conflicting, and suggest, as Dr. Payne writes,
that the authors "set down only a part of what they knew."
W. Y. Fullerton in 1920, and John Carlile in 1933, published
biographies of Spurgeon sympathetic to his side of the controversy. Both had been friends and students of Spurgeon's,
but neither followed him out of the Union in 1887, and both

Baptist Union was sharpened by two factors; first,

Spurgeon's great personal prestige, and second, the

---

later served as presidents of that organization, so their
attitude toward the Baptist Union could not be described
as hostile. Dr. John Clifford, who was president of the
Baptist Union in 1888, was dissatisfied with the Fullerton
account and dictated a lengthy memorandum setting down his
side of the controversy; this memorandum was used by Sir
James Marchant in his biography of Clifford. In 1954,
Willis B. Glover devoted a chapter of his Evangelical Nonconformists and Higher Criticism in the Nineteenth Century
to the controversy. Glover's account is highly critical
of Clifford's role in the controversy, and accuses the
officers of the Union of "dishonest trifling" toward Spurgeon. (p. 172) The Glover version prompted Dr. Payne
to write the lengthiest analysis yet of the controversy
based upon the records of the Baptist Union. This unpublished paper was deposited at the Baptist Church House in
London in 1955. It was the basis for a somewhat abridged
account of the controversy in Payne's The Baptist Union,
A Short History, which was published in 1959. Dr. Payne
contends that the controversy was not a personal struggle
between Clifford and Spurgeon (as Glover maintains), but
rather grew out of Spurgeon's suspicions concerning certain
younger members of the denomination. His version, not
unexpectedly, is more sympathetic to the Union than to
Spurgeon. One missing link in the controversy is Spurgeon's
personal correspondence. In the years preceding Spurgeon's
break with the Union, a number of letters passed between
Spurgeon and Samuel Harris Booth, the Secretary of the
Union, concerning the theological soundness of certain members of the denomination. These letters were the substance
for Spurgeon's charges of heresy, but were never published,
and were finally destroyed. Fullerton says in his biography
of Thomas Spurgeon that it was Thomas who burned the letters; John Carlile says in his biography of Spurgeon that
it was Charles Spurgeon; Mrs. Spurgeon implies that she
destroyed the evidence--apparently all had a hand in the
business. These letters, wrote Dr. Carlile in 1934, "were
well-known to me and to others," (Spurgeon, An Interpretive
Biography, p. 244), but they cannot be reproduced, and the

conservative reputation of the denomination. The Baptists,
regarded by many as the most theologically conservative of
the sects, seemed an unlikely source of heresy. A perceptive analysis of the Baptists appearing in the Westminster Review in 1871 had characterized the denomination
as "dead to ideas that are moving the time and forming the
mode of the future."[14] The writer noted that one name
which occurred whenever the Baptists were mentioned was
that of Spurgeon, a man "who bestrides the denomination
like a Colossus; his influence is immense everywhere within
its borders . . . and thousands think him the greatest
preacher that ever expounded a text."[15] Although the

---

gap in the evidence remains. The latest account of the
controversy, Ernest Bacon's Spurgeon: Heir of the Puritans
(London, 1967) is sympathetic to Spurgeon's position and
sharply critical of "the cancer of unbelief and rational-
ism" which destroyed the evangelical basis of the Union.
I was able to find some new material relating to the controversy in the Spurgeon papers at Spurgeon's College,
but I am convinced that many vital documents no longer
exist.

[14]"The Baptists," Westminster Review, XL (October
1871), 426.

[15]Ibid., 436.

Westminster Review lamented the theological backwardness
of the majority of Baptist congregations, hints were
dropped of an "infant liberalism" that was beginning to
be voiced in Baptist pulpits. Even the Baptists, concluded the writer, were "beginning to doubt eternal damnation. . . . There is a growing tendency to regard Christ
more as an example than a sacrifice."[16] Prominent Baptists
such as William Landels (who had joined with Spurgeon in
founding the London Baptist Association) were openly
questioning "the mercantile view of atonement."[17] The
writer predicted that even Spurgeon--"the mere loud-voiced
echo of narrow Puritan divines"--was not influential
enough to halt the inevitable liberalization of the denomination. "The wedge has entered which has riven religions
and forms of religion one after another."[18]

The prediction of the Westminster Review that
modernism would eventually infiltrate the ranks of the
conservative Baptists proved true. In 1863, the Baptist
Union had passed a formal resolution condemning the views

---

[16]Ibid., 441.   [17]Ibid., 434.

[18]Ibid., 442.

of Bishop Colenso that certain parts of the Pentateuch
were unhistorical and of later origin than Moses; twenty
years later, "such a resolution would have been impossible
for many,"[19] writes their historian. A growing number of
Baptist schools (most notably Rawdon College) were turning
out preachers trained in the new approaches to Biblical
criticism and hostile to the mechanical views of election,
the atonement, and scriptural infallibility which characterized the teachings of the Pastor's College. It was
natural enough that many of these younger preachers
resented what they believed to be Spurgeon's reactionary
influence within the denomination. He, in turn, saw in
their preaching a deviation from the gospel and a threat
to the theological soundness of Baptist congregations.
This was the situation which spawned the Downgrade
Controversy and led to Spurgeon's withdrawal from the
Baptist Union.

Long before Spurgeon's formal break with the Union
in the winter of 1887, there had been rumors that he

---

[19]Ernest Payne, "The Downgrade Controversy," an
unpublished paper deposited in the Baptist Church House,
London, in January 1955.

sensed the spread of modernism in Baptist pulpits. In
1873 the Union had voted to drop from its Basis of Union
the phrase, "the sentiments usually denominated evangelical," to describe the beliefs of member churches. The
reason advanced for the decision was that since all Baptist
churches were evangelical, the phrase was redundant and
unnecessary; but Spurgeon, who had opposed the decision of
the majority, looked back later and saw in this decision
the beginnings of a drift away from evangelical principles.[20]
Nevertheless, in 1877, he was still optimistic: "The
Baptists are coming together. . . . Never were the signs
more hopeful. . . . We see everywhere the true evangelic
spirit, in happy contrast with other quarters where
intellect is idolized and novelty of doctrine sought after."[21]
The following year, speaking before the Baptist Union, he
noted with pride, "We are the least clannish of all denomi-
nations--we do not, certainly run into one mold."[22] Spurgeon

[20]Payne, The Baptist Union, p. 130. See also,
Spurgeon's article "Ministers Under False Colors," in Sword
and Trowel, VII (1870), 70-73.

[21]Sword and Trowel, XIII (1877), 284.

[22]Pike (ed.), Speeches, p. 179.

had often maintained that the loose structure of the denomination suited him perfectly; yet in his last years he began to see that this loose framework coupled with the traditional Baptist hostility to written creeds had produced a situation allowing a much wider margin for theological deviations than in rigidly structured church organizations having a fixed set of articles or creed. He found it easy to praise the Baptists for not all running into one mold, so long as the denomination accepted a common set of evangelical beliefs, but it was much more difficult for him to praise nonconformity when those traditional beliefs were questioned. Spurgeon was a Calvinist, but he was willing to tolerate the Arminian General Baptists; a believer in open communion, he conceded the right of other Baptist congregations to limit their communion table--these were the sorts of differences within the denomination he was willing to accept. He was not willing to remain in a union in which the traditional evangelical teachings on the atonement, future punishment, or the plenary inspiration of the scriptures were regarded as debatable.

In 1881, Spurgeon suggested his growing
dissatisfaction with denominational developments in a
speech before the annual Baptist Union meeting at Portsmouth. The year had been a bad one for him; ill much of
the time, he conceded that he had frequently felt in
"deep-waters of mental depression."[23] The question of his
health is relevant, for his opponents in the Downgrade
Controversy were to suggest that his ill health and subsequent depression led him to make his charges of heresy; he
heatedly denied these gentle hints of senility. In his
speech, Spurgeon openly referred to his fears that certain
members of the denomination were moving away from basic
evangelical doctrine. "I am afraid that as to matters of
doctrine I would not like to bring a loose charge against
any, but I would say that there are some churches that have
gone aside from Christ. . . . There are sermons which have
very little of the atonement in them; and, if you leave
out the atonement, what Christianity have you got to
preach?"[24] His speech prompted rumors that he was about

---

[23]Sword and Trowel, XVII (1881), 92.

[24]The Baptist, November 4, 1881.

to quit the Union, a suggestion that he felt compelled to deny in print. Calling such a break "a monstrous leap," he affirmed that "no one more heartily desires the prosperity of the Union than I do; no one is more satisfied with its designs and plans. If there be any mutterings or tempest, they certainly do not arise from me."[25] In spite of this vigorous denial, Spurgeon was plainly alarmed at what he felt to be the drift away from evangelical doctrine by some Union members, and his alarms were sufficiently well known to provoke discussion concerning his intentions toward the Baptist Union. Certainly in 1881, Spurgeon was not ready to take "the monstrous leap" out of the Union, but he had already commenced upon a course which brought him inevitably to that position.

Interestingly enough, when Spurgeon journeyed to Portsmouth to address the Baptist Union, he was the house-guest of Canon Basil Wilberforce, a son of the very Bishop Wilberforce who had once denounced Spurgeon in the House of Lords. Bishop Wilberforce did not live to appreciate the irony of this curious friendship, and one wonders what he

---

[25]Fullerton, C. H. Spurgeon, p. 309.

might have thought about this communication from his son

to Spurgeon:

> Your visit was such a joy to me--that union of the
> spirit! how sweet how <u>real</u> it is--I felt when we
> knelt together that there is nothing which really
> separates those who love the Lord. We can "tongue-
> bang" each other about methods and externals but
> after all they are <u>carnal</u> however necessary to our
> present condition--when on true church grounds ie on
> our knees together we are <u>one</u>
> > With true affection
> > I am ever yours
> >
> > Basil Wilberforce[26]

Quite apart from the irony of the friendship, however, the

ties between the two men are indicative of another impor-

tant development in Spurgeon's career. As a young man

Spurgeon had been fiercely denominational, and in the

course of championing one of the doctrines of his denomi-

nation had been led into a bitter controversy with the

Evangelicals. As he grew older his priorities changed.

"Surely, to be a Baptist is not everything. If I disagree

with a man on ninety-nine points, but happen to be one with

him in baptism, this can never furnish such ground of unity

----

[26]Ms. letter from Basil Wilberforce to Spurgeon,
November 19, [1881] in the Spurgeon Papers, Spurgeon's
College.

as I have with another whom I believe in ninety-nine points, and only happen to differ upon one ordinance."[27] As he became increasingly critical of the theological tendencies of his own denomination, he drew closer to the Evangelicals in the Church of England, for he recognized that in the larger fight they were better allies than many members of his own Baptist community. His staunchest supporters during the Downgrade Controversy were the Church of England Evangelicals, the very group he had once charged with hypocrisy. Conversely, many of the Baptists who had stood with him in 1864, condemned him in 1887. The situation produced some strange crossfire; William Landels, who had written a pamphlet in defense of Spurgeon during the Baptismal Regeneration Controversy, wrote one condemning him during the Downgrade Controversy, and Canon Francis Cruse, who had written a pamphlet denouncing Spurgeon in 1864, published a sermon defending him in 1888. In 1864, Spurgeon had withdrawn from the Evangelical Alliance in order to form stronger denominational ties with the London Baptist Association; during

---

[27] Sword and Trowel, XXIV (1888), 83.

the Downgrade Controversy he withdrew from the London Baptist Association while praising "the hearty support of the Evangelical Alliance," which twice invited him to preach before the group on the topic, "The Unchanging Gospel," and greeted him with a reception so tumultous that tears streamed down the preacher's face.[28] In 1891, one year before his death, Spurgeon withdrew from the Liberation Society. He had come to believe that the disestablishment fight was less important than the fight to preserve evangelical doctrine. As he lost old friends and allies in his denomination, he gained new friends and allies in the Establishment. He became the house-guest of a Wilberforce, a friend of bishops and archbishops; championed in his hour of need by an old adversary, the Evangelical paper, The Rock, he seemed unsinged by any coals of fire. At the grave of this great champion of voluntaryism, Randall Davidson, a future Archbishop of Canterbury, pronounced the final benediction.

---

[28]E. J. Poole-Conner, Evnagelicalism in England (London, 1951), p. 247.

Spurgeon's last personal appearance before the Baptist Union came in 1882 when the group met at Liverpool. He preached an eloquent sermon which was followed by a spontaneous collection for his orphanages. He did not attend the meeting at Leicester in 1883, but his correspondence shows that he was greatly disturbed over the proceedings there. A mayoral reception had been held in honor of the visiting Baptists, and the well-known Unitarian preacher, the Reverend Mr. Page Hopps, had spoken. The episode had not been planned by the Union officials, but Spurgeon seemed to think that they should have used this social occasion to denounce Unitarianism. The president-elect of the Baptist Union in 1883 was Richard Glover of Bristol, a man who, according to his son, "was frankly interested in Darwin."[29] His sermon welcoming the delegates was printed in the Baptist paper, The Freeman, and Spurgeon carefully clipped and underlined certain passages. Glover had said,

I am glad to believe that Christ will smile upon many who cannot call him God, but who will, perhaps, at last be glad to wake up and find that He was Divine.[30]

[29]Payne, The Baptist Union, p. 128.
[30]The Freeman, October 5, 1883. Scrapbook clipping.

Spurgeon saw in this passage clear evidence of the growing laxity of Baptist doctrine. Had Glover not, in fact, hinted at universal restitution? If so, the fundamental evangelical doctrine of future punishment of the wicked was being denied by the president of the Baptist Union. Spurgeon wrote asking Glover's meaning, and Glover, in reply, sought to clear himself of suspicion. "The smile I meant was his smile here. . . . The waking up I meant was waking up in the next world where the glory of the saviour will be unmistakable."[31] Spurgeon was unconvinced by this kind of reasoning. "Every sign of the times warns us of a desperate conflict for all that is precious and vital in our religion," he wrote. "It behooves all lovers of the old faith to be valiant for truth."[32] Already some of the more impetuous and doctrinaire of his old students were beginning to write to him urging that he speak out against the growing heresy of the denomination. Archibald Brown, a member of the Council of the Baptist Union and pastor

---

[31]The Ms. of Glover's answer is enclosed in a letter to Spurgeon from Archibald Brown, October 13, 1883, at Spurgeon's College.

[32]Sword and Trowel, XIX (1883), Preface.

of London's second-largest Baptist congregation, wrote

three letters to his old teacher relating all of the heresies

he had uncovered at the Leicester meeting. "'The spirit of

the age' seems to have found a welcome in our midst, but

in my humble judgment--it is a spirit of anti-Christ--there

is nothing left for those loyal to Christ except to pro-

test against it and refrain from all fellowship with it."[33]

Spurgeon replied, evidently urging caution, for Brown's

next letter assured Spurgeon that "you may rely upon my

not being impetuous." The letter ended with Brown's plea

to Spurgeon to speak out: "Praying . . . that yours may

be the arm to strike down the vaunting 'zeit geist.'"[34]

It is clear from the correspondence surrounding

the Baptist Union meeting at Leicester in 1883 that Spurgeon,

although disturbed by rumors of heresy in the denomination,

was still reluctant to make any formal charges. Because

of his reputation within the denomination, he was the

logical choice of conservative Baptists to head the

---

[33]Ms. letter, Archibald Brown to Spurgeon,
October 11, 1883, Spurgeon's College.

[34]Ms. letter, Brown to Spurgeon, October 13, 1883,
Spurgeon's College.

crusade against modernism. He was besieged by
correspondents urging him to speak out against the heresies
which were eroding the denomination. His scrapbooks for
the period 1883-1887 are filled with letters from clergy
and laity alike all over Britain and even from the United
States, reporting the spiritual failings and doctrinal
heresies of local preachers. These waspish, unctious, tale-
bearing letters do not make particularly edifying reading,
but it is easy to see that the sheer cumulative effect of
them must have been to convince Spurgeon that he had been
chosen to lead the fight against the "vaunting zeit-
geist." When he made his decision to lead the crusade and
issued his call to arms, he was shocked to discover how few
he was leading, and indeed, how many of those who had
urged him to speak now demurred at the step he had taken.
Some of those who had written outlining doctrinal deviations were to charge him with speaking without evidence.

In October 1883, following the meeting at Leicester,
Spurgeon wrote to the Secretary of the Union, Samuel Harris
Booth, concerning some of his suspicions. Booth replied
in a telegram suggesting a special meeting of the Council
of the Baptist Union, and urging Spurgeon to "do nothing

until I have seen Mr. Brown and yourself."[35] An editorial

in the Sword and Trowel the following month criticized

officials of the Union for "the welcome given to a denier

of our Lord's Godhead," and commented pointedly on "the

loudness of loose thinkers" present.[36] A few days later,

a letter appeared in The Christian World challenging the

editorial. The letter was signed by two young Baptist

preachers, J. G. Greenhough and James Thew.[37] During the

subsequent controversy, Spurgeon was frequently asked to

name names, but he always refused to do so. Had he named

names, the names of these two young men would probably

have headed his list, for they were typical of those

younger Baptist clergy who were beginning to discard many

of the old teachings concerning hell and eternal damna-

tion. Greenhough had once preached a sermon (carefully

clipped and underlined by Spurgeon) in which he had said,

"Our preaching of hell wins none but the base and cowardly.

. . . Hopes are much larger than creeds."[38] Evidently

---

[35]Post office telegram, Booth to Spurgeon, October 27,
1883, Spurgeon's College.

[36]Sword and Trowel, XIX (1883), 607.

[37]The Christian World, November 8, 1883.

[38]Scrapbook clipping. Payne admits that Greenhough
was the Council member most likely to have been discussed
by Booth and Spurgeon.

Greenhough and Thew were aware that Spurgeon had suspicions
concerning their commitment to evangelical doctrine, for
in November 1883, they sent two telegrams to Spurgeon
requesting a meeting to explain their views.[39] He refused.

By the beginning of 1884, Spurgeon was considering
a break with the Baptist Union. Another former student,
William Cuff, wrote to him urging that he call a meeting of
"our own men. . . . Many of us could not, and would not
have fellowship with men who held such views and sneered
at what they call the ignorance of those who denounce
them."[40] In a second letter, Cuff warned Spurgeon that
"they have thrown down the gauntlet with a vengeance," and
assured him that the old College men were "ready to issue
a manifesto at a word."[41] This, in fact, was not the case.
A significant number of "our own men" had become "tainted"
by modernism and refused to follow "the Guv'nor" out of

---

[39]The two telegrams are in Spurgeon's scrapbook,
Spurgeon's College.

[40]Ms. letter from William Cuff to Spurgeon,
October 16, 1883, Spurgeon's College.

[41]Ms. letter from Cuff to Spurgeon, November 9,
1883, Spurgeon's College.

the Union. Even the loyal Cuff finally felt moved to say

later, "I'll stand by you, Guv'nor, but I don't understand

what you're at."[42] Of the one hundred members of the

Council of the Union in 1887, ten were graduates of the

Pastor's College, but only one of the ten dissented when

the Council passed a resolution censuring Spurgeon for

making charges of heresy.[43]

The Baptist Union met at Swansea in 1885. Spurgeon

was disturbed over the implications of a sermon delivered

before the delegates by Thew, and announced that he would

make no more appearances before the Baptist Union, since he

could "have no fellowship with modern doubt."[44] He was

moving away from his old friends, preaching sermons on the

lonely nobility of Elijah while he compiled dossiers on the

modern priests of Baal. It was at this time that he began

a correspondence with Samuel Booth concerning the theological

views of certain members of the Council. A number of letters

---

[42]Payne, "Downgrade Controversy," p. 60. Many could
not afford to leave the Union, for the salary of poorer
preachers was supplemented by Union funds.

[43]Ibid., p. 35.

[44]The Freeman, November 13, 1885.

passed back and forth, naming names and citing sermon passages. When Spurgeon finally made his accusations of heresy, Booth pleaded with him not to quote his letters, and Spurgeon honored the request, even though their correspondence constituted the only real "evidence" he had. The result was to make Spurgeon look very foolish, making vague charges of heresy while refusing to name the heretics. The experience was not a pleasant one, and Booth's reluctance to finish what he had started embittered Spurgeon's followers. Booth, of course, was perfectly justified from his point of view in refusing to allow his personal correspondence to be cited as "evidence" in a heresy trial. Booth preferred the Union with its heretics to no union at all. Spurgeon chose the way of Elijah.

The publicity given to the "heresy trial" at Andover in December 1886, during which five professors were dismissed from their positions for deviating from the school's creed perhaps set Spurgeon to thinking how his own denomination might purge the heretics from its midst. In January 1887, Spurgeon was ill and recuperating at Mentone. He remained at Mentone through much of the year, and his absence from London during the crucial winter of 1887 helped to aggravate the circumstances. One of his biographers has speculated that the events of 1887 might have ended differently had Spurgeon had access to a telephone; as it was, he remained virtually incommunicado through the crucial period from October to December 1887.[45] When he did return to London in January 1888, he had already withdrawn from the Baptist Union, and compromise was unlikely.

The Downgrade Controversy took its name from a series of articles on "the downgrade in religion" which appeared in Sword and Trowel in the spring of 1887. The first article was published in March, the work of Robert Shindler, the pastor of a Baptist church in Addlestone.[46] The first Downgrade article was concerned with the eighteenth-century drift away from evangelical principles, especially among the Calvinist sects. Although the author drew no contemporary parallels, the implications were clear--if modernism spread, the evangelical sects would

---

[45]Fullerton, op. cit., p. 315.

[46]"The Downgrade," in Sword and Trowel, XXIII (1887), 122-126.

drift into scepticism, just as the eighteenth-century
sects had drifted into Unitarianism. The second of
Shindler's articles, which appeared the following month,
made the point even more forcefully, emphasizing the principle that "as went the preacher, so went the people":
"The tadpole of Darwinism was hatched," according to
Shildler, "at the old chapel in High Street, Shrewsbury,"
where Darwin's father and grandfather had been misled by
a preacher who preached "full-blown Socinianism."[47]
Spurgeon was so impressed with Shindler's argument that
he had the articles reprinted as penny tracts and sent
one to every Baptist minister in England.

The following month, Spurgeon contributed his own
opinions concerning the Downgrade question. For any who
might have missed the implications of the two "historical
surveys," Spurgeon pointed them out. Nineteenth-century
evangelical Protestantism was on the downgrade because
certain preachers were "giving up the atoning sacrifice,
denying the inspiration of the Holy Scriptures, and casting

[47] Ibid., 168.

slurs upon the justification by faith."[48] In August 1887,

he added "Another Word Concerning the Downgrade":

> No lover of the gospel can conceal from himself the
> fact that the days are evil. . . . A new religion has
> been initiated which is no more Christianity than
> chalk is cheese. . . . The atonement is scouted, the
> inspiration of scripture is derided, the Holy Spirit
> is degraded into an influence, the punishment of sin
> is turned into fiction, and the resurrection into a
> myth, and yet these enemies of our faith expect us to
> call them brethren and maintain a confederacy with
> them. . . . If for a while the evangelicals are doomed
> to go down, let them die fighting.[49]

The challenge had been issued. Unless the confederacy--

the Baptist Union--would purge itself of those members who

persisted in denying what Spurgeon believed to be essential

evangelical teachings, then he would no longer call them

brothers.

Spurgeon was dismayed to discover that what he

considered a stirring manifesto for reform was dismissed

as an old man's alarmism by many younger members of the

Baptist Union. The Union met at Sheffield in October 1887,

and while there was no formal discussion of Spurgeon's

---

[48]Ibid., 195.

[49]Ibid., 397.

charges, there was a great deal of informal discussion concerning his intentions. The younger men were inclined to dismiss his articles as foolish, and, according to The Freeman, treated the whole subject of a Downgrade as a joke. Spurgeon's older friends on the Council were saddened that he believed the denomination to be drifting away from evangelical principles, and felt that if he had proof he should present it before the Council rather than make vague charges of apostasy. "The general opinion," summed up The Freeman, "is that Mr. Spurgeon either says too much or he does not say enough."[50] Spurgeon was deeply hurt, and his response was immediate. On October 28, he resigned from the Baptist Union. "I have done my duty, even if all men forsake me," he wrote to his wife from Mentone. "What a providence that I am here, out of call! Luther was best at the Wartburg was he not?"[51]

The reaction of the religious and secular press to Spurgeon's sensational break with the Baptist Union was mixed. He received little support for his action from

---

[50]The Freeman, August 1887, clipping.

[51]Autobiography, IV, 256.

the Nonconformist press. The Freeman and the Baptist Magazine both criticized his action, as did The Nonconformist, The Christian World, and R. W. Dale's The Congregationalist Review. On the other hand, Spurgeon was supported by The Rock, The Record, and Church Bells, three Church of England publications. The Pall Mall Gazette, edited by W. T. Stead--a close friend of John Clifford, the president-elect of the Baptist Union--published a series of articles on the Downgrade Controversy highly critical of Spurgeon; yet, surprisingly, his ancient adversary the Saturday Review took his side, declaring he was "a competent witness." Spurgeon's older friends within the Union, disturbed by his action, sought without success to patch together a compromise which would bring the nation's most famous Baptist back into the Union. Some of the younger men, however, doubtless muttered "good riddance." Voicing the bitterness that many of the younger men in the denomination felt concerning Spurgeon's action, J. G. Greenhough wrote in The Christian World that Spurgeon had taken the position of a would-be Pope: the Sword and Trowel, Greenhough wrote, "is little read except by members of his own school." He dismissed Spurgeon's charges of heresy with

434

the observation that they might have been occasioned by Spurgeon's poor health. "Perhaps physical weakness has something to do with his mental irritation." In any event, Spurgeon's charges were "shamefully abusive and unjust," and his pretensions "little short of papal. . . . In many ways he misunderstands and perverts the great thoughts of Jesus."[52]

"I am suffering enough just now to drive a man out of his mind," Spurgeon confided to a friend in November, "but abuse and scorn have not the sting in them which is found in the hesitancy of friends."[53] Spurgeon was discovering how few of his "friends"--many of them former students--were willing to follow him out of "that confederacy of evil." Meanwhile, the Council demanded that Spurgeon produce names and cite cases, and Booth had refused to allow Spurgeon to quote their correspondence. The Tabernacle congregation stood firmly behind their pastor, but the College was split in two over the

_____

[52]The Christian World, September 8, 1887.

[53]Ms. letter, Spurgeon to Rev. Lockheart, November 19, 1887, Spurgeon's College.

controversy. Although seriously ill, Spurgeon was
indignant at the suggestion that his gout had prompted
his decision to break with the Union. His critics were
seeking to "detract from the truth by pointing to the
lameness of its witness. . . . Do our critics think that,
like Achilles, our vulnerable point lies not in our head,
but in our heel?"[54] Tragically, Spurgeon had become isolated by his reputation. He had traveled a long distance
from the "Boy Wonder" days. Once in the vanguard, an
innovator criticized for his "sensationalism," he was now
looked upon by many as an established, old-fashioned
figure. At fifty-three he was already an old man and out
of touch with the aspirations and convictions of a younger
generation of preachers. A prisoner of his past, he still
listened to an ancient tune, and few could hear it save he.

The period from Spurgeon's resignation in October
1887, to the next meeting of the Baptist Union in April
1888, was one of great activity, as Union officials worked
to find a formula which would lure Spurgeon back into the
organization. It was not until compromise failed in April

Sword and Trowel, XXIII (1887), 462.

that Spurgeon finally realized that great though his reputation was, he could not dictate terms to the Union, and that his "charges"--so very real to him--would be regarded as hearsay by others unless he produced some concrete evidence. "What is wanted is not wild rumor, but evidence," wrote John Clifford. Give us "not the gossip of careless and malevolent tongues, but fact; not anonymous postcards written by theological pessimists, but tested evidence on which the accused himself has been fully heard."[55] After April 1888, there was little expectation that Spurgeon would return to the Baptist Union and only speculation that he might seek to found a new denomination.

In the months following his resignation from the Baptist Union, Spurgeon elaborated and expanded his original charges of heresy. Originally he had accused certain preachers of rejecting three cardinal doctrines--the plenary inspiration of the scriptures, the atonement, and eternal punishment. On the first and last of these charges there is substantial contemporary evidence that Spurgeon was

[55]"Mr. Spurgeon's Appeal to Christendom," Pall Mall Gazette, XLVII (February 13, 1888), 5.

correct in maintaining that some Baptist preachers had
abandoned the traditional view of scriptural infallibility
and eternal damnation. But the Council insisted on
hearing the names of those who were preaching the sermons
Spurgeon objected to, and he was equally adamant about
"not going into personalities." He certainly could have
"named names"; he did in fact consider doing so, but was
apparently stopped by the threat of libel action. He
offered at one point to pay for a lawyer's opinion on the
subject, but the officials of the Union, fearing publicity,
declined. As he became more and more frustrated by the
legal technicalities of the situation, his heresy charges
grew more and more diffuse. Ministers were accused of
going to the theater and ignoring prayer meetings. His
emphasis began to shift from doctrinal error to worldliness; as Willis Glover observes, "he spoke of the fre-
quenting of theaters by ministers as though it were an
error on a par with the denial of revelation or theological
unsoundness."[56]   Desperate to "prove his case," he went

---

[56]Glover, op. cit., p. 165.

to the absurd lengths of challenging his critics to bear witness "to the sound doctrine of our entire ministry."[57]

Spurgeon argued that the only way for the Baptist Union to purify itself would be to draw up a formal statement of evangelical principles held in common by all members. Those who could not subscribe to the statement should leave the Union. "Declare the Baptist Union is a confederation of Evangelical churches, that it holds the truths commonly known as Evangelical, and that persons who do not hold these truths are not rightly in the Union."[58] What else is to be done, he argued, now that "strange children" have entered the Union?[59] The Council was willing to declare a vague commitment to evangelical principles, but was unwilling to spell these principles out or to force a creed upon all members. Dr. James Culross, the president of the Union in 1887, pointed out to Spurgeon

---

[57]Sword and Trowel, XXIII (1887), 462.

[58]Ms. correspondence between Spurgeon and Culross, November 22, 26, December 2, 5, 1887, in scrapbooks, Spurgeon's College. It is interesting to note that at this time, Spurgeon began to keep copies of his letters to Union officials.

[59]Autobiography, IV, 263.

that creeds were futile in preventing heresy,[60] and

Spurgeon interpreted this to mean that the Union had

closed the door against him.

> I am unable to sympathize with a man who says he has
> no creed; because I believe him to be in the wrong.
> . . . He ought to have a creed--he must have one,
> even though he repudiates the notion. . . . The
> objection to a creed is a very pleasant way of con-
> cealing objection to discipline, and [reveals] a
> desire for latitudinarianism. What is wished for is
> a Union, which will, like Noah's Ark, afford shelter
> for the clean and unclean, for creeping things and
> winged fowls.[61]

In a final attempt to come to terms with Spurgeon, four

officials of the Union offered to journey to Mentone to

discuss matters with him. "If it means they will surrender

it is well," he wrote to his wife, "but if it is meant to

fix on me the odium of being implacable, it is another

matter."[62]

The suggestion came to nothing, neither side was

willing to "surrender," and when Spurgeon returned to

London in January 1888, he met the deputation from the

Union at the Tabernacle. He signed a statement declaring

---

[60]Ms. letter, December 2, 1887, Spurgeon's College.

[61]Sword and Trowel, XXIV (1888), 82.

[62]Autobiography, IV, 257.

that the Baptist Union was not "knowingly so" a "confederation of evil," but he refused to give any names to the Union, since, as he put it, at present the Union had no authority to get rid of heretics anyway.[63] Five days later, the Council of the Union met--it consisted of six officers and one hundred members, of whom twenty-seven were laymen,--formally accepted Spurgeon's resig-nation, and passed a resolution offered by Dr. Landels condemning Spurgeon for making his accusations. Only five votes were cast against the resolution, and only one of the five was a Pastor's College man.[64] Spurgeon's brother, James, cast one of the five dissenting votes, and then left the meeting in protest. He did not, however, withdraw from the Union, and was president-elect of the organization in the year of his death.

The resolution condemning Spurgeon was quickly labeled "the vote of censure," and caused great bitterness between the two factions. The Union officials maintained that the resolution was not a vote of censure, but it is

---

[63]Payne, The Baptist Union, p. 135.

[64]Payne, "The Downgrade Controversy," p. 35.

certainly difficult to see how else it might have been construed. Spurgeon's partisans planned an appeal from the Council to the Assembly of the Union, due to meet in April in London. Spurgeon failed to understand how accurately the Council votes reflected the general sentiment of the members of the Union, and was confident that his forces would reverse the Council action when it came before the Assembly. In February he wrote to a friend, "They keep on clamouring for <u>names</u>. You can give me names. I don't want anyone to be drawn into person- alities; but if they cry 'names,' we shall have enough to give them!"[65] Spurgeon was warned by his brother that if he did name "heretics," he would be open to libel action, and he did not redeem the promise of this letter. Although he refused to give any specific instances of heresy, he was still optimistic. A few days before the Assembly met he wrote, "There are signs of a better spirit with some on the Council, and I am hopeful."[66] On February 21, the Council met and adopted a declaration of evangelical

---

[65]Copy of a letter to "Joseph," February 8, 1888, Spurgeon's College.

[66]Copy of a letter to Mr. Stockwell, February 14, 1888, Spurgeon's College.

principles held in common by Baptists, but specifically denied in the preamble to the declaration any authority to enforce the principles upon any member.[67] Spurgeon declared that the preamble "gives it another meaning altogether," and refused to accept the declaration as a substitute for a creed.[68] On April 23, the Assembly met in Dr. Parker's City Temple, and after listening to a speech from the new president, John Clifford, defending the Union against Spurgeon's charges, accepted the Council's resolutions without any serious debate from the floor. It was clear to the Assembly as it was to Spurgeon that a vote to uphold the Council was a vote against Spurgeon. The motion passed with only seven dissenting votes, and the results were greeted with "tumultous cheering, and cheering and cheering yet."[69] Spurgeon's hopes were shattered. "I feel so ill and utterly crushed by last Monday that I feel I am only acting like a sensible man if I keep out of all Unions and associations henceforth. . . . We are sold, not betrayed but entrapped by

---

[67] Payne, The Baptist Union, pp. 137-138.

[68] Ibid., p. 138.

[69] E. J. Poole-Connor, Evangelicalism in England (London, 1951), p. 247. See also, Bacon, op. cit., pp. 140-141.

diplomatists."[70] Spurgeon, honest to the point of
bluntness, was impervious to a subtler form of reasoning.
"I cannot speak sponges," he once said. "I feel better
now that my mind is made up never to return to a company
so extremely clever in the use of language," he told a
friend. "I should never know what they meant, and like
the good people at the Tower of Babel I should soon be on
the move."[71]

After April 1888, Spurgeon made no more overtures
to the Union. At the end of April he withdrew from the
London Baptist Association which he had helped to found in
1865. The following month, the Pastor's College Conference, an association of all Pastor's College graduates, was
disbanded and re-chartered as the Pastor's College Evanel-
ical Association after adopting a creed similar to that
Spurgeon had suggested to the Baptist Union.[72] Eighty of
his old students refused to join the new association, the

---

[70]Copy of a letter to Mr. Wright, April 27, 1888,
Spurgeon's College.

[71]Copy of a letter to Mr. Wright, May 4, 1888,
Spurgeon's College.

[72]For the creed, see Sword and Trowel, XXVII
(1891), 446.

most bitter blow Spurgeon had to bear. "I feel that my
candle has been snuffed," he told his son, Charles.[73] "I
have suffered enough for one lifetime from those I lived
to serve," he wrote.[74] To a friend he confided, "I cannot
tell you by letter what I have endured in the desertion of
my own men. Ah me! Yet the Lord liveth, and blessed by
my rock!"[75] As the prophet, he had souncded the call

> . . . Come ye out from among them, and be ye separate,
> saith the Lord, and touch not the unclean thing; and
> I will receive you, and will be a father unto you,
> and ye shall be my sons and daughters, saith the Lord
> God Almighty.

Some refused to hear his call, and he was saddened; yet he
never faltered in his resolve. "I shall live if I am
quite alone; in fact I shall live all the better, for the
more associations, the more care and trouble."[76] Spurgeon's
journey had taken him full circle, and he was back where
he had started, in an Independent parsonage.

---

[73]Letter to son Charles, September 20, 1888, in
Letters, p. 85.

[74]Copy of a letter to Mr. Near, February 22, 1890,
Spurgeon's College.

[75]Copy of a letter to Mr. Near, February 21, 1888,
Spurgeon's College.

[76]Ms. letter to a "friend," October 12, 1888,
Spurgeon's College.

CHAPTER IX

LAST YEARS

Autumn begins to lay its hands upon all things. The
vigor of the year is past, and the sabbath season of
the woods has come. . . . Every falling leaf is a
sermon. "Far from the city's dust and din" we wander
till our feet are arrested by the tiny tarn which
gives drink to bird and beast; and by its brink we
sit us down and muse upon a fading world, and the
generations of its life which rise like the waves of
the sea only to die upon the shore. Yet life abides
and death cannot drive it from its throne. The
leaves fall, but the forest lives on: men perish,
but the race survives. Better still, the Lord of all
things lives; and as his watchful eye watches over
the floweret which blooms in the innermost wood, so
does he care for me. Lost as I might well be amid
these pathless forests, yet he broods around me, and
I am at home in him. When, like a faded leaf, I hang
upon the tree awaiting my end, I will not fear; for
when the time shall come for me to flutter to the
ground, he will be with me, and direct my way, as
surely as though I were the only creature he ever
made.

. . . CHS

Inevitably, Spurgeon's circle of friends and

associates narrowed as a result of his break with the

Baptist Union. In "one dark hour" he felt "as if no man

would stand with me,"[1] although there was no danger that
he would be left friendless. Many of his friends took
his side, but some did so because they were personally
loyal to Spurgeon; not all of them shared his fears that
the Baptist denomination was theologically unsound. Many
of his most vocal supporters did share his conservative
views, and their influence on him in his last years was
not always beneficial. G. Holden Pike, who knew and
admired Spurgeon, conceded that in the preacher's last
years, "he came under the influence of men of narrower
minds than his own was naturally."[2] Surrounded by men who
grasped only one side of the controversy, he grew more and
more convinced of the complete righteousness of his position.
Unwilling to concede that his opponents might be motivated
by principle, he began to evidence signs of persecution
mania, speaking of "conspiracies of evil," and charging
that the press was engaged in "a conspiracy of silence,
or else have culled from their correspondence letters

---

[1]Sword and Trowel, XXV (1889), 307-308,

[2]Pike, Life, III, 95.

unfavorable to the truth."[3] Even Spurgeon's most ardent
admirers have admitted that he was never at his best in
controversy. "Spurgeon was not formed for controversy,"
wrote G. Holden Pike; "he was most effective opposing error
when he simply proclaimed the truth."[4] "Spurgeon was not
a great controversialist," said John Carlile; "he hated it,
wrote badly at it."[5] W. Y. Fullerton, a close associate,
admitted, "Mr. Spurgeon was too earnest, too intent upon
the eternal meaning of things, too sure of his own standing,
to be a good controversialist. . . . He was a witness,
not a debater."[6] And yet in spite of his lack of skill as
a controversialist, Spurgeon seemingly could not avoid
controversy. He was a figure of controversy from the day
he arrived in London until the day he died in Mentone.

Spurgeon had few confidantes and few close friends
among his peers. He was happiest with his students, in a
situation in which he was both mentor and father, and less

---

[3]Sword and Trowel, XXIV (18880, Preface.

[4]Pike, II, 265.

[5]Carlile, op. cit., p. 248.

[6]Fullerton, op. cit., p. 307.

at ease in the company of those whose reputation equalled
his own. It is certainly significant that Spurgeon had
few close friends among the most famous preachers of his
day, and that, indeed, he deliberately antagonized many of
them. Few of his contemporaries measured up to his
standard of orthodoxy. Of the theologically conservative
Canon Farrar, he wrote: "We do not feel he is a safe
guide or in the least helpful to spiritual life."[7]
R. W. Dale, who had doubts concerning eternal damnation,
had "embraced modern error," according to Spurgeon.[8] While
he conceded that Beecher was "a much bigger man than I
am," he declared that "I make up for it," by offering "a
great deal more gospel."[9] Later he was even harsher in his
opinion of Beecher. Spurgeon believed every rumor that
wafted across the Atlantic concerning Beecher's conduct,
and when Beecher's friend, Joseph Parker, invited him to
preach at the City Temple, Spurgeon declared that the
pulpit had been "desecrated." Dr. Parker, like Spurgeon,

---

[7]Sword and Trowel, XXI (1885), 377.

[8]Ibid., XIV (1878), 33.

[9]Williams, op. cit., p. 34.

believed in an inerrant Bible, but even Parker was not

orthodox enough for Spurgeon. Reviewing Parker's The

Priesthood of Christ, Spurgeon declared it to be "the most

evil piece of writing it was ever our misery to read."[10]

In earlier days, Parker and Spurgeon had exchanged pulpits

frequently, but when Parker sanctioned ministers attending

the theater, Spurgeon anathematized him. Parker and

Spurgeon were the two leading exponents of conservative

evangelical Nonconformity in England, yet as Willis Glover

has pointed out, "the amazing fact is that the most bitter

quarrel in which Parker and Spurgeon were engaged in the

crucial period between 1887 and 1892 was a quarrel with

each other."[11] When Parker invited Spurgeon to participate

in a conference on preserving evangelical truths, Spurgeon's

reply was a blunt refusal: "I do not think your past

course of action entitles you to be considered a champion

of the faith. . . . The Evangelical faith in which you and

Mr. Beecher agree is not the faith which I hold; and the

view of religion which takes you to the theater is so far

---

[10]Sword and Trowel, XIII (1877), 42.

[11]Glover, op. cit., p. 244.

off from mine that I cannot commune with you therein."[12]
Spurgeon wrote to the Congregationalist, Newman Hall, that
he had "declined a certain invitation to confer as allies
respecting Gospel truth and conduct because his own views
were opposed to those of H.W.B., and because he disapproved
of Christian ministers sanctioning by their presence the
theatrical exhibitions of the day."[13]

Cut off from any liberalizing influences, Spurgeon
saw evil everywhere he looked. By 1888 he was convinced
"there are many more rotten men in the Union than I dreamed
of."[14] Turning his attention briefly from the Baptists to
the Methodists he announced "the gentlemen just now to the
front in Methodism are no more Methodists than we are
Dutchmen."[15] Even those who shared his theologically
conservative outlook were the frequent targets of his
criticism. General Booth's pronouncements on modernism

---

[12]Ibid.

[13]Newman Hall, An Autobiography (London, 1898),
p. 297.

[14]Copy of a letter to Mr. Near, June 16, 1888,
in Spurgeon Papers, Spurgeon's College.

[15]Sword and Trowel, XXVII (1891), 342.

were almost identical to those of Spurgeon, but the two men were not close, and failed to make a common cause in defense of their views. Privately, Spurgeon expressed the opinion that Booth was a fool for "playing at soldiers," while Booth, scandalized by Spurgeon's remarks on tobacco, had serious reservations about the moral fitness of the Pastor of the Tabernacle. Even Moody, while declaring in public, "I have for years thought more of him than any other man preaching the gospel,"[16] grumbled to his associates that he resented Spurgeon's patronizing attitude and his attempts to "take over" Moody's London campaigns. He was furious when Spurgeon urged that his converts be re-baptized.[17] All too often, the evidence suggests, the most prominent evangelicals wasted their energies carping at one another over petty differences, and, in the process, lost sight of their main objective--the defense of evangelical truth. Their bickering prevented their rallying around a common spokesman or giving much more than lip-service to a common cause.

[16]Autobiography, IV, 170.

[17]J. C. Pollock, Moody, A Biographical Portrait (New York, 1963), p. 153.

Relevant to the subject of Spurgeon's narrowing circle of friends was his relationship to John Clifford. Of all the personal issues raised by the Downgrade Controversy, the nature of the quarrel between Spurgeon and Clifford remains the most controversial. Dr. Clifford was a cosmopolitan man, a Liberal and a Fabian, active in politics and a prominent spokesman for the social gospel movement in Britain. After Spurgeon, he was probably the most prominent Baptist in the country. In 1888, he served as president of the Baptist Union, and played a significant part in the maneuvering which led to the Baptist Union's resolution censuring Spurgeon in April. Prior to the "vote of censure," Spurgeon's relations with Clifford appeared, on the surface at least, to be amiable. Spurgeon was suspicious of Clifford's views on free will, but in a meeting at the Tabernacle with Clifford in January 1888, Spurgeon told him, "As you know we differ, but we hold vital evangelical truth in common."[18] (Though with his usual forthrightness, Spurgeon added, "I do not like your

---

[18]In a letter to F. A. Jones, February 1888, cited in Payne, The Baptist Union, p. 129.

last book.") According to Clifford's later account of the
meeting, Spurgeon, although differing with him on free will,
felt he was sound on other points. When Spurgeon told
Clifford in January that the two were in accord, he had not
yet been censured by the Baptist Union. His statements
about Clifford after the vote of censure are indicative
of his bitterness at the action of the Union, and an indication that he held Clifford personally responsible.

In 1887, Spurgeon wrote to Clifford, "You and I
understand each other,"[19] but in 1889 he told a correspondent, "Cliffordism will ruin the General Baptists if generally adopted and many of them see it."[20] When Dr. Clifford
addressed a meeting in a Unitarian chapel in 1889, Spurgeon
was quick to point out that the president of the Baptist
Union had addressed a group gathered in a room graced with
plaques bearing the words of Voltaire, Jesus, Paine, and
Zoroaster.

_____

[19]Ibid., p. 315.

[20]Copy of letter to Mr. Near, June 23, 1888,
Spurgeon's College. (The original is in the Angus College
Library, Oxford.)

> The blasphemous association of Our Lord with Thomas
> Paine and Voltaire creates an indescribable feeling
> in the Christian mind, and makes us wonder how a man,
> professing to be a servant of the Lord Jesus, could
> associate himself with such a place. Well might the
> Union resent our complaints against its most obscure
> wanderers, when its President, before he closed his
> year of office, would publically associate himself
> with the deniers of Our Lord's divinity.[21]

In his zeal to condemn Clifford, Spurgeon had apparently

forgotten the sensational young preacher who had provoked

bitter criticism for preaching at race tracks and music

halls. But that young preacher had become an embittered

old man.

In 1890, W. T. Stead published a program for "the

Church of the Future," and Clifford wrote a preface to the

volume giving Stead's ideas his qualified endorsement.

Stead was something of an amiable crank on religious ques-

tions—he admitted to having been converted three times and

he later embraced spiritualism—and his ideas for

"restoring Christ to Christianity" were calculated to

enrage traditionalists. "My ideal Church will include

atheists, it will run a theater, and it will be the

---

[21]Sword and Trowel, XXV (1889), 244.

455

proprietor of a public house."[22] Spurgeon's reaction to such a "church" was predictable. He devoted a sermon and an editorial in the Sword and Trowel to attacking "this monster." Dr. Clifford's statement that he was "completely sympathetic with the spirit and aim" of Stead's proposals, and that he saw in them "a return to the Christianity of Christ Jesus,"[23] seemed conclusive proof to Spurgeon that, under Clifford, the Baptists were headed for disaster. As for Stead, Spurgeon spoke of him in terms he usually reserved for the emissaries of the Pope or the forerunners of the Anti-Christ. Five years before, Spurgeon had defended Stead when the controversial editor had been jailed for publishing an expose of the white slave trade in the Pall Mall Gazette. He wrote a letter defending Stead's actions which was read at an Exeter Hall rally held by Stead's supporters. He had, Stead later wrote, "rendered me yeoman service. . . . When the Pall Mall Gazette was being howled at by all the prurient prudes

---

[22]W. T. Stead, "The Church of the Future," in Great Thoughts (January 3, 1891), p. 8.

[23]Ibid., p. 40.

and alarmed adulterers, Mr. Spurgeon spoke up manfully in

our defense."[24] But five years before, Spurgeon and

Clifford "understood one another." By 1890, Spurgeon was

consumed by a fire which sacrificed old ties to orthodoxy.[25]

In the last two years of his life Spurgeon was

surrounded by syncophantic listeners anxious to reassure

him that his war against modernism was a valiant crusade

against "the vaunting zeit geist." Dr. Parker, an old

friend now denounced as a heretic, made one last attempt

to reach Spurgeon in the form of an "open letter," published

in The British Weekly. Parker warned Spurgeon that he was

guilty of "the heterodoxy of one-sidedness," "a want of

spiritual discrimination," and "a bluntness which can only

be accounted for by the worst kind of spiritual ignorance.

The universe is not divided into plain black and white, as

---

[24]Review of Reviews, V (1892), 117.

[25]Spurgeon's answer to Stead was preached in a ser-
mon, "Our Manifesto," delivered April 25, 1890. In
December 1890, Stead sent Spurgeon a copy of his recently
published Portrait Album, and noted "whatever else the
Review of Reviews may have done or not done, it has in no
way whatever impaired the circulation of the Sword and
Trowel." Telegram, December 19, 1890, William Jewell
College.

you suppose. It is not your function to set some people
on your right hand and the rest on your left." Pointedly,
Parker urged Spurgeon to "widen the circle of which you
are the center. You are surrounded by offerers of
incense. They flatter your weaknesses, they laugh at
your jokes, they feed you with compliments. My dear
Spurgeon, you are too big a man for this. . . . Scatter
your ecclesiastical harem."[26] Perhaps because there was
much truth in the charges, Spurgeon's supporters were
enraged. Only Spurgeon's edict that the "open letter" be
ignored prevented his supporters from rushing to dismember
Parker in print. When Parker died in 1902, Spurgeon's son,
Thomas, admitted that it was only standing at the "open
grave" that he was able to forgive the "open letter."[27]

The last chapter in Spurgeon's great career was a
tragic one. On his fiftieth birthday in 1884 he had
appeared at the very pinnacle of his chosen profession--
admired, respected, the idol of thousands, a man whose word
might influence elections and whose sermons work miracles.

---

[26]"An Appeal to Spurgeon," The British Weekly,
April 25, 1890.

[27]Fullerton, Thomas Spurgeon, p. 301.

Three years later he had broken with his party and his denomination, had become alienated from old friends and associates, and, as a final blow, had begun to lose the marvelous energy and confidence which had sustained him through so many battles in the past. In 1888, his mother died and his wife was seriously ill. His own health was beginning to deteriorate at a rapid rate, and this time there were no sources of untapped energy left to draw upon, and there would be no more miraculous recoveries. "I am broken-backed and broken-kneed," he wrote to his brother. "No dealer would buy me except for cat's meat, and I'm not worth so much for that as I was, for I am many pounds lighter."[28] Spurgeon had been afflicted with a chronic form of Bright's Disease for years, and his body was beginning to evidence the symptoms that the disease was in the terminal stages. Gout spread from his feet to his head and hands, and he was rarely free from disabling swelling and the accompanying pain. For weeks at a time he suffered what his doctors described as "acute delirium" and "nervous debility." He was unable to eat most solid

[28]_Letters_, p. 66.

food and was finally reduced to a diet of oatmeal. A Boston minister, Dr. George Lorimer, who visited Spurgeon ten months before his death, found him prematurely old. "His shoulders were bent, he leaned heavily on a chair when he preached, he walked with painful slowness . . . he evidenced many marks of extreme old age."[29]

His physical infirmity, coupled with the emotional strain of the Downgrade Controversy, produced in Spurgeon a deep sense of melancholy. "Only those who knew his sufferings," wrote a student, "know how utterly low his spirits were often brought."[30] Left with too much time to brood, in one dark hour Spurgeon slipped back to the doubts of his youth and once more questioned his own salvation. This strong-minded, strong-willed man, whose greatest authority was grounded in the absolute conviction of his faith was so reduced by circumstances that he wondered aloud if he might not be "only a waiter, and not a guest, at the Gospel feast."[31] In gloomy moments he felt "such a sense

---

[29]George Lorimer, Charles Haddon Spurgeon (Boston, 1892), pp. 18-19.

[30]Williams, op. cit., p. 221.

[31]Fullerton, C. H. Spurgeon, p. 113.

of unworthiness . . . as to make him dread being numbered among the unworthy servants."[32] Spurgeon had always been too busy and too confident to put much stock in millennial visions. He warned his students against becoming so absorbed with the doctrine of the second coming "that you neglect to preach the first."[33] In 1877 he said: "If I knew our Lord would come this evening, I should preach just as I mean to preach, and if I knew he would come during the sermon, I would go on preaching until he did. Christian people ought not to be standing with their mouths open, gazing up into heaven and wondering what is going to happen."[34] Though he had often cautioned against speculating on the "dates and seasons" of the Lord's Coming, in his last years he saw evidence that the Second Coming was imminent. "I believe the Second Coming of Christ will be very soon," he told the students at his last College conference.[35]

---

[32]Williams, p. 51.

[33]Ibid., 166.

[34]Sermon number 1,231, preached July 5, 1877, in Metropolitan Tabernacle Pulpit.

[35]Williams, p. 199.

Spurgeon's final illness coincided with his struggle with the Baptist Union, and his opponents in the controversy frequently suggested that illness had warped his mind and embittered his outlook. His supporters, on the other hand, argued that the controversy aggravated his illness, and after his death, they were to cast him in the role of a "martyr for truth." His private secretary, J. W. Harrald, sounded this theme when he spoke at Spurgeon's funeral service: "Within that olive casket lies all that remains of a martyr for Truth's sake. That great controversy killed him."[36] Spurgeon, wrote his wife, had died "Christ's faithful witness and martyr."[37] Was Spurgeon a martyr? The medical evidence suggests that his relatively early death was inevitable. He had a chronic and incurable disease, had suffered its ravages for years, and would finally have succumbed to its effects even if he had remained at peace with the Baptist Union. Perhaps the controversy, by disturbing him emotionally,

---

[36]James T. Allen, Charles H. Spurgeon (London, 1931), p. 47.

[37]Autobiography, II, 259.

depleted his physical resources and hastened his death, but the controversy did not kill him. At the same time, it appears that Spurgeon almost welcomed the possibility of martyrdom. He believed that it was the controversy and not the disease which was killing him. "To be free from all ecclesiastical entanglements is to the Christian minister a blessing worth all it has cost, even though an almost fatal illness might be reckoned a part of the price," he wrote.[38] When a former student departed to a ministry in Australia in March 1891, Spurgeon's last words to him were, "Goodbye, Ellis, you will never see me again, this fight is killing me."[39] Spurgeon had always been fascinated by the example of martyrdom. He prided himself on his descent from "that martyred Spurgeon of long ago," and since childhood had found inspiration in Foxe's Book of Martyrs. "I believe the Church has scarcely ever increased except through the blood of her martyrs," he declared,[40] and he proclaimed in one of his earliest sermons that "it

[38]Sword and Trowel, XXVIII (1892), 93.

[39]Autobiography, III, 152.

[40]C. H. Spurgeon's Prayers (London, 1905), p. 178.

would be the greatest dignity I could ever attain to, if
the enemy would place the blood-red crown of martyrdom
around this brow."[41] He assured his congregation that
before he embraced the heresy of modernism, "May these
bones be picked by vultures, and this flesh rent assunder
by lions, and may every nerve in this body suffer pangs
and tortures."[42] Spurgeon realized that the day was past
when a Christian would be thrown to the lions or burnt at
the stake for his views, yet when he suffered the "pangs
and tortures" of disease he attributed his suffering to the
strain of the controversy in which he as engaged. Perhaps,
too, in speaking and preaching beyond his physical endurance,
he was unconsciously seeking martyrdom. "I am overdone and
half-dead," he told his borther in May 1891, "I am so
longing to rest."[43]

It was clear by the summer of 1891 that he had
reached the end of his physical limits. On May 17, he
attempted to preach a sermon, and for the first time in

[41]The New Park Street Pulpit, I (1855), 366-367.

[42]Autobiography, II, 275.

[43]Letters, p. 66.

his life, found himself unable to preach. He broke down
and had to be assisted from the platform. On June 7, he
preached what was to be his last sermon at the Tabernacle.
Perhaps sensing the end, he chose a prophetic text:

> For David, after he had served his own generation by
> the will of God, fell on asleep.

On the following day, he made a last pilgrimage to Stambourne, hoping to find in that pastoral setting some
release from the tensions of controversy. But even there he
could find no peace. Becoming ill, he was taken back to
London where he remained in "an acute delirium" for over
a month. Messages poured in from the Prince of Wales,
Gladstone, the Duke of Argyll, the Earl of Aberdeen, the
Archbishops of Canterbury and York, the Bishops of Liverpool, Ripon, Rochester, and Winchester. When he did
recover consciousness he found that the illness had brought
"a _faraway_ tone" to his voice. That remarkable voice,
one of the greatest of the age, was gone forever, and all
that remained was a feeble echo of its former power. There
was still optimistic talk of improvement; the deacons
urged him to go abroad, and accepting their advice, the
ailing preacher, accompanied for the first time by his

beloved "Susie," journeyed to Mentone in hope that the Riviera sun would work its old magic.

"Time is not a thing to be killed as fools have dreamed, or to hang heavy on one's hands, as idiots have maundered," he once mused. "It is as priceless as it is fleeting, and alas! all too short for zeal and love, all too hurried for peace and rest, and all too uncertain for high designs and lofty purposes."[44] Time was flying for him now and he knew it. Looking back upon a life filled with honors and accomplishments, he regretted that he had achieved so little. "I beseech you," he entreated a favorite student, "to live not only for this age, but for the next also. I would fling my shadow through eternal ages if I could."[45] "Be ye faithful unto death, and your crowns will not be wanting," he told his studnets, "but oh! let none of us die out like dim candles, ending a powerless ministry in everlasting darkness."[46] On January 17, 1892, Spurgeon spoke briefly at a small family service gathered

[44]Sword and Trowel, III (1867), Preface.

[45]Williams, pp. 85-86.

[46]Sword and Trowel, XXV (1889), 421.

together in a hotel room at Mentone. It was the last service he ever conducted. Two days later he returned from a drive with a chill. He went to bed, fell into a deep sleep, and never regained consciousness. His death was peaceful, but there were no "last words" or "parting testimony" for those who kept the vigil around his bed. He died on Sunday, January 31, just before midnight. "The only pulpit name of the nineteenth century that will be remembered is no longer the name of a living man," wrote his old adversary, Joseph Parker. "That great voice has ceased."[47]

A heavy rain fell all day long on February 8, 1892, when Spurgeon's body was returned to Victoria Station. Students carried his coffin into the Tabernacle where his body lay in state for three days as more than 60,000 people filed by in a last tribute to the memory of the great preacher. On February 11, Spurgeon's body was carried out of the Tabernacle for its final journey through the familiar streets of South London. His funeral parade was two miles long, and over 100,000 people lined the five

---

[47]_The Times_, February 3, 1892.

miles from the Tabernacle to the cemetery in Upper

Norwood. His empty brougham followed the hearse, in imi-

tation of a military funeral parade, but in place of the

sword, his Bible rested upon his coffin. All along the

funeral route flags flew at half-mast, shops were closed,

and even the public houses closed their doors. He had

requested a simple marker for his grave. Perhaps recalling

the example of John Wesley, he had asked that only a plain

stone bearing the initials, "C.H.S.," be erected. His

wishes were overruled, however; and an elaborate tomb

marks his grave. Carved upon its face are the words of

his favorite hymn:

> E're since by faith I saw the stream
>   They flowing wounds supply,
> Redeeming love has been by theme
>   And shall be till I die.

CONCLUSION

Spurgeon's death left a void in the popular religious tradition of England that no one could fill. He left no successors capable of continuing his work. His two sons divided his clerical responsibilities--Thomas Spurgeon, who died October 20, 1917, took over the Tabernacle pulpit; Charles Spurgeon, who died December 13, 1926, became the director of the Orphanage. They were both dedicated, capable men; but they lived their lives in the shadow of their father's reputation. Devoted to their father's principles, they lacked his genius and failed to attract his audience. Over the years, the Tabernacle congregation grew smaller, and what had been a London institution became merely another half-empty neighborhood church.

No one of stature arose in England to take up Spurgeon's banner in defense of traditional evangelical doctrine. Although scattered pockets of resistance to modernism continued, England developed "no strong school of fundamentalist Bible scholars and no close-knit

468

fundamentalist factions in the major denominations."[1]
Dr. Parker survived Spurgeon by ten years, but at his
death the pulpit at City Temple passed to R. J. Campbell,
a modernist.[2] The Congregationalist Newman Hall, one of
the few contemporaries Spurgeon regarded as theologically
sound--"we are two of an old school,"[3]--came to question
the absolute inerrancy of scripture, and refused to dogmatize on eternal damnation.[4] "In his noble zeal," Hall
said of Spurgeon, "he overrated the declension" of
evangelical principles.[5] The Baptist denomination continued its steady drift toward modernism--in 1920,
H. W. Robinson, a modernist, became the head of Regent's
Park College, and in 1925, T. R. Glover was elected the
president of the Baptist Union. The denomination survived
the Downgrade Controversy, concludes Willis Glover, because
a majority of Baptists did not agree with Spurgeon that

---

[1]Glover, op. cit., p. 219.

[2]Ibid., p. 244.

[3]Newman Hall, Autobiography (London, 1898), p. 298.

[4]Glover, p. 166.

[5]Good Words, XXXIII (1892), 234.

the acceptance of higher criticism constituted the denial of evangelical principles.[6]

It is not entirely coincidental that much of Spurgeon's support during the Downgrade Controversy came from areas outside Britain. During the single month of August 1888, strong resolutions praising Spurgeon were passed by Baptist associations in Kentucky, Nova Scotia, New Brunswick, and Prince Edward Island.[7] It was on the other side of the Atlantic that Spurgeon's challenges struck a responsive chord. It was to be in America rather than in his own country that Spurgeon's combination of conventional evangelical doctrine and unconventional homiletical style were to survive into the twentieth century. In a symbolic gesture, Susannah Spurgeon presented Spurgeon's pulpit Bible to D. L. Moody. "This Bible has been used by my beloved husband, and is now given with unfeigned pleasure to one in whose hands its service will

---

[6]Glover, pp. 174-175; Bacon, op. cit., pp. 144-146; Poole-Conner, op. cit., pp. 249-252.

[7]Sword and Trowel, XXV (1884), 447.

be continued and extended."[8] Ten years later the rest of

Spurgeon's library crossed the Atlantic. When his library

was offered for sale in 1905, it was the trustees of an

American Baptist College who raised the funds to purchase

what Spurgeon had regarded as his most treasured possession.

The Baptists of Britain paid belated homage to Spurgeon's

memory by erecting a statue of the preacher in the Baptist

Church House, London, in 1934, but few in the denomination

paid more than lip service to the views Spurgeon had

championed.

D. L. Moody, with his seventh-grade education and

his no-nonsense sermons, was even less pretentious than

Spurgeon in his approach to preaching the gospel. Moody

lacked Spurgeon's rhetorical power and gift of language;

his sermons were simple, straightforward, and blunt. If

by Victorian standards, Spurgeon was self-educated, Moody

was uneducated. Spurgeon was secretly amused by Moody's

pronunciation--he told a friend that Moody was the only man

he knew who could reduce the word, "Mesopotamia," to two

---

[8]W. R. Moody, The Life of Dwight L. Moody (New York, 1900), 447.

syllables. Yet Moody, with his wide audience on two
continents, was the logical successor to Spurgeon as the
leader of the crusade against modernism. It was a task
he did not wish and attempted to avoid. Moody, like Spurgeon, believed in an infallible Bible. When asked if the
story of Jonah and the whale was a myth, Moody's reply,
"I stand by Jonah,"[9] was unequivocal enough for Spurgeon.
Yet Moody was much less doctrinaire than Spurgeon and had
no denominational ties to bind him. In 1899, he complained
that there was too much hairsplitting among Christians
and the Church was losing ground in consequence. "Under
these conditions the question of the authorship of individual books of the Bible has become of less immediate
importance than knowledge of the Bible itself; the question
of the two Isaiahs less urgent than a familiarity with
the prophecy itself."[10] He urged critics to "agree to a
truce, and for ten years bring out no fresh views," so
that ministers could "get on with the practical work of

[9]Ibid., p. 496.

[10]Ibid., p. 497.

the kingdom."[11] Such a pragmatic approach to the issues
of higher criticism would have been impossible for Spurgeon,
and even Moody was to find his efforts to steer a middle
course difficult. Although at his death both modernists
and fundamentalists were to claim him as one of them, his
most recent biographer has concluded that "the evangelist's personal ability to bridge the gap was a tenuous
achievement."[12]

Reuben Torrey, who succeeded Moody as head of the
Moody Bible Institute, was much less willing than his
predecessor to compromise upon doctrinal questions. There
is more than an echo of Spurgeon in Torrey's pronouncements concerning hell--"I believe the old-fashioned Bible
doctrines regarding hell"--or the evils of social dancing--
"there is a contact between the sexes that is permitted
nowhere else in decent society. I have never seen a
decent dance."[13] In common with Spurgeon, Torrey professed
great faith in the good sense of the untutored common man.

---

[11]James F. Findlay, Dwight L. Moody, American
Evangelist (Chicago, 1969), p. 412.

[12]Ibid., p. 413.

[13]McLoughlin, op. cit., p. 373.

"In ninety-nine out of a hundred cases, the meaning that a plain man gets out of the Bible is the correct one."[14] In the twentieth century the torch passed from the Tabernacle to the Moody Bible Institute.

Had Spurgeon survived into the twentieth century, he would have been appalled at the pulpit antics of the converted baseball player, Billy Sunday, but Sunday was merely the jazz-age version of the nineteenth-century popular preacher. Certainly Sunday's ministry, although frequently bizarre, occasioned no more controversy than the early career of Spurgeon. "I am perhaps vulgar," the Boy Preacher had written in 1855, "but I must and will make the people listen." This was an argument that would have made sense to Billy Sunday. "We must," Spurgeon told his students, "use what Whitefield called 'market language' if we would have all classes of the community listening to our message."[15] "I want to reach the people, so I use the people's language," declared Billy Sunday.[16] The "market language" of each community changes from age to age, and

---

[14]Ibid., p. 372.

[15]The Soul-Winner, p. 228.

[16]McLoughlin, op. cit., p. 373.

what would have shocked Spurgeon did not necessarily shock

the typical member of Sunday's congregation. It is, after

all, only a small semantic leap from Spurgeon's observation

that Jesus was "no namby-pamby milksop," to Sunday's

contention that Jesus was "no dough-faced lick-spittle

proposition."[17]

There is much truth in Emerson's observation that

the religion of one age becomes the literary entertainment

of the next. Few figures offer the social historian such

tempting targets as popular preachers. "Who art thou

that judgest another man's servants," Spurgeon reminds

us. "Do these workers of many sorts and divers manners

win souls? Then they are wise; and you who criticize

them, being yourself unfruitful, cannot be wise, even

---

[17]An interesting analogue can be found in the
sermons of the late Clarence A. Jordan of Americus, Georgia,
who according to a report in The Associated Press, August 16,
1967, brought 7,000 cheering students to their feet with
his comments before a national convention of the Lutheran
League: "I'm tired of seeing Jesus Christ portrayed as a
man who kept his nails nice with polish. . . . The only
reason Peter followed him is that Jesus could beat him
fishing. . . . Jesus was a first-class mule rider. He rode
a mule that no man had ever sat--and that was down main
street with everybody throwin' palm branches."

though you affect to be their judges."[18] By what standards shall Spurgeon be judged? In the eighty years since his death, the world has moved far away from the standards he would recognize or accept. Even in his own time many regarded him as an anachronism, a judgment which left him unperturbed. He once said that the highest praise he had ever received had been the words of a critic: "Here is a man who has not moved one inch forward in all his ministry and at the close of the nineteenth century is teaching the theology of the first century, and in Newington Butts is proclaiming the doctrines of Nazareth and Jerusalem current eighteen hundred years ago." "Those words," Spurgeon declared, "did please me!"[19]

It is easy to characterize Spurgeon as theologically illiterate; to see him as a man who reduced the gospel to its lowest common denominator in order to appeal to masses of simple-minded people. Many of his contemporaries made the same charges. Yet for every Matthew Arnold, lamenting the limitations of the Nonconformist Philistine, or every

---

[18]The Soul-Winner, p. 238.

[19]Pike, Life, III, 109.

477

Fitzjames Stephen, ridiculing the foibles of "the Anabaptist
Caliban," there were many thousands like the Scots house-
wife who began every week with the words, "dinna forget
Spurgeon." Spurgeon was intelligent and shrewd, and his
genius was practical rather than theoretical. It is unfair
to judge him as a theologian or as an original thinker, for
he did not claim these roles. "I am content to live and
die as a mere repeater of scriptural teachings; as a person
who has thought out nothing and invented nothing," he
declared.[20] If we are to judge Spurgeon he must be judged
as a preacher and as a philanthropist, and here the verdict
will be more charitable, for in his chosen vocation he was
perhaps without peer--an innovator in the pulpit, a man
whose original and pithy sermons offered the comforts of
a common-sense gospel to the thousands who could comprehend
no other truth than the simple truth he proclaimed. Spurgeon
clung to the end to old-fashioned doctrines, but as
Dr. Parker observed, those old-fashioned doctrines "created
mission societies, Sunday schools, hospitals, orphanages,
and refuges for penitence; they gave every child a new

---

[20]Messages to the Multitudes, p. 269.

value, every father a new responsibility, every mother a
new hope, and constituted human society into a new
conscience and a new trust."[21] A modern theologian has
written, "Critics ought to see in this man Spurgeon the
shepherd who was content to allow his robes--including his
clerical robes--to be torn to tatters by the sharp thorns
and stones as he clambered after the lost sheep, at times
seeming to be engaged more in training for a cross-country
race than in liturgical exercises. Worldly preaching is
impossible without the earth leaving its traces on a man's
wardrobe."[22]

It was Spurgeon's tragedy that he lived long enough
to witness the comfortable intellectual assumptions of
evangelicalism disrupted by the twin challenges of science
and higher criticism. He saw his task as one of resistance
rather than reconciliation, and he devoted his last
energies to a fruitless crusade against modernism. That
decision has impaired his reputation with posterity, for
the future belonged to his opponents. He failed to stem

---

[21]Parker, Autobiography, p. 99.

[22]Thielicke, op. cit., p. 41.

the tide against the future, and his life ended on a note of defeat, but it was not the defeat of silence or of resignation. "If for a while the evangelicals are doomed to go down," he said, "let them die fighting!" Spurgeon at least kept that vow.

BIBLIOGRAPHY

The following is a partial list of works consulted for this study.

Manuscripts

British Museum--Gladstone Papers; scattered Spurgeon manuscripts in the general collection.

Spurgeon's College Collection (London)--There are a number of Spurgeon manuscripts at Spurgeon's College. The papers were not catalogued. Some are in boxes, others pasted into the more than fifty volumes of Spurgeon's scrapbooks. The college is attempting to make copies of all known Spurgeon correspondence. In general, the scrapbooks are arranged in chronological order, but there are many exceptions.

William Jewell College (Liberty, Mo.)--Spurgeon's library of over 7,000 volumes is in Liberty, Mo. Many of the theological works have Spurgeon's annotations, but the majority of works in the library are not annotated. There are a few manuscripts in the collection.

Newspapers

(All London)

The Daily News   The Standard

The Daily Telegraph   The Times

481

Periodicals

American Church Review

Andover Review

The Baptist

The Baptist Magazine

The British Weekly

Cambridge Historical Journal

The Christian Observer

The Congregationalist

The Congregational Review

Contemporary Review

The Freeman

Good Words

The Hornet

Journal of Theological Studies

Living Age

Macmillans

New Englander

Nineteenth Century

The Nonconformist

North American Review

Pall Mall Gazette

Punch

Review of Reviews

Saturday Review

Spectator

Sunday At Home

Sword and Trowel

Victorian Studies

Westminster Review

Works by Spurgeon

Spurgeon, C. H. Able to the Uttermost, twenty gospel
    sermons. London: Marshall Brothers, 1922.

_____. An All-Round Ministry, addresses to ministers
    and students. London: Passmore and Alabaster, 1900.

_____. Anecdotes. James Ellis (ed.). London: Pass-
    more and Alabaster, 1892.

Spurgeon, C. H. Anecdotes and Stories. Oliver Creyton (ed.). London: Houlston and Wright, 1866.

_____. C. H. Spurgeon's Autobiography, compiled from his Diary, Letters, and Records by his Wife and his Private Secretary. 4 vols. London: Passmore and Alabaster, 1897-1900.

_____. Baptismal Regeneration, A Sermon Preached June 5, 1864. London: Passmore and Alabaster, 1864.

_____. Barbed Arrows from the Quiver of C. H. Spurgeon. London: Passmore and Alabaster, 1896.

_____. The Bible and the Newspaper. London: Passmore and Alabaster, 1878.

_____. The Claims of God, an Address to Men of Business. London: Passmore and Alabaster, 1877.

_____. The Clue of the Maze. London: Passmore and Alabaster, 1884.

_____. Come Ye Children, a book for parents and teachers on the Christian training of children. London: Passmore and Alabaster, 1897.

_____. A Double Knock at the Door of the Young. London: Passmore and Alabaster, 1875.

_____. The Early Years, 1834-1859, a revised edition of the first two volumes of Spurgeon's Autobiography. London: The Banner of Truth Trust, 1962.

_____. Eccentric Preachers. London: Passmore and Alabaster, 1879.

_____. Exeter Hall Sermons. London: James Paul, 1856.

_____. Farm Sermons. London: Passmore and Alabaster, 1882.

Spurgeon, C. H. Feathers for Arrows, or Illustrations for preachers and teachers. London: Passmore and Alabaster, 1870.

_____. A Good Start, a book for young men and women. London: Passmore and Alabaster, 1898.

_____. Gospel Temperance. London: National Temperance Publication Depot, 1886.

_____. The Greatest Fight in the World. London: Passmore and Alabaster, 1896.

_____. Illustrious Lord Mayors, A Lecture. London: Passmore and Alabaster, 1861.

_____. John Ploughman's Pictures and More of His Talk. London: Passmore and Alabaster, 1880.

_____. John Ploughman's Talk. London: Passmore and Alabaster, 1868.

_____. Lectures to My Students. 3 vols. London: Passmore and Alabaster, 1875, 1893, 1894.

_____. Lectures to Young Men. London: James Nesbit, 1859.

_____. The Letters of C. H. Spurgeon. Charles Spurgeon (ed.). London: Marshall Brothers, 1923.

_____. Messages to Multitudes. London: Sampson, Low, Marston, and Co., 1892.

_____. The Metropolitan Tabernacle, Its History and Work. London: Passmore and Alabaster, 1876.

_____. My Run to Naples and Pompeii. London: Passmore and Alabaster, 1873.

_____. My Sermon Notes. London: Passmore and Alabaster, 1895.

Spurgeon, C. H. The Old Gospel and the New Theology,
     Twelve Sermons. London: Passmore and Alabaster,
     1879.

_____. Only a Prayermeeting. London: Passmore and
Alabaster, 1901.

_____. Prayers. London: Passmore and Alabaster, 1905.

_____. Revival Year Sermons Preached at the Surrey
Gardens During 1859. London: Banner of Truth Trust,
1959.

_____. The Salt Cellars, being a collection of
proverbs together with homely notes thereon. 2 vols.
New York: A. C. Armstrong and Son, 1890.

_____. The New Park Street Pulpit, 1855-1860. London:
The Banner of Truth Trust, 1963-1964.

_____. Sermons. American edition, 11 vols. New York:
Sheldon, Blakeman, and Co., 1857-1874.

_____. A Textual Index of C. H. Spurgeon's Sermons,
Vols. I-XXXII. London: Passmore and Alabaster, 1887.

_____. The Soul-Winner. Grand Rapids: William
B. Eerdmans Publishing Co., 1963.

_____. Speeches at Home and Abroad. G. Holden Pike
(ed.). London: Passmore and Alabaster, 1878.

_____. The Teachings of Nature in the Kingdom of Grace.
London: Passmore and Alabaster, 1896.

_____. What the Stones Say or Sermons in Stones.
London: Christian Herald Publishing Co., 1894.

_____ and Benjamin Beddow. Memories of Stambourne.
London: Passmore and Alabaster, 1892.

Biographies of Spurgeon

Allen, James T. Charles H. Spurgeon. London: Pickering and Inglis, 1931.

Anon. Charles Haddon Spurgeon, A Biographical Sketch and Appreciation by One Who Knew Him Well. London: Andrew Melrose, 1903.

Bacon, Ernest. Spurgeon: Heir of the Puritans. London: Allen and Unwin, 1967.

Barnes, R. H. and C. E. Brown. Spurgeon, The People's Preacher. London: Walter Scott, 1892.

Burley, A. Cunningham. Spurgeon and his Friendships. London: Epworth Press, 1933.

Carlile, J. C. C. H. Spurgeon, An Interpretive Biography. London: The Religious Tract Society, 1933.

Conwell, Russell. Life of Charles Haddon Spurgeon, the World's Greatest Preacher. New York: Edgewood Publishing Co., 1892.

Fry, Edmund. Life and Labors of the Reverend C. H. Spurgeon. London: William Arthrop, 1855.

Fullerton, W. Y. C. H. Spurgeon, A Biography. London: Williams and Norgate, 1920.

Lorimer, George C. C. H. Spurgeon, the Puritan Preacher. Boston: James Earle, 1892.

Pike, G. Holden. Charles Haddon Spurgeon, Preacher, Author, Philanthropist. New York: Funk and Wagnalls, 1892.

_____. The Life and Work of Charles Haddon Spurgeon. 3 vols. London: Cassell and Co., 1892.

_____. Seven Portraits of the Reverend C. H. Spurgeon. London: Passmore and Alabaster, 1879.

Ray, Charles. The Life of C. H. Spurgeon. London: Passmore and Alabaster, 1903.

Shindler, Robert. From the Usher's Desk to the Tabernacle Pulpit, the Life and Labors of Charles Haddon Spurgeon. New York: A. C. Armstrong and Co., 1892.

_____. From the Pulpit to the Palmbranch. London: Passmore and Alabaster, 1892.

Stevenson, George. Sketch of the Life and Ministry of the Reverend C. H. Spurgeon. New York: Sheldon, Blakeman, and Co., 1857.

Williams, William. Personal Reminiscences of C. H. Spurgeon. London: The Religious Tract Society, 1895.

Pamphlets

I have omitted from this list the more than one hundred pamphlets on the Baptismal Regeneration Controversy. They are gathered together in three bound volumes at Spurgeon's College. The British Museum Catalogue lists nearly sixty pamphlets on the Controversy.

Anon. An Apology for Spurgeon. London: Pattie, n.d.

_____. A Chat About Spurgeon in a Railway Car. London: John Caudwell, 1865.

_____. The Flying Angels, Spurgeon and the Cathedrals. London: Partridge, 1857.

_____. The Popular Preachers: The Reverend C. H. Spurgeon, his Extraordinary 'sayings and doings.' London: C. Kerbey, 1856.

_____. The Popularity of the Reverend C. H. Spurgeon. London: Daniel Oakey, 1858.

_____. The Reverend C. H. Spurgeon, His Friends and Foes. London: James Paul, 1855.

Anon. The Reverend C. H. Spurgeon, Twelve Realistic Sketches. London: James Clarke, 1877.

Bayne, Peter. Terrorism for Christ's Sake, or Mr. Spurgeon and Dr. Campbell. London: Simpkin, Marshall, and Co., 1860.

Campbell, John. The Modern Whitefield, Remarks on Mr. Spurgeon's Oratory. London: James Paul, 1863.

Clergyman of the Church of England, An Estimate of the Reverend C. H. Spurgeon's Ministry. London: Wertheim and MacIntosh, 1856.

Convert, Awful Progress of Infidelity in Southwark: Scriptural Prophesies Fulfilled. London: T. Jones, n.d.

Higgs, W. Miller. The Spurgeon Family, being an account of the descent and family of C. H. Spurgeon with notes on the family in general, particularly the Essex branch from 1465 to 1905. London: Elliot Stock, 1906.

Landels, William. Baptismal Regeneration, Remarks on the Controversy. London: Passmore and Alabaster, 1864.

_____. The Reverend C. H. Spurgeon and the Baptist Union. Edinburgh: Andrew Elliot, 1888.

Mayers, W. J. Who Led Charles H. Spurgeon to Christ? London: Morgan and Scott, 1927.

Morgan, Nicholas. The Phrenological Characteristics of the Reverend C. H. Spurgeon. London: Passmore and Alabaster, 1873.

Noel, Wriothsley B. Letter to the Reverend C. H. Spurgeon Respecting His Attack Upon the Evangelical Ministers of The Church of England. London: James Nesbet, 1864.

Price, Seymour J. The Spurgeon Centenary, Gleanings from the Minutebooks. London: The Kingsgate Press, 1934.

Shaftesbury, the Earl of. Religious Services in Theaters. London: 1860.

Stead, W. T. The Church of the Future. London: A. W. Hall, 1891.

Steinmetz. Andrew. A Chance Visitor, the Tabernacle on Easter Sunday with the Reverend C. H. Spurgeon. London: William Clark, 1873.

Weaver, Richard. A Complete View of Puseyism. New York: Collins, 1843.

_____. A Voice from the Coalpit; Or Six Addresses to the Working Classes by a Converted Collier. London, 1861.

Wilberforce, Samuel. 'The Giant of Voluntaryism,' or Mr. Spurgeon in the House of Lords. London: Simpkin and Marshall, 1868.

Published Memoirs and Diaries

Asquith, Herbert. Memories and Reflections, 1852-1927. Vol. I. London: Cassell and Co., 1928.

Benson, A. C. The Life of Edward White Benson. Vol. II. London: Macmillan, 1899.

Cross, J. W., ed. George Eliot's Life. Vol. III. London: Blackwoods, 1885.

Dale, A. W. W. The Life of R. W. Dale of Birmingham. London: Hodder and Stoughton, 1898.

Davies, C. Maurice. Orthodox London. London: Tinsley, 1876.

_____. Unorthodox London. London: Tinsley, 1876.

Evans, Joan and John Howard Whitehouse. The Diaries of John Ruskin. Vol. I. Oxford: Clarendon Press, 1958.

Haldane, Elizabeth. From One Century to Another. London: Alexander Maclehose, 1937.

Ellis, S. M., ed. A Mid-Victorian Pepys, The Letters and Memories of Sir William Hardman. London: Cecil Palmer, 1923.

Hall, Newman. An Autobiography. London: Cassell and Co., 1898.

Hodder, Edwin. The Life and Work of the Seventh Earl of Shaftesbury. London: Cassell and Co., 1892.

Kingsley, Charles. His Letters and Memories of his Life, edited by his wife. New York: Scribner, Armstrong and Co., 1877.

Lathbury, D. C. Correspondence on Church and Religion of W. E. Gladstone. 2 vols. London: Macmillan, 1910.

MacLaren, Ian. (Dr. John Watson). His Majesty Baby and Some Common People. London: Hodder and Stoughton, 1902.

Morley, John. Recollections. Vol. I. New York: Macmillarn, 1917.

Parker, Joseph. Autobiography. London: Hodder and Stoughton, 1899.

Raymond, E. T. Portraits of the Nineties. London: Unwin, 1921.

Reminiscences of the Revival of 'Fifty-Nine and the 'Sixties. Aberdeen: The University Press, 1910.

Russell, George W. E. The Letters of Matthew Arnold. 2 vols. London: Macmillan, 1905.

Walling, R. A. J., ed. John Bright's Diaries. London: Cassell and Co., 1930.

Wilberforce, Reginald G. The Life of the Rt. Reverend
    Samuel Wilberforce. Vol. III. London: John Murray,
    1883.

Zetland, the Marquis of. The Letters of Disraeli to
    Lady Bradford and Lady Chesterfield. London:
    Ernest Benn, 1929.

                    General Works

Addison, W. G   Religious Equality in Modern England.
    London: Macmillan, 1944.

Arnold, Matthew. Culture and Anarchy. J. Dover Wilson
    (ed.). Cambridge: The University Press, 1960.

Balleine, G. R. A History of the Evangelical Party in
    the Church of England. London: Longmans, 1933.

Beecher, H. W. Twelve Lectures to Young Men. New York:
    Appleton, 1890.

_____. Yale Lectures on Preaching. 3 vols. New York:
    J. B. Ford, 1872-1874.

Bell, G. K. A. Randall Davidson, Archbishop of Canterbury.
    New York: Oxford Press, 1952.

Bevington, Merle Mowbray. The Saturday Review, 1855-1868.
    New York: Columbia University Press, 1941.

Blackwood, James. The Soul of Frederick W. Robertson.
    New York: Harpers, 1947.

Booth, Charles. Life and Labor in London. Series three,
    "Religious Influences, South London." Vol. IV.
    London, 1902.

Bowen, Desmond. The Idea of the Victorian Church. Montreal:
    McGill University Press, 1968.

Briggs, Asa. _Victorian People_. Chicago: University of Chicago Press, 1955.

Brastow, L. O. _Representative Modern Preachers_. New York: Macmillan, 1904.

Carlile, John C. _The Story of the English Baptists_. London: James Clark, 1905.

Clark, G. Kitson. _The English Inheritance_. London: SCM Press, 1950.

_____. _The Making of Victorian England_. London: Methuen and Co., 1962.

Conwell, Russell. _Every Man His Own University_. New York: Harpers, 1917.

_____. _How a Soldier May Succeed After the War_. New York: Harpers, 1918.

Cross, Robert D., ed. _The Church and the City, 1865-1910_. New York: Bobbs-Merrill, 1967.

Dale, R. W. _Nine Lectures on Preaching Delivered at Yale_. London: Hodder and Stoughton, 1877.

Davies, Horton. _Worship and Theology in England from Newman to Martineau, 1850-1900_. Princeton: The University Press, 1962.

Dawson, Joseph. _William Morley Punshon_. London: Charles H. Kelly, 1906.

Findlay, James. _Dwight L. Moody, American Evangelist_. Chicago: The University of Chicago Press, 1969.

Forman, R. C., ed. _Great Christians_. London: Ivor Nicholson and Watson, 1933.

Fullerton, W. Y. _Thomas Spurgeon, A Biography_. London: Hodder and Stoughton, 1919.

Glover, Willis B. Evangelical Nonconformists and Higher Criticism in the Nineteenth Century. London: Independent Press, 1954.

Hanham, H. J. Elections and Party Management, Politics in the Time of Disraeli and Gladstone. London: Longmans, 1959.

Heasman, Kathleen. Evangelicals in Action. London: Geoffrey Bles, LTD., 1962.

Hofstadter, Richard. Anti-Intellectualism in American Life. New York: Alfred A. Knopf, 1963.

Hughes, Thomas. The Manliness of Christ. 16th edition. Boston, n.d.

Inglis, K. S. Churches and the Working Classes in Victorian England. London: Routledge and Keagan Paul, 1963.

James, Walter, The Christian in Politics. London: Oxford Press, 1962.

Kellett, E. E. Religion and Life in the Early Victorian Age. London: The Epworth Press, 1938.

McCown, Chester Charlton. The Search for the Real Jesus, a Century of Historical Study. New York: Scribners, 1940.

McLoughlin, William G. Modern Revivalism: Charles Grandison Finney to Billy Graham. New York: The Ronald Press Company, 1959.

Magnus, Philip. Gladstone, A Biography. London: John Murray, 1954.

Martin, R. B. The Dust of Combat: A Life of Charles Kingsley. London: Faber and Faber, 1959.

Moody, William R. D. L. Moody. New York: Macmillan, 1930.

Newsome, David. _Godliness and Good Learning_. London: John Murray, 1961.

Nias, J. C. S. _Gorham and the Bishop of Exeter_. London: S.P.C.K., 1951.

Niebuhr, H. Richard. _Christ and Culture_. New York: Harpers, 1951.

Norman, E. R. _Anti-Catholicism in Victorian England_. London: Barnes and Noble, 1968.

Parker, Joseph. _Pulpit Notes_. London: Strahan and Company, 1873.

Payne, Earnest A. _The Baptist Union, A Short History_. London: The Kingsgate Press, 1959.

_____. "The Downgrade Controversy," an unpublished paper deposited at the Baptist Church House, London, in January 1955.

Plumb, J. H., ed. _Studies in Social History_. London: Thomas Nelson, 1963.

Pollock, J. C. _Moody, A Biographical Portrait_. New York: Macmillan, 1963.

Poole-Conner, E. J. _Evangelicalism in England_. London: Henry Walter LTD., 1951.

Price, Lucien. _Dialogues With Alfred North Whitehead_. New York: Mentor Books, 1956.

Robson, Robert, ed. _Ideas and Institutions of Victorian Britain_. New York: Macmillan, 1967.

Rourke, Constance. _Trumpets of Jubilee_. New York: Harcourt Brace, 1927.

Semmel, Bernard. _Democracy Versus Empire_. New York: Anchor Books, 1969.

Shannon, R. T. Gladstone and the Bulgarian Agitation 1876.
    London: Thomas Nelson, 1963.

Thielicke, Helmut, ed. Encounter With Spurgeon. Phila-
    delphia: The Fortress Press, 1963.

Thompson, E. P. The Making of the English Working Class.
    New York: Vintage, 1963.

Trilling, Lionel. Matthew Arnold. New York: W. W. Norton,
    1939.

Underwood, A. C. A History of the English Baptists.
    London: The Kingsgate Press, 1947.

Vincent, John. The Formation of the Liberal Party, 1857-
    1869. London: Constanble and Company, 1966.

Webb, R. K. Harriet Martineau, A Radical Victorian.
    New York: Columbia University Press, 1960.

Whitehead, Alfred North. Science and the Modern World.
    New York: Mentor Books, 1956.

Wilkinson, William C. Modern Masters of Pulpit Discourse.
    New York: Funk and Wagnalls, 1905.

Wood, H. G. Belief and Unbelief Since 1850. Cambridge:
    The University Press, 1955.

Young, G. M., ed. Early Victorian England, 1830-1865.
    2 vols. Oxford: The University Press, 1951.

Note on Additional Bibliography

A number of works in Victorian religious history published since this study was completed have contributed to a better understanding of the popular religious history of the nineteenth century and the social environment in which it existed.[1] But there has been no new published work on Spurgeon's ministry itself. An unpublished dissertation by Albert Roger Meredith, "The Social and Political Views of Charles Haddons Spurgeon,"[2] is a study of Spurgeon's views of politics and society as reflected in his published works. Meredith feels that most biographies of Spurgeon have underestimated the extent of his political activity. G. I. T. Machin, Politics and the Church in Great Britain, 1832--1869,[3] is concerned with the period before Spurgeon became politically active, but Machin's work is important for an understanding of the relationship between Gladstone and the Nonconformists, and for the crucial decade of the 1860's when the Liberal-Nonconformist alliance was formed. Stephen Koss, Nonconformity in Modern British Politics,[4] carries the story of this alliance into the twentieth century, and demonstrates the way in which the Nonconformists, and certainly the Baptist denomination, continued to be a force of political significance. Hugh McLeod, <u>Class and Religion in the Late Victorian City</u>,[5] addresses the question, "who went to church?" and offers in answer a sociological analysis of the city as an entity divided into separate worlds having almost no communication with one another. He argues that church attendance, (as distinguished from religious <u>belief</u>), was largely a matter of social status and class membership. His statistical evidence on the Baptists supports my analysis of Spurgeon's congregation: that the denomination drew the bulk of its support from the lower middle class, and particularly the people described as "respectable artisans."

John Kent, <u>Holding the Fort: Studies in Victorian Revivalism</u>[6], reviews the part played by American religious revivalists in the religious world of nineteenth-century Britain. Kent's book is the best account available of the revival of 1859, which he views as a failure. His work supports my conclusion that Spurgeon, although benefitting from the revival, had personal resources and a denominational base, allowing him to survive the collapse of the movement. Kent argues that the general trend of revivalism after 1870 was pre-millennial, and therefore opposed to social and political action. In opposition,

organized Nonconformity became less-revivalist, and more
political. The millenarian tradition is seen as the basis
for the emergence of fundamentalism by Ernest Sandeen in
Roots of Fundamentalism: British and American Millenarianism,
1800--1930.[7] His work is a revision of the common view that
fundamentalism was born in the 1920's. It is his contention
that fundamentalism was a religious movement before, during,
and after this decade, and that it was millenarianism which
gave life and shape to the fundamentalist movement. Sandeen
does not deal with Spurgeon, but he notes the close connection
between American fundamentalists and the Tabernacle in the
twentieth century, a connection underscored by the fact that
two American fundamentalists held the position of pastor of
the Tabernacle after Spurgeon's death.

Footnotes

[1]For a review of recent literature, see Hugh McLeod, "Recent Studies in Victorian Religious History," Victorian Studies, 21 (Winter, 1978), pp. 245-255.

[2]Albert Roger Meredith, "The Social and Political Views of Charles Haddon Spurgeon" (PhD. diss., Michigan State University, 1973).

[3]G. I. T. Machin, Politics and the Churches in Great Britain, 1832--1868 (Oxford, Clarendon, 1977).

[4]Stephen Koss, Nonconformity in Modern British Politics (London, Batsford, 1975).

[5]Hugh McLeod, Class and Religion in the Late Victorian City (London, Croom Helm, 1974).

[6]John Kent, Holding the Fort: Studies in Victorian Revivalism (London, Epworth Press, 1978).

[7]Ernest Sandeen, The Roots of Fundamentalism: British and American Millenarianism, 1800--1930 (Chicago, University of Chicago Press, 1970).

INDEX

Arnold, Matthew   303-308, 476.

Ashley-Cooper, Anthony (Seventh Earl of Shaftesbury)   84,
      133, 161, 361-362.

Beecher, Henry Ward   80, 95, 115, 227, 252, 283, 448, 450.

Benson, E. W. (Archbishop of Canterbury)   138, 157, 175,
      215, 298, 464.

Baptists, the
      badly split in Spurgeon's youth   59.
      reputation for unlearned ministry   61.
      growth in membership   69.
      movement toward Modernism   413-417, 422-428, 436-438,
         469.

Baptist Union, the   69. See also, "Downgrade Controversy."

Baptismal Regeneration Controversy, the   236, 254-281, 385.

Church of England, the
      Spurgeon's influence upon   84-85, 100.
      Spurgeon's views on doctrine   30-31, 261-272.
      supports Spurgeon in Downgrade Controversy   419-420.

Clifford, John   65, 410, 433, 436, 442.

Dale, R. W.   38, 64, 77, 161, 199, 216, 253, 259, 323, 338,
      356, 433, 448.

Disestablishment   294-320, 420.

Disraeli, Benjamin   245, 335, 337, 345, 360.

Downgrade Controversy, the   170, 254, 279-281, 408-444,
      452, 259, 469-470.

Education Act of 1870   321-330.

Eliot, George   115, 124-125.

Gladstone, W. E.   11, 128, 186, 245, 257, 283, 286-287,
      299-302, 314-315, 319, 321, 332-336, 341-344,
      351-355, 357-358, 360, 464, 470.

Great Revival, the 68, 142-143, 146, 248, 497-498.

Hall, Newman 130, 161, 469.

Home Rule 287, 356-358.

Landels, William 64, 280, 412, 219, 440.

Metropolitan Tabernacle Congregation 128-138, 497.

Moody, D. L. 64, 101, 116, 133, 143, 165, 186, 194, 248,
    251, 358, 373, 451-456, 470-474.

Parker, Joseph 24, 197, 247, 291, 374-375, 406, 442, 448-
    449, 469, 477.

Pastor's College 163-164, 168-169, 194, 434-435, 443-444.

Ruskin, John 125-128, 146.

Sankey, Ira David 104, 143, 248.

Spurgeon, Charles (son) 108, 444.

Spurgeon, Charles Haddon

    biographies of 2-5, 26.
    physical appearance of 33-34, 79, 107, 215-216.
    early years 8, 13-30.
    education 27, 30, 32, 50, 61-65, 366.
    conversion 35-42.
    joins the Baptists 42-43.
    begins preaching 51-54.
    first ministry at Waterbeach 55-66.
    invited to London 67-68, 70.
    Pastor at New Park Street Chapel 44, 67-71.
    Exeter Hall Campaign 83-85, 126-127.
    Surrey Gardens disaster 87-92, 137-138.
    Moves to the Metropolitan Tabernacle 85, 142, 146,
        147, 150-155, 254, 273, 280.
    Marriage 106-110.
    early press opinion of 110-111, 117-124, 140-142, 189.
    preaching style of 56-57, 71-75, 82, 95-98, 139, 178-
        180, 184-200, 203-206.
    influence within the denomination 156, 254, 273, 280,
        405, 411-412.
    views on church government and services 155-160, 209-
        219.
    success of printed sermons 2, 98, 185, 233-249.

influence of Puritans upon 20-23, 44, 63, 103, 148, 153-154, 210-211, 225, 297, 370, 380-82.
embodiment of middle-class virtues 148, 165, 167-168, 216-217.
anti-intellectual attitudes 201-203, 232.
his library 211, 232, 366-368, 471.
attitudes toward smoking and drinking 219-224, 231-232.
on higher criticism 13, 200, 374, 389-395, 399, 406-417, 478.
political activism of 279, 282, 286-361.
anti-Catholicism of 21-22, 49-50, 265-267, 331.
as a Calvinist 47-49, 60, 111-116, 232, 415.
illness 81, 338 n., 358, 387-388, 428, 434-435, 458.
mental depression 93-94, 416, 459-460.
resigns from Baptist Union 432.
death 466.

Spurgeon, Eliza (mother) 8, 36, 43.

Spurgeon, James (grandfather) 8, 13-14, 18-19, 23, 25, 48, 62.

Spurgeon, James Archer (brother) 136-137, 173-174, 294, 440-441, 468.

Spurgeon, John (father) 8, 33, 40-44, 62, 123, 174.

Spurgeon, Susannah (wife) 4, 75-76, 92-93, 106-110, 126, 187-188, 367, 465.

Spurgeon, Thomas (son) 95, 109, 177, 457, 468.

Spurgeon's Orphanage 170-171, 421, 468.

Stead, W. T. 21, 147, 204, 239, 243, 360, 377, 302, 303, 433, 454-457.

Sword and Trowel 4, 118, 171-172, 429-433.